LANGUAGE IN SOCIETY 19

Linguistic Variation and Change

Language in Society

GENERAL EDITOR
Peter Trudgill, Professor in the Department of Language and Linguistics,
University of Essex

ADVISORY EDITORS
Ralph Fasold, Professor of Linguistics, Georgetown University
William Labov, Professor of Linguistics, University of Pennsylvania

Linguistic Variation and Change

On the Historical Sociolinguistics of English

James Milroy

BLACKWELL
Oxford UK & Cambridge USA

First published 1992

Basil Blackwell Ltd
108 Cowley Road, Oxford, OX4 1JF, UK

Basil Blackwell, Inc.
3 Cambridge Center
Cambridge, Massachusetts 02142, USA

Library of Congress Cataloging in Publication Data
Milroy, James.
Linguistic variation and change: on the historical
sociolinguistics of English/James Milroy.
p. cm. — (Language in society; 17)
Includes bibliographical references and index.
ISBN 0–631–14366–1. — ISBN 0–631–14367–X (pbk.)
1. English language—Grammar, Historical. 2. English language-
Social aspects. 3. English language—Variation.
4. Sociolinguistics. I. Title. II. Series: Language in society
(Oxford, England); 17
PE 1101.M55 1922
306.4′4—dc20   91–18703
                                                CIP

Typeset in Ehrhardt 11 on 13 pt
by TecSet Ltd
Wallington, Surrey
Printed in Great Britain by Hartnolls Ltd, Bodmin

This book is printed on acid-free paper.

Contents

Editor's Preface

The impressive and exciting breakthroughs developed in this book are due not only to the fact that the research presented here is very much in historical sociolinguistics, as opposed to historical linguistics pure and simple, but also to the fact that it involves work where, more than in any other previous historical linguistic research, a consistent distinction is drawn between linguistic systems, on the one hand, and speakers on the other. Obviously, languages without speakers do not change. Linguists, however, have not always drawn the correct conclusion from this truism, namely that it is speakers who change languages. A language changes as a result of what its speakers do to it as they use it to speak to one another in everyday face-to-face interactions. One of the emphases of this book is therefore on the use of detailed analyses of data, derived from empirical observations of vernacular language varieties in actual everyday use, to shed light on historical linguistic problems, some of them associated with the interpretation of historical data from English and other languages, most of which is derived, of course, from non-vernacular written sources.

Further vital insights are due to an insistence on making a distinction between linguistic innovations and linguistic changes, and a related distinction between speakers as innovators and speakers as 'early adopters'. Crucial, too, is the emphasis on the importance of weak social ties between individuals in the spread of linguistic innovations.

Most impressive in this book, however, is the way in which it combines erudition in historical–linguistic, sociolinguistic and social theory with a detailed knowledge of linguistic varieties that can come only from the experience of working closely with speakers themselves – as sociolinguists do – rather than with languages as purely abstract systems that one may or may not have intuitions about. Linguistic change constitutes one of the great unsolved mysteries of linguistic science, and the puzzle of the causation and function of language change is a challenge that generations of linguists and philologists have wrestled with. Perhaps the biggest mystery of all, especially as far as sound change is concerned, is what we have come to call, following the seminal 1968 paper by Weinreich, Labov and Herzog, the *actuation problem*. We have become quite expert at explaining why particular linguistic changes occur, and why certain changes are more to be expected than others. We are still very inexpert, however, at accounting for their actuation: why do particular changes occur in a particular language variety at a particular time, and not in other varieties or at other times?

Professor Milroy would not claim to have answered this question here. Indeed, he makes it clear that the final answer to this question, if we ever achieve one, will be extraordinarily complex. His book, however, does penetrate further than any other research that I am familiar with into the heart of this problem. For what Jim Milroy has done in this book is to ensure that, henceforth, in seeking the answer to this question, we shall be looking in the right place. We will not in future be wasting our energies in seeking purely linguistic explanations for what, as he has shown with exemplary clarity, is a supremely sociolinguistic phenomenon.

As an acknowledged expert on the history of the English language *and* as one of the best-known of all the world's practising empirical sociolinguists, Jim Milroy is uniquely equipped to tackle the massive problems associated with the study of change in human language. It should not surprise us, therefore that he has produced a work that future generations of scholars will surely come to regard as one of the most important works on linguistic change ever written.

Peter Trudgill

Preface

This book is undertaken as a result of a long-term interest in the task of explaining how linguistic change comes about. In particular, it is an attempt to explore the extent to which language change can be said to be a social phenomenon, and it is focused mainly on variation in the English language.

In this task I rely quite heavily on a generation of work in social dialectology extending back to the 1960s, and especially on the sociolinguistic research projects that I undertook at Queen's University, Belfast, between 1975 and 1982. The specific purpose of these was to study social aspects of language change by investigating spoken vernacular English systematically in social and situational contexts of use. These projects were based on a 'coming-together' of a number of my own research interests, and they were designed as part of a longer-term research programme. It is appropriate here to sketch in briefly the relationship between the Belfast work – including the ideas behind it and the continuing work that has arisen out of it – and the general topic of this book. This is further justified by misunderstandings that have arisen about the responsibility for, and scope of, this research.

I was chief investigator in the first project (1975–7) and jointly chief investigator with Lesley Milroy in the second project (1979–82). The work was undertaken on the basis of prior interests in language change, language standardization and historical English dialectology, extending back over a number of years, and some ideas about linguistic norms and language maintenance that I had derived from these interests. I had been particularly interested in language standardization and prescription, and the way in which vernacular norms seem to oppose these processes, presumably in an identity-maintaining function. These observations suggest that norm-enforcement in language might often come about in a non-institutional way, through informal pressures within social groups in order to maintain the vernacular, and I thought it might be worth investigating these things empirically. Orthodox historical linguistics, however, appeared at that time to have no place at all for such matters as prescription and norm-enforcement, even though these must be in some way implicated in language change. But as non-standard norms are not codified in books, the only way in which vernacular norm-enforcement can be investigated is by exploring language in the community – hence the particular form that the Belfast projects took.

My main interest in undertaking this work was in explaining how non-standard norms are maintained by social pressures, and the relevance of this to linguistic change and the history of English; this is broadly the topic of this book. For a number of reasons – which may have had to do with the fact that these ideas were unfashionable at the time – I found it difficult to get support for the proposed projects. In 1975, I was finally successful in obtaining a modest research grant from the Social Science Research Council. Lesley Milroy joined me at the preparatory stage, and together we prepared the detailed design of the inner-city project.

It is the interest in language *maintenance* (as a basis for studying language *change*) that chiefly differentiates this research from other quantitative sociolinguistic projects of that time, in that this particular interest controls the research design and the methodology adopted. If language maintenance is emphasized, questions of the following kind become accessible to investigation: why do different dialects remain divergent from 'mainstream' norms of language despite the low status usually accorded to them (why do they not all become 'standard-ized'?), and why do many of these divergent forms and varieties persist for generations and even for centuries? These questions have a broader applicability, of course, to bilingual and multilingual situations, to the question of how minority languages survive and to many associated social, legal and educational issues. We always had these possible applications in mind, but in this book I shall be focusing mainly on historical English language studies. Within this narrower scope, we can pose further questions: why, for example, do changes in the 'prestige' norm over the centuries seem to originate in 'lower-status' varieties of English rather than in elite ones? The rise of urban varieties (such as London English in the late Middle Ages and the 'new' dialects of nineteenth-century industrial cities) are relevant to historical developments in English: therefore, using Belfast as a general case-study, I was additionally concerned with exploring the rise of urban vernaculars to see what kinds of thing happen in 'live' urban vernacular development. Traditional historical descriptive linguistics has no satisfactory answers to the questions I have raised in this paragraph: to attempt to answer them, we focused in our socio-historical work on language in day-to-day interaction rather than on past records of language.

Because of the concern with language maintenance we studied in the first phase of the research the forms of speech and social interaction that differ most from 'mainstream' norms, that is, highly divergent and non-standard forms of the language. We studied inner-city locations before extending the analysis in later stages to the outer city (we were of course concerned with *non-institutional* norms of language, which I shall discuss further in chapters 1 and 4). However, it is important to notice that, unlike Labov's (1966) work, our research did not depend in the first place on projecting a stratificational social class model on to the linguistic data collected. Thus, our interpretation of the sociolinguistic patterns does not depend on this either. During the course of the inner-city research, we looked around for a social variable that we might adapt to quantitative use to measure language maintenance, and decided jointly to use *social network* in connection with other social variables, rather than place prior emphasis on social class. I shall look at the relationship of class and network in chapter 7.

The findings of the projects depended on collaboration between a number of people. The main day-to-day task throughout most of these years was the quantitative linguistic analysis of the data, which was carried out at Queen's University. I am grateful to Rose Maclaran, Domini O'Kane, Linda Policansky, John Harris, Brendan Gunn, Anne Pitts, and Zena Molyneux, all of whom worked – either full-time or part-time – on the data as research assistants in my department at Queen's, and to Máire Burke, who carried out the Andersonstown fieldwork; the late Sue Margrain gave statistical help and advice, and Irene Dempster helped for many years as typist and secretary to the projects. Most of all, I am grateful to Lesley Milroy.

She and I shared the main tasks equally and are jointly responsible for all aspects of the work. Decisions on research design, sampling, fieldwork strategy, linguistic analysis, use of speaker variables, quantitative analysis, and on all other matters, were in practice taken collaboratively. More importantly, we developed the *ideas* in the research collaboratively also. But as some division of labour was necessary in practice, my main day-to-day task was to direct and carry out the linguistic side of the work, and Lesley's was mainly on the ethnographic and social side. These two sides of the work are of course interdependent, and our findings depend on both.

These comments are fuller than I would have liked, but they are necessary because the Belfast research has now been quite commonly misrepresented as wholly or mainly the work of my colleague, Lesley Milroy. In fact, her book *Language and Social Networks* develops the ethnographic side of the argumentation within the general framework of the joint research, and is dependent for its linguistic database on my analysis of the language. It also depends on my interests in many other ways, particularly in the emphasis on language norms and maintenance. In Chapters 3 and 4, I shall review the central concerns of the Belfast research, focusing on the linguistic interests rather than ethnography, and emphasizing the methodological independence of the linguistic analysis, on the one hand, from the socially-based interpretation, on the other.

A few comments are also required here on the treatment of linguistic change in this book. I am concerned with change in the basic structural parts of language, and – following Neogrammarian concerns – mainly with sound-change. Sound-change has always been the testing-ground of historical linguistic theory, chiefly because – in a language-internal account – sound-change, more so than other kinds of change, appears at first sight to be quite mysterious: there is no obvious reason why it should happen at all. In a sound-change from [a] to [o], for example, there is apparently no 'improvement' in the language – we cannot demonstrate by empirical methods that the new state of language brought about by this change is 'better' or 'more efficient' than the state that went before. It is more difficult to explain why sound-change should happen than to explain some other aspects of language change, and I am keeping the mystery of sound-change very much in mind at every point throughout this book. The book is also intended to contribute to the development of historical sociolinguistics, a field of interest that Romaine (1982a) labels *socio-historical linguistics*. It will be evident that my approach is rather different from hers.

I am extremely grateful to the Social Science Research Council (now renamed ESRC) for their generous financial support. The first project (HR 3771: 'Speech Community and Language Variety in Belfast' – the inner-city work) was directed by me and carried out between 1975 and 1977; the second project (HR 5777: 'Sociolinguistic Variation and Linguistic Change in Belfast') was directed by both of us and carried out between 1979 and 1982. I also acknowledge with gratitude the support of Queen's University and the Ulster Polytechnic (at which Lesley Milroy was then a Senior Lecturer). Since 1982 we have of course continued to work on matters arising from these projects, and many chapters of this book draw on my continuing collaboration with Lesley. Chapters 6 and 7, in particular, are largely based on jointly-authored papers written since we completed the analytic work in the Belfast projects, and this is acknowledged in the text. In the projects themselves, however, so many people gave advice and help that I cannot acknowledge all of them here: I hope they will know that I am grateful. But I would particularly like to mention Roger Lass for the much-needed encouragement that he has always given to me, and Peter Trudgill for his constant support and, more recently, his immense patience as editor in dealing with an increasingly wayward author. My thanks also to Philip Carpenter for his patience. But there is one other person without whose help the Belfast research could hardly have got off the ground. I owe a special debt of gratitude to William Labov for his example and inspiration, and for his unfailing personal support and encouragement.

James Milroy
March 1991

1

Introduction: Language Change and Variation

1.0 Language Change

One of the most important facts about human language is that it is continuously changing. Everyone knows that languages have changed in the course of history: it is easy to see from a distance in time that there are differences between Shakespeare's English and present-day English, but it can also be shown from close at hand that language is continuing to change in the present just as it did in the past. At this very moment changes are being implemented and diffused: old varieties are dying out and new varieties are springing up; pronunciations are changing, new words and constructions are being adopted and old ones adapted to new uses. Sometimes change is rapid, and sometimes it is slow, and at any given time some linguistic structures are changing while others remain stable. Indeed, change seems to be inherent in the nature of language: there is no such thing as a perfectly stable human language.

It is also true that at any given time a language is *variable*. Languages are never uniform entities; they can be observed to vary geographically and socially, and according to the situational contexts in which they are used. In the study of linguistic change, this heterogeneity of language is of crucial importance, as change in progress can be detected in the study of variation. It is also important to remember this when we look at past states of language: we have to accept that, just as language is variable when observed at the present day, so it must also have been variable in the past. The history of any language is therefore not the history of one 'variety', but is a multidimensional history.

It follows, therefore, that at any time we care to look at a language – or a dialect – it is variable and in a state of change. We may, of course, choose to ignore this and treat language for descriptive purposes *as if* it were a uniform and unchanging phenomenon, and there are often good practical reasons for adopting this convenient idealization. For instance, we may want to write a grammar of English for the use of foreign learners, and it will be more helpful to our readers if we focus on what is constant rather than what is changing. However, the idea that language is static or uniform has also penetrated into the roots of theory, and much of the linguistic theory of this century has been based on the perceived need to treat language *as if* it were static and uniform. It should, however, be borne in mind that technological advances since the earlier part of this century have made it much more feasible for us to focus on variable states of language than it was for de Saussure, Sapir and Bloomfield.

1.1   Uniformity and Variation

Early in the century de Saussure emphasized the priority of synchronic descriptions and from that time onwards the dominant trends in language description were synchronic: they focused on states of language *at given times* as finite entities. Historical (or *diachronic*) linguistics was relegated to a subsidiary role and was often conceived of as an exercise in *comparing* these finite states of language at different times. From this point of view we can liken a synchronic description to a still photograph and a historical description to a comparison of a series of still photographs taken at different times. In reality, however, the history of language is a continuous process: it is not a series of stills, but a moving picture. If we are to come closer to understanding why and how languages change, we need to bear this in mind.

It has often been pointed out (for example, by Bynon, 1977: 104–7) that Saussurean structuralism can lead to a paradox for historical linguistics. According to the Saussurean view, a language is at any given time a system *où tout se tient* – in which everything holds together in a coherent self-contained structure of interdependent parts. Historical linguistic inquiry then proceeds by comparing different states of language that have been attested from different periods. However, a difficulty arises in the (unattested) intervening stage between one state (state A) and another (state B), as it appears that in this transitional stage the cohesiveness of the state A structure has been to some extent violated. From this point of view, therefore, we may be inclined to think of language as being perfectly structured at some times but flawed at other times. Now, if linguistic change were an abnormal state of affairs, this would not be an unreasonable way to look at language: change could then be seen as something that strikes a language from time to time like a disease. We could talk of healthy languages (where everything holds together) and sick languages (where it does not). But this is not how things are: no real language state is a perfectly balanced and stable structure, linguistic change is always in progress, and all dialects are transitional dialects. Synchronic states, as we observe them at a given time, are therefore changing states, and stable states of language of the kind postulated in Saussurean theory are idealizations.

The same, of course, applies to *uniform* states of language. As Sapir observed long ago (1921: 147): 'everyone knows that language is variable'. No language is ever uniform. Linguistic theorizing, however, has often proceeded *as if* languages were uniform entities. Indeed, according to Weinreich, Labov and Herzog (1968), it has gone further than this and has assumed that structuredness is found *only* in uniformity: thus, variability in language has often been discounted as unstructured. In fact, the equation of uniformity with structuredness or regularity is most evident in popular (non-professional) attitudes to language: one variety – usually a standard language – is considered to be correct and regular, and others – usually 'non-standard' dialects – are thought to be incorrect, irregular, ungrammatical and deviant. Furthermore, linguistic changes in progress are commonly perceived as 'errors'. Thus, although everyone knows that language is variable, many people believe that invariance is nonetheless to be desired, and professional scholars of language have not been immune to the consequences of these same beliefs. We have discussed these points elsewhere (J. Milroy & L. Milroy, 1985a), and I shall return to them in later chapters. Here my concern is merely to point out that uniform states of language are idealizations and that variable states are normal; furthermore, variation in language may itself be structured and regular. Languages are not in reality completely stable or uniform, and there is absolutely no reason why they should be.

The discussion above has raised some basic questions about language. Is a language actually a system *où tout se tient*, in which all the structural parts are interdependent? Is variation in a language also totally structured and systematic? Finally, if languages are actually like this, how can change occur at all? In this book, I shall take the view that these structuralist assumptions are not self-evidently true and that to establish the degree to which language is structured within itself – without reference to outside (for example, social) factors – is an empirical task. Indeed, if language states are not to some extent open-ended – if there are no 'leaks' in the system – it is difficult to see how linguistic change can take place.

1.2 Foundations for the Social Modelling of Language Change

One way of investigating these matters is to focus on the social nature of language change, and this is the purpose of this book. My aim is to examine the extent to which the origins of linguistic change can be shown to be social; to put it in a slightly stronger form, I want to examine the thesis that linguistic change is a product of speaker-activity in social contexts, which cannot be wholly explained from within the properties of language systems themselves. This approach is justified on the grounds that language is a social phenomenon: it is used by speakers to communicate with one another in social and cultural contexts in which the language system (narrowly defined as a 'grammar') is not the sole means of communication and personal interaction. Furthermore, it is commonly observed that *languages which have no speakers do not change*;[1] therefore, it seems reasonable to inquire into the role of speakers in language change. As socially-based arguments of this kind have not been widely favoured by historical linguists over the last century or so, I shall attempt in Chapter 2 to relate this social theme to the context of intra-linguistic historical argument. First, however, I want to explain more directly why I have felt justified in developing this socially-based approach to historical linguistics. The key point to bear in mind here is that language throughout history has been primarily a spoken, and not a written, phenomenon – my thesis is largely a matter of following out the implications of that fact.

'The drama of linguistic change', according to Wyld (1927: 21), 'is enacted not in manuscripts nor inscriptions, but in the mouths and minds of men', and historical linguists have generally insisted that the history of language is primarily the history of spoken language. Traditionally, however, it was not possible to follow this out very thoroughly because investigators did not have the technology to study spoken discourse *in extenso*, and could hardly have imagined how complex the patterning of spoken interaction in situational contexts would actually turn out to be when it did become possible to analyse it. As a result of these limitations, much of the generally accepted body of knowledge on which theories of change are based depends on quite narrow interpretations of written data and decontextualized citation forms (whether written or spoken), rather than on observation of spoken language in context ('situated speech'). However, it is in spoken, rather than in written, language that we are able to detect structural and phonetic changes in their early stages; for this reason and others, our understanding of the nature of linguistic change can be greatly enhanced by observing in a systematic way recurrent patterns of spoken language as it is used around us in day-to-day contexts by live speakers. I would therefore like to suggest here three general principles, or foundations, for the social modelling of change that arise directly from this emphasis on spoken interaction, and that I have used as guidelines in research into language change.

Speech is a social activity in a sense that writing is not, and the primary locus of speech is *conversation*. Conversations take place between two or more participants in social and situational contexts, and linguistic change is one type of phenomenon that is passed from person to person in these situations. The first principle for a socially-based model of language change therefore concerns the *observation* of language in use: it is the principle that speech-exchanges can be observed only within social and situational contexts – they can never be devoid of such a context. To express this more fully:

Principle 1 As language use (outside of literary modes and laboratory experiments) cannot take place *except* in social and situational contexts and, when observed, is *always* observed in these contexts, our analysis – if it is to be adequate – *must* take account of society, situation and the speaker/listener.

This first principle carries with it a number of implications, the most important of which is that generalizations about language structure depend on a process of abstracting 'language' from the situational contexts in which it naturally occurs. We do not actually observe 'the language' or 'language' in the abstract: we observe people talking. In a social account of language change, therefore, we have to explain how changes get into this abstract structure that we call language (which we cannot observe directly) as a result of the activities of people talking (which we can observe more directly). Furthermore, unstructured observations of very selective phenomena will not be enough here: our descriptions of sociolinguistic patterns will depend on observing recurrent patterns and will have to be systematic and accountable to the data. In chapter 2 I will suggest a distinction in principle between *system* and *speaker*, which arises from this discussion; it is a distinction that I think we need to bear in mind when we are analysing language in use. It also follows from this first principle that close attention to methods of data collection and analysis (and the relation of one to the other) is crucial; we regarded this as very important in our work in Belfast, which I describe more fully in chapters 3 and 4.

Whereas Principle 1 concerns the impossibility of *observing* language independently of society, Principle 2 concerns the impossibility of *describing* language structures independently of society. This is not as controversial as it may seem.

> *Principle 2*   A full description of the structure of a variety (whether it is 'standard' English, or a dialect, or a style or register) can only be successfully made if quite substantial decisions, or judgements, of a social kind are taken into account in the description.

The word 'social' here does not mean social class or prestige – the decisions (or judgements) we are talking about are decisions (or judgements) about the 'norms' of the variety concerned, and these norms are social in the sense that they are *agreed on* socially – they depend on consensus among speakers within the community or communities concerned and will differ from one community to another. The accuracy of the linguist's description must therefore be judged on how closely it coincides with the socially agreed norm for the relevant community.

Most language description encounters this problem of 'norms', and although it is not always acknowledged, it can be detected in many descriptive accounts of English. Even a statement that Received Pronunciation (RP) of English has a long diphthong with an open first element in such words as *tie* and *tight* depends on observing a sample of people who are considered to be speaking this variety and on the linguist's judgement that this vowel is the majority usage among these persons. But as a more general example of judging the norm, let us consider Palmer's (1965: 72–7) characterization of the English perfect tense/aspect. Palmer cites sentences in which the adverbs *just* and *already* occur with the perfect, but he gives no examples of their occurrence with the simple past tense. Thus, forms like 'I just did it' and 'I did it already' are not given as possible sequences. A normative judgement is implicit here, and this is probably a correct judgement for many varieties, chiefly southern English ones. However, it is certainly not correct for all varieties: the [past tense + just/already] collocation is frequently observed in American, Irish and Scottish English. Therefore, the accuracy of Palmer's characterization has to be assessed, not in terms of some absolute standard of 'grammaticality' of the construction, but in terms of the speech community to which it is relevant. It is not a matter of grammaticality or ungrammaticality of the usage for all speakers of English; it is a matter of accurately describing what is agreed on by speakers in the community concerned as the consensus norm of that community.

The interpenetration of social and linguistic judgements is easily demonstrated in the work of linguists who are ostensibly non-social in their approach. Smith (1989: 111–12), for example, comments that 'for most speakers of (British) English' *He ate the pie already* is 'barely acceptable', whereas *He has eaten the pie already* is 'fine'. This involves the same kind of normative judgement that I have discussed above, and it is more or less correct for English in England and Wales. But much more dubiously, Smith further comments that 'for *all* speakers' (my italics) *He has eaten the pie yesterday* is 'ungrammatical'. However, this construction does occur in SBE (Southern British English). As Trudgill (1984a: 42) points out, 'The rules governing the use of the present perfect in Standard English seem to be altering somewhat, and there appears in particular to be an increase in the usage of such forms as: *I've seen him last year; He's done it two days ago.*' Noting that [perfect tense + *yesterday, last year* etc.] is spreading in SBE and is 'grammatical' in other languages, such as French, it is advisable to side with sociolinguists and not with Chomskyan linguists. We are not dealing with ungrammaticality, but with a change in the norms of usage for some part of the community. What this demonstrates is how easy it is for the non-social linguist to appear to propose *prescriptive* judgements. These typically appeal to some idealized superordinate norm which is part of the 'standard' or literary language, rather than a consensus community norm, but, although they are not enunciated as social, they are also social judgements.

But what is true of 'standard' English norms (as described by Palmer, Trudgill and Smith) is also true of non-standard norms, no matter how violently deviant they appear to be to the prescriptively-inclined observer. For example, if everybody in a social group says *we was there*, then *we was* is the consensus norm. To take one of our own examples, it is clear that for many Belfast speakers (and indeed for many speakers of Irish English generally), the pronoun *yous* (plural) is categorical, contrasting with *you* (singular): 'So I said to our Trish and our Sandra: "Yous wash the dishes." Sure, I might as well have said "You wash the dishes", for our Trish just got up, put her coat on and went out.' The categorical distinction here between *you* and *yous* can be said to be a norm for some community of speakers. The difficulty that arises for the descriptive linguist is not so much to determine the extent of what is 'grammatical' (on which see especially Labov, 1973), as to determine the extent of the community of speakers within which this particular structure is the *consensus norm*. It is clear that many people in Belfast have categorical *yous*, but that many others vary in the plural between *you* and *yous*; indeed, there are some who have categorical *you* (as in standard English). Therefore, a description which states that *yous* (plural) is categorical in Belfast English will be valid for some part of the community, but not for all speakers or all styles, and the variability in *you/yous* usage will certainly exhibit a socially structured pattern.

Thus, although linguists have generally described differences between varieties of language as *linguistic* facts, these differences are also social facts. The preference for 'I did it already' in dialect A as against 'I've done it already' in dialect B, for example, arises from differences in speaker-agreement within communities and is to that extent a social fact. It follows from this that all language descriptions, no matter how objective they are, must be *normative*. But although linguists have often equated *normative* with *prescriptive*, no such equation is intended here. Language descriptions are normative because to be accurate they have to coincide as closely as possible with the consensus norms of the community concerned. To be normative, the linguist's account of a variety does not have to be prescriptive; that is, it does not have to prescribe how people in a community *should* speak. The distinction I am making here can be described as the distinction between *observing* a norm for descriptive purposes and *enforcing* a norm prescriptively; but as this is not a familiar distinction, I should perhaps discuss it a little more fully.

Linguistic scholars commonly contrast 'descriptive' with 'prescriptive'. Daniel Jones, for example, has this to say in the preface to his *English Pronouncing Dictionary* (1955): 'No attempt is made to decide how people *ought* to pronounce; all that the dictionary aims at doing is to give a faithful record of the manner in which certain people do pronounce.' This is as good a statement of the descriptivist position as I can think of, and it seems to me to be irrelevant to point out (as Haas, 1982, does) that people will nevertheless treat the dictionary as prescriptive: they will use it to find out how they *ought* to pronounce. If they do, this will not be because the presentation is prescriptive, but because the pronunciation that happens to be described here is viewed as one that it is desirable to acquire. If some other dialect had been described, people would not use the description prescriptively. I doubt, for example, if many people will use my own description of Belfast pronunciation (1981) in order to acquire fluency in inner-city Belfast English, although in principle they could. Jones's *English Pronouncing Dictionary* is therefore descriptive, and not prescriptive, in exactly the same way as the description of any other dialect is. But it is also normative (as all such descriptions must be) in the sense that it attempts to reflect the socially agreed norms of some particular community of speakers – in this case the community (and social network) of RP speakers.

These first two principles can be described as requirements to acknowledge the importance in language descriptions of: (1) the social and situational context of speech-exchanges, and (2) consensus on linguistic norms of usage within speech communities. There is a third principle, which can be seen as an extension of the idea of consensus norms into the diachronic dimension, and it is based on the notion of language *maintenance*. If we assume that the natural tendency of language is to diverge, relatively convergent states can be described as arising from language maintenance through agreement on, or acceptance of, particular norms of usage in the community. To the extent that linguistic changes take place in speech communities, however, they take place against a background of language maintenance, and the extent to which they are successful depends on the interplay of these two sets of social influences – those that encourage maintenance (or stability), on the one hand, and those that encourage change (or divergence), on the other. Principle 3 is fundamental to the design of the Belfast research projects which were initiated in order to follow out some arguments about linguistic change. Our various discussions since then, about 'language loyalty', 'focusing', 'social identity', social network and related matters, all grow directly out of the idea of language maintenance in the research design itself.

1.3   Language Maintenance and Language Change

The third principle can be stated thus:

> *Principle 3*   In order to account for differential patterns of change at particular times and places, we need first to take account of those factors that tend to maintain language states and resist change.

This is closely related to the *actuation problem*, which we discuss more fully in chapter 2, and the emphasis on language maintenance is the most salient difference between the way I have approached historical linguistic change and the approach of most other historical linguists. It also differentiates our sociolinguistic research from other work in that subject, including the large urban projects (such as Labov, 1966) that influenced the Belfast research in the first place. It gives rise to a number of consequential differences in approach. Historical linguists do not generally describe patterns of *maintenance*: they tend to focus on those things that are known to have changed and ignore those things that have not, and they can often explicate historical changes very elegantly without any reference at all to the social embedding of the changes concerned. What strikes me as important here, however, is the fact that if we focus exclusively on change and ignore maintenance, these non-social procedures can be quite easily justified: we can indeed propose sophisticated descriptions and highly constrained theories of linguistic change, without taking any account of social factors, and this is frequently done. However, if we pose the more basic question why some forms and varieties remain stable while others change, we cannot avoid reference to society. This is one of the justifications for Principle 3 in a socially-based model of change. Let me clarify it briefly.

If we are interested in how language states can remain stable and how speech communities *resist* change, we have almost no alternative but to take account of social factors. Suppose we notice that the structure of language X has remained stable for a century: it is not very interesting to point this out and then to leave it at that. We naturally want to know why it has remained stable when other states of language have changed, but in order to do this we have to study the social and speaker-based reasons that may account for the fact that it has *not* changed. In reality, languages change at given times in some ways and not in others, sometimes they change rapidly and sometimes slowly, some varieties are divergent and some convergent, and so on. Thus, the third principle that I have proposed above is clearly relevant in a range of very diverse language situations, and at widely differing levels of generality, and I shall have much more to say about this in later chapters.

I noted above that our Belfast research projects depended especially on this third principle. It is the idea of language maintenance that is most immediately relevant to the *historical* interests of this research, and that is what this book is also about. If you look at historical states of English, it is clear that some characteristics of the language have persisted through time while others have changed, and it is also clear, even in written documents, that early states of English were variable just as present-day English is. Therefore, we want to know how divergent forms and varieties of the language can be maintained across considerable periods of time, and how structured variability can persist through time. These interests influenced the original design of the Belfast research, and there were some other related interests (including dialectological interests, such as cross-dialectal comprehension and the question of access of non-standard speakers to so-called 'standard' languages). What these situations all have in common is the maintenance of distinctive norms of language and (very often) persistence of divergent varieties through time, but historical linguistic theorists haven't shown much interest in matters like this. Therefore, as a historical linguist, I thought that we might get a better understanding of what linguistic change actually is, and how and why it happens, if we could also come closer to specifying the conditions under which it does not happen – the conditions under which 'states' and forms of language are maintained and changes resisted.

This means, amongst other things, that we can see some of the traditional problems of historical explanation in a different light: for example, we might want to ask why apparently 'low prestige' varieties of language can persist over centuries, and why dialects of the same language can be maintained for long periods in forms that differ so much from one another that they are mutually incomprehensible. But the most general consequence of an interest in maintenance is the one I have mentioned above: it forces us to ask questions about *society* and to investigate the structure of the societies in which norms of language are maintained and changes implemented. If we focus on change alone, we can propose explanations that are language-internal without systematic reference to social processes, *but we cannot do this if we focus on maintenance: our answers have to be in some way socially based.*

Of course, none of this implies that historical linguists *never* appeal to social explanations: sometimes they do, but the appeals tend to be *ad hoc* appeals to 'prestige', 'the standard language' and the like, which assume the existence of speaker-links and power-structures in society, but which do not investigate these systematically. This has various consequences, but the one I need to call attention to here is that, as a result of the superficiality of the social analysis, accounts of the histories of particular languages have often been very heavily coloured by the social attitudes of the investigators themselves. Frequently, the researchers have not been able to observe social structures and processes in an impartial way: their subjective social attitudes have often been based on ideological positions which they have simply assumed to be 'common sense', and so not easily open to rational examination. They have then imposed these ideological positions on to the analysis 'from above', as in the following: 'Just as fashions in dress are binding upon all members of a given class and are imitated by all who look up to that class, so fashions in language are binding upon all people of culture and are followed by other members of the community to the best of their ability' (Sturtevant, 1917: 26). This is a unidimensional imposition of standards from the top; it is basically elitist, but quite mildly expressed. In some cases, as we shall see, the standard language ideology is much more strongly expressed, and in some accounts 'non-standard' forms and varieties are rejected as if they were not really 'language' at all. In chapter 5 we shall discuss the effects of standard-based attitudes on historical descriptions of English.

What we seem to need, therefore, is a theoretical orientation to the study of language maintenance that takes full account of social processes and therefore of social theories. Such an orientation, in contrast with theories that have focused on change alone, is in the fullest sense *sociolinguistic*. In this book I shall explore the social side of our subject more fully than has been usual, and in chapters 6 and 7 I shall attempt to develop an integrated social model for the interpretation of language change. In section 1.4, we first acknowledge the importance of the 'empirical foundations' of Weinreich, Labov and Herzog (1968).

1.4   The 'Empirical Foundations'

Whereas the three principles proposed above can be seen as basic in a context of language stability and maintenance, the 'empirical foundations' of Weinreich, Labov and Herzog (1968) are quite specifically directed towards a theory of language *change*. Furthermore, whereas our three principles are very definitely about the *social* nature of language variation, their principles are in practice more directly focused on locating the *linguistic* patterns of change. They are devoted to supporting the claim that linguistic innovations move in an orderly manner through space (social, geographical, historical) affecting linguistic structure also in an orderly manner. Thus, although there is no necessary contradiction between their principles and ours, we have tended over time to reinterpret their principles in the light of our own experiences in social and sociolinguistic analysis. The essential difference here can perhaps best be understood by recalling that whereas Labov's New York City study was specifically directed towards locating linguistic changes, our inner-city study of Belfast was primarily a study of maintenance, and therefore necessarily social for the reasons given above. Although it is assumed that change is in progress at any time in any speech community, we would not have been greatly concerned if, in this limited study, we had not found any evidence for change at all: we would have expected it to appear at some later stage.

According to Weinreich, Labov and Herzog, the task of explaining linguistic change is best divided into five parts – the problems of *constraints, embedding, evaluation, transition* and *actuation*. The first three of these are interrelated and we have tended to treat them as aspects of the same thing. The problem of the universal constraints on linguistic change would, if it were solved, specify which changes are possible and which are impossible, and predict which changes would happen in particular circumstances: much historical linguistic theorizing has been directed towards a solution to this problem. Here, however, we need to notice that although the term 'constraints' has often been understood as intra-linguistic, it is obviously possible to speak also of social constraints on change. Let us consider this briefly.

'Avoidance of homophony' (following Martinet's (1955) arguments, and see further chapter 2) may be considered to be an intra-linguistic constraint on change. In this spirit, I have pointed out (J. Milroy, 1976a) that the development of [eː] (as in *bait, sane*) in Belfast vernacular (henceforth BV) to [eɪ] (as in RP) may be blocked by the fact that the vernacular pronunciation of the word-class of *bite, sign* is already pronounced with [eɪ] in BV. Thus, if the RP-like pronunciation were adopted, there would be merger of two distinct lexical sets. However, following Principle 2 (which is concerned with consensus norms), the decisive constraint here and elsewhere is just as likely to be social as linguistic, because despite homonymic clash (of the *meat/meet* type), mergers do commonly occur in languages. Furthermore, in this case there would have to be some social motivation for moving in the RP direction in the first place. Our evidence suggests, however, that there is little or no such motivation: throughout most of the Belfast community there is no discernible movement in *phonetic* realization towards RP. Therefore, we can suggest very plausibly that the so-called 'prestige' motivation to adopt RP forms is overridden here by the solidarity constraint, which requires the speaker to conform to local community norms rather than to norms that are viewed as 'external'. It is very striking, after all, that in our inner-city work there were no examples at all of RP-like [eɪ] in closed syllables of the type *bait, sane*, and very similar points can be made about a number of other vowels (for further discussion see chapter 3).

In the Weinreich, Labov and Herzog programme, all aspects are said to be both social and linguistic, but it is the *evaluation* problem that is most clearly designated as social. This pertains principally to social responses to language change 'at all levels of awareness, from overt discussion to reactions that are quite inaccessible to introspection' (Labov, 1982: 28). It embraces notions of prestige, attitudes to language (both overt and covert), as well as linguistic stereotyping and notions of correctness. In practice, we have taken a rather wider view of what goes on in speech communities than the Weinreich, Labov and Herzog principles imply, and have tried to look at evaluation within the context of broader structural principles such as power and solidarity (Brown and Gilman, 1960), and interactional factors such as 'politeness' (Brown and Levinson, 1987) and 'accommodation' (Giles and Smith, 1979, Trudgill, 1986a). We have also been interested in how speech communities can reach consensus on the evaluation of linguistic forms and how this consensus can shift in the course of time.

It seems, however, that the problems of evaluation and constraints can be viewed as constituent, or contributory, parts of the more general problem of explaining the *embedding* of linguistic changes in pre-existing states of language and society. Labov's original contribution here (principally in the New York City study) has been to provide a general model of the social location of a linguistic innovation and of the manner in which it spreads from a central point upwards and downwards through a speech community. But clearly, this overlaps conceptually with the *transition* problem, in so far as the transition from one state to another must be described here also. Thus, the graphs and diagrams of the quantitative paradigm, when they show stable patterns, can be interpreted as displaying aspects of the linguistic *embedding* of a variable; when there is a crossover pattern, however, they also display transition.

Transition concerns 'the intervening stages which can be observed, or which must be posited, between any two forms of a language defined for a language community at different times' (Weinreich, Labov and Herzog, 1968: 101). Transition is what most historical description has been about, mapping (as it has usually done) the transition between state A at one period and state B at a later one.

Quantitative analysis here allows a gain in sophistication: the process by which one form gradually gives way to another can be demonstrated in fine-grained detail in what is generally an orderly progression through different social groups and speech-styles (for a study of this kind, see Eckert, 1980).

The fifth problem – actuation – is a very different kind of problem from these others, and I shall not consider it here. We shall return to it in Chapter 2 and later chapters, and I shall suggest that a solution to it must be based on the behaviour of speakers rather than primarily on the properties of languages. Here, it is appropriate to comment on some general differences that seem to exist between the Weinreich, Labov and Herzog methods of accounting for change in language systems and our own approach to it. The chief difference, as I have suggested above, is that whereas their programme and Labov's work within it are based on first being able to locate linguistic changes in progress, our work has been more generally based on describing variation in the speech community and accounting for differing patterns (whether or not they exhibit change in progress) in social terms. In other words, our notion of the embedding of change in the speech community is broader, and as a result our idea of what a linguistic change actually is is broader and less traditional than Labov's view appears to be. It also raises the question of what a sound-change actually is: how do we know when we have located one, and how does the pattern of a change differ from other patterns that we might locate?

I shall discuss these matters more fully in later chapters, but I can lay some of the groundwork here. Traditional codifications of sound-change have generally focused on sound-segments as they 'change' across time. Thus – to simplify – a linguistic change can be described as a change from A to B in some lexical set, such as that of Old English [aː] in *stān, hām*, which in the course of time 'becomes' an [oː]-like vowel in PresE (Present English) *stone, home*. The transitional stages can be postulated in the Middle English period or studied directly, as in Kristensson's (1967) study of onomastic sources from abround 1300, from which figure 1.1 is compiled, showing the northward progress of the 'new' rounded vowel in this set at that time (the rounded vowel has penetrated further northward in the west, that is, in Lancashire and the West Riding, than in the east, that is, in Lincolnshire). Labov's treatment of sound-change seems to be quite similar to this traditional treatment in that a change

OE *āc, brād, Brāding, *cā, dā, drāf, hān, hlāford, *hlāfording, (ge)lād, rā, rāp, stān*
ON *blár, gás, grár, pá, skáli, vrá* in uncompounded names and ME *pācok/pōcok*

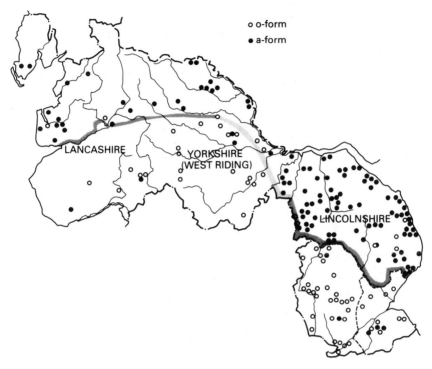

Figure 1.1   Northward progression of ō for OE ā (in words of the type *āc*: 'oak') *c.*1290–1350. (Adapted from Kristensson, 1967)

is generally located by comparative methods (comparing different social groups in real and apparent time) within a single segment or a very limited class of sounds.

We have also used these methods, but our conceptualization of linguistic change is broader and is largely based on the normative principle that I proposed above: linguistic change is to be understood more broadly as changes in consensus on norms of usage in a speech community. During the process there will be some disagreement or conflict on norms at some levels in the community, but if a change is ever 'completed', then it will be possible to say that some community of speakers agrees that what was formerly A is now B. But this can apply at different levels of generality – from a single sound-segment up to a language state as a whole. Thus – to take a much more generalized case than, say, post-vocalic /r/ in New York City – if a language state is observed to become more (or less) homogeneous within itself in the course of time, then the trend to greater or lesser homogeneity is itself a pattern of linguistic change that has to be accounted for in terms of consensus or conflict amongst speakers within the speech community.

We might wish to look, for example, at Australian English in this way. It is much more homogeneous than British English, even though the early settlers came from many different places. If it has moved from an early heterogeneous state to a more homogeneous one, this is itself a linguistic change relevant to the history of Australian English and aspects of colonial language development in general. Thus, many of the detailed patterns that we are likely to find in sociolinguistic inquiries will not be unidimensional (as more traditional work often suggests), but bidimensional or multidimensional, showing trends towards greater agreement or greater disagreement on norms within the communities (see further J. Milroy, 1982b, and chapters 3 and 4).

1.5   Synopsis

The purpose of chapter 2 is to place the general theme of this book in perspective by considering the relationship between historical linguistic explanations of a non-social kind and sociolinguistic explanations of language change. I do not attempt to review all current intra-linguistic work on change, as my main aim is to propose a different (social) way of looking at change, but I discuss some of the main trends. Following out my social arguments and Principle 1, I shall focus on conversational settings as the locus of change, and I shall suggest that language change is made possible to the extent that it is passed from person to person in speaker encounters, in which the apparently dysfunctional nature of language change is counteracted by features of the communicative context (this idea is developed from our early work in Belfast on speech and context: L. Milroy and J. Milroy, 1977).

Chapters 3 and 4 are chiefly about analysing language in the community and interpreting the patterns revealed, bearing in mind Principles 2 and 3 (on linguistic norms and language maintenance). The main database is the Belfast research, from which I have selected examples. My purpose is to build the general foundations in these chapters, starting with the observation and analysis of language in the community. In chapter 5, I extend the perspective backwards in time, and consider some case-studies of language maintenance over periods of time that are relevant to historical interpretation. In this chapter we have to consider what we mean by a sound-change in history, and we conclude with a brief discussion of Neogrammarian views on how sound-change is implemented.

Chapters 6 and 7 are the main theoretical chapters and are devoted to the social modelling of linguistic change. In chapter 6, I outline a social model which is derived from the social network model that we have used to study language maintenance, and I propose a model of 'weak ties' to account for the possibility of language change. As this model does not account for broader social structures and processes, I explore in chapter 7 the links between network and social class in an attempt to build up a more comprehensive social model for the interpretation of language change.

2

Social and Historical Linguistics

2.0   Explaining Language Change

The ultimate aim of historical linguistics is to explain the *causation* of linguistic change. The question of causation is beset with difficulties, but we can focus on it here by stating Weinreich, Labov and Herzog's formulation of *the actuation problem* (1968: 102): 'Why do changes in a structural feature take place in a particular language at a given time, but not in other languages with the same feature, or in the same language at other times? This *actuation problem* may be regarded as the very heart of the matter.' In attempting to solve the actuation problem we are concerned with no less than the origin of change: we want to locate its beginnings and by any means possible attempt to explain why that particular change was initiated and diffused at some particular time and place. It seems clear that to tackle it, we must take account of how *speakers* initiate changes, and I shall treat it in later chapters in these terms.

The actuation problem, however, is so challenging that historical linguists do not usually address it directly; this is hardly surprising as, when it is formulated in this way, it is actually insoluble: a solution to it implies the capacity to *predict*, not only what particular change will happen, but also when and where it will happen. However, the probability of any event in life actually taking place at some particular and specified place and time is close to zero. Weather prediction is a convenient analogy here: we can predict from meteorological observations that it will rain on a particular day with a high probability of being correct, but if we predict that in a particular place it will start raining at one minute past eleven and stop at six minutes past twelve, the probability of the prediction being correct is vanishingly low. Nevertheless, we would be bad meteorologists if we did not try to improve the accuracy of our predictions, and of course this greater accuracy includes the ability to specify the conditions under which something will not happen as well as the conditions under which it will happen. In view of all this, we have no excuse as linguists for not addressing the actuation problem.

The Weinreich, Labov and Herzog formulation has several implications that are important for a theory of language change, and some of these can be understood fairly readily if we cite as an example a kind of sound-change that is frequently observed in languages and is sometimes called 'natural'. So let us consider here the palatalization of /k/ before front vowels. Suppose it happens (as it often does) that one particular language (or dialect) undergoes this palatalization, whereas a closely related language (or dialect) of very similar structure does not. Following the Weinreich, Labov and Herzog principles, we have to ask why it happened in one variety but not in the other. We also have to ask why it should have happened at some particular time and not at some other time, when the structure of the relevant language presumably exhibited suitable conditions for the change at times when it did not happen as well as at the time when it did. There are, of course, well-known examples of varying developments of this kind: amongst the continental Scandinavian languages, Swedish and Norwegian have palatalization of Old Norse /k/, whereas Danish now usually has a velar; Old English underwent palatalization before front vowels whereas Old High German and Old Norse did not: hence PresE *cheese* for German *käse* and English/ Norse doublets in PresE such as *shirt/skirt*; many Hiberno-English dialects (J. Milroy, 1981, and elsewhere) have [k]-palatalization in words of the type *car, cart*, whereas most other English dialects do not.[1] What we observe here are conflicting patterns of change and stability in languages and dialects of similar structure. In these examples it seems that the proximity of the velar consonant to a front vowel may be a *necessary* condition for palatalization, but as it does not happen in every case, it is not a *sufficient* condition. We need to find out what the other conditions favouring or preventing the change might have been, and it seems that in cases where the change was adopted the *social* conditions must have been favourable; conversely, when it was not adopted, it may again have been social conditions that prevented the change. This suggests that to make progress in understanding actuation we must take into account the activities of speakers in social contexts in addition to the internal structural properties of language.

Indeed, although linguistic changes are observed to take place in *linguistic systems*, they must necessarily come about as a result of the activities of *speakers*. As we have noted in chapter 1, languages which have no speakers (or – sometimes – writers) do not change, and so these remarks may well seem uncontroversial to any non-specialist who has given thought to the matter. After all, there is no point in having a language if it is not used by human beings. It seems to be specialists, rather than non-specialists, who think that language change can be explained without reference to society. Within orthodox historical linguistics, the emphasis has generally been on the properties of linguistic *systems*, and speaker-roles have been referred to indirectly and sometimes very vaguely. As Lass (1980: 120–2) points out, historical linguists have tended to regard language as an 'autonomous formal system' or natural object and have preferred to believe that it is 'languages that change and *not* speakers that change languages'. Thus, historical descriptions and theories of historical change have generally focused on the structural properties of language and not on its speakers. This tendency is very deeply embedded in historical theorizing, and it is appropriate to look at it a little more closely here.

2.1   System-based Accounts of Change

The orthodox position as stated by Lass (1980) is not entirely a twentieth-century phenomenon: the separation of language from speakers has an ancient and honourable pedigree, and the nineteenth-century emphasis on the independent 'life' of language is by present-day standards very striking. According to Trench (1888: 223–4), language has a life 'as surely as a man or a tree', and creativity in language in developing new forms is attributed by Max Müller (1881: 33) not to the creativity of speakers, but to the 'marvellous power of language' itself: according to him (1861: 36) 'it is not in the power of man either to produce or prevent' linguistic change. Müller's adoption of the biological metaphor is so strongly stated that for him it does not seem to have been a metaphor at all: linguistics, according to Müller, is literally a *physical* science on a par with geology, botany and biology, and not a *historical* science, such as art, morals or religion. 'Physical science', including linguistics, 'deals with the works of God' whereas 'historical science deals with the works of man' (1861: 22). Language therefore does not have *history*, it has *growth*. The metaphor has weakened since Müller wrote, but there have been many publications on language history since then that have been based on the idea of the independent 'life' of language. Indeed, the metaphor is by no means dead: this is amply demonstrated by continued references in recent work to 'language birth', 'language death' and the 'roots' of language.

Of course, it is not true that language is a living thing (any more than swimming, or birdsong, is a living thing): it is a vehicle for communication *between* living things, namely human beings. Hence, the metaphor has been largely replaced since the nineteenth century by a new metaphor based on the machine age: language is now more often seen as a self-contained *system*, like a working machine. The acceptance of this metaphor is widespread enough for it to appear in the title of a book on linguistics – *The Twitter Machine* (Smith, 1989) – and it is clearly greatly encouraged by developments in computer modelling of language. However, whereas the nineteenth-century metaphor could readily incorporate the idea of change (as language was said to have 'growth' within it, like a plant), this system-based approach cannot so easily do so. Internal combustion engines, for example, do not initiate structural changes within themselves. From this point of view, therefore, the system-based model may seem to be an unsuitable one to use as the basis for studying language change. What is certainly clear is that within this perspective our attempts at explanation continue to be essentially language-internal. When speakers are referred to, they are decontextualized and asocial abstractions.[2]

Possibly as a result of the emphasis on internal language systems, descriptive accounts (such as histories of English) commonly separate the *internal* history of a language from its *external* history (that is, the political, social and attitudinal contexts of language). Thus, some historical accounts of English, such as Wyld (1927), have been mainly internal (typically focusing on sound-change and morphological change), whereas others (such as McKnight, 1928) have been about the external history of the language, discussing, for example, speaker-attitudes to variation as they were expressed by seventeenth- and eighteenth-century commentators. Both of these approaches can of course yield insights; however, it is commonly believed that the 'real' history of a language is its internal system-based history and that the external history is relatively unimportant. The traditional position on internal and external histories has again been clearly stated by Lass (1987: 34–5), who claims quite explicitly that in most respects 'external' accounts do not help to explain changes in linguistic structure. According to him, 'there was nothing in the 17th century English political or social climate' that could account for, for example, the merger of the formerly distinct vowels in words of the type *bird, fern, hurt*; he further states that 'at the structural level there is no connection between language and society' and that 'the internal life of language is close to autonomous.' My position, which I shall further develop below, is – on the contrary – that we cannot hope to explain change *without* inquiring into social factors.[3]

One reason for this is that intra-linguistic arguments with only vague references to speakers, or accounts that explicitly reject speakers, are not in themselves capable of dealing with *actuation*, as it is speakers who actuate changes. Nevertheless, the causes of change (like the causes of illness) are multiple; therefore, we need to take both speakers and systems into account and, if possible, specify the link between speaker-activity and change in language systems. As for intra-linguistic theorizing, its main contribution has been to specify in a more and more refined way the linguistic *constraints* on change, not its causes. In order to exemplify the mode of argument used in system-based accounts, we can consider here Kiparsky's recent review (1988) of progress in the study of phonological change.

This account is system-based and set in the traditional controversy about whether sound-change operates blindly and without exceptions (the Neogrammarian *exceptionlessness hypothesis*), or whether other approaches over the last century (such as *lexical diffusion*) have invalidated the hypothesis. The lexical diffusion model (Wang, 1969) holds that sound-changes may be lexically gradual: thus, in a change from /eː/ to /iː/ (such as the EModE (Early Modern English) change in words of the type *meat, peace, leave*), items are transferred to the new class at differential rates, often leaving a residue of items that do not get transferred (in this case such words as *great, break, steak*). Neogrammarian theory, however, has generally been interpreted to mean that the relevant class of items all undergo the change at the same time, that is, that sound-change is phonetically gradual and lexically sudden.

Kiparsky reconciles these approaches by arguing in terms of *lexical phonology*: those changes that appear not to fit into the Neogrammarian hypothesis (including instances of lexical diffusion, in which items in a class are not affected simultaneously by a change) are part of the *lexical rule* component, whereas Neogrammarian exceptionless change is accounted for by *post-lexical rules*. There is more to his argument than this, but I am not concerned here, of course, with the precise content of the argument – although I have tried not to do any gross injustice to it – but with its intellectual background, and specifically its intra-linguistic nature. In this argument, certain points are evident. First, the argument is system-oriented and not speaker-oriented (specifically, it is about phonological rules), and its goal is a 'grammar' of linguistic change; the activities of speakers are not given prominence in the argument. Second, it is set in the traditional controversy about the regularity of sound-change in language systems (and certain other binary distinctions that arise from it, which attempt to specify constraints on change: for example, whether sound-change is lexically gradual or sudden). Third, it is proposed that the two patterns of change can be accounted for by fitting them into a new binary taxonomy based on lexical phonology. Thus, the discussion casts new light on an old controversy by redefining the controversy within a non-social system-based linguistics; it specifies the problem in a more refined and elegant way, and its proposals are then subject to critical discussion, testing and further refinements.

But this account, like many others, does not primarily address the actuation problem, and the question why (and how) *speakers* initiate changes is not central to the intellectual context in which it is conceived. It is true that there are two pages on 'causes of sound change' that acknowledge the work of sociolinguists in this area – particularly Labov, Yaeger and Steiner (1972) and Kroch (1978) – but the discussion of 'causes' does not form the backbone of the account. The main aim of historical phonology, as represented here, is the construction of sophisticated system-based *grammars* of change, and the problem of how speakers *actuate* changes is not directly addressed. It is interesting (and much to be welcomed), therefore, that Kiparsky includes an extensive and skilful discussion of the Labov–Sankoff *variable rule* paradigm. The significance of this here is that variable rules are, of course, themselves explicitly *system*-based (Cedergren and Sankoff, 1974, and see chapter 6, below, for a fuller discussion of this point): they are grammars of language and not accounts of actuation. Thus, whereas speaker-based studies cannot easily be incorporated into orthodox system-based accounts, variable rules can fit in perfectly and add sophistication to grammars of change.

A second quite recent example of intra-linguistic argumentation is Lass's *On Explaining Language Change* (1980), to which I have referred above. Lass states that linguists have proceeded language-internally and have taken the view that it is languages that change, not speakers that change languages. But he is also critical of sociolinguistic accounts of change and seems to dismiss them. He says that when attempts have been made to introduce the speaker into explanations of language change, these attempts have been 'superficial and otiose', and he considers (p. 121) even Labov's notion of 'speech community' to be 'a very tenuous abstraction' (more on this below). Taking his cue from the tradition, he points out that the most fruitful results for theories of language change have come about precisely because historical linguistics has studied 'formal objects and their mutations over time, not . . . their inventors or users'.

The point that great advances in the past have come about through intra-linguistic argumentation cannot be disputed. One thinks especially of the great innovators of the nineteenth century, such as Bopp, Rask, Grimm and Verner, but also of modern advances, such as work on language universals, lexical phonology and many other areas. However, it plainly does not follow from any of this that we should therefore neglect the role of speakers in linguistic change. If we do not know what role speakers play, it seems appropriate that we should investigate it empirically.

Before we look at this more fully, however, we need to notice that it would not be correct to infer from what Lass says that older generations of scholars always neglected the role of speakers. On the contrary, there are several great names who assumed that linguistic change must have social origins (amongst others) and who did not think it beneath them to write extensively on this, while at the same time contributing fully to system-based accounts of language. Among these are Henry Sweet, H. C. Wyld, E. H. Sturtevant and Otto Jespersen. In Sturtevant's *Linguistic Change* (1917), we find an emphasis on the idea of social norm-enforcement, childish errors and slips of the tongue, and (incidentally) a plea for the study of universals of language change. All this is presented in a framework that distinguishes *primary change* (compare our idea of *speaker-innovation*) from *secondary change* (effectively, linguistic change as admitted into grammars of language). Thus, a speaker/system distinction similar to that which we have proposed (J. Milroy and L. Milroy, 1985b) is considered by Sturtevant, and he attempts to integrate the two sides of the question. Jespersen's *Language* (1922), which is a better-known book, reads in places like a research proposal for modern sociolinguistics and language acquisition studies: the possible causes of change include features of children's language, sex-differences (there is a chapter on 'The Woman'), taboo and euphemism (unfashionable at the moment, but unquestionably very important), language contact, and Pidgin and Creole development.

It seems that if speaker-based arguments have since that time been found unsatisfactory, there may have been contingent reasons for this. The correct generalization seems to be, not that speakers are irrelevant to change in language systems, but simply that it has in the past been extremely difficult to study speaker-behaviour in a systematic and accountable way. As we noticed in chapter 1, early investigators, such as Wyld, did not have the necessary technology – in particular they did not have tape-recorders. So, until about 1960 it was very difficult to explore their ideas further by experiment or systematic observation and impossible to study conversational interaction in a reliable way. Dialect investigations were usually limited to single-word citation forms, and the empirical study of discourse in situational contexts could hardly have been contemplated. This, clearly, is no longer true. Although we are still interested in 'formal objects and their mutations over time', advances in data collection from live speakers, and the analysis of such data, have put us in a position to inquire into the role of speakers in change. If we do not know what role speakers play in implementing changes, we can inquire further into that role – we do not need any longer to dismiss it as impossible to explain.

Before we go on in the next section to amplify this discussion by looking at the *functions* of change, we can draw together the strands of the argument so far. Historical linguistics in this century has largely depended on the idea that language is a self-contained system, and investigators have generally not systematically addressed the question of how *speakers* can introduce changes into the structural parts of language. Thus, complaints about the superficiality of 'external' explanations of change are in a sense self-fulfilling prophecies. Clearly, if you concentrate exclusively on abstract systems of language and do not develop a coherent and accountable theory of the social embedding of language change, your comments on the possible social reasons for changes will inevitably be *ad hoc* and superficial.

But although the above remarks are concerned with theory rather than description, they are relevant to descriptive accounts also: for example, to historical descriptions of English. It is impossible to write a reasonably full history of English without making at least some reference to social categories, such as class, and to institutional aspects of language, such as standardization. Indeed, system-based accounts, such as that of Lass (1987) himself, do routinely make reference to 'class', 'prestige' and other socially-based 'external' categories. What most of these histories of language have done is to refer to these social matters in an *ad hoc* way, without contemplating an accountable theory of the social embedding and motivation of language change. Indeed, as we noticed in chapter 1, some invest-igators, being themselves embedded in a social matrix, have filtered their social explanations through their own 'common sense' views of social class and social prestige, without clearly acknowledging that these are themselves complex theoretical concepts, and certainly not 'common sense'.

There seems to be no reason why we should not inquire further into social structures and processes as part of an inquiry into linguistic change, and no reason why we should not also think of linguistic change as being an aspect of social change in general, that is, to think of it in an entirely new perspective. But to do these things is not to exclude the possibility of also developing sophisticated internal accounts of language change. Both kinds of approach are needed – and one should contribute to the other – because although linguistic change must be initiated by speakers (and is therefore a social phenomenon) it is manifested as internal to language. Bearing these questions in mind, therefore, I shall move on in section 2.2 to consider in what senses linguistic variation and change can be shown to be *functional*. It is important to consider this question, because from an intra-linguistic point of view variation and change can actually appear to be *dysfunctional*.

2.2   The Functions and Malfunctions of Change and Variation

In the introductory sections of chapter 1, we were mainly concerned with structural aspects of language, exploring the apparent conflict between the structuralist axiom – that a language is a coherent self-contained system of interdependent parts – and the fact that language is continuously changing. In what follows I am concerned with *function*: I want to consider whether linguistic change is functional, that is, whether it serves a purpose of some kind, and if so in what sense it is functional. Here we need to recall that it is very widely asserted by linguistic scholars that a language system is at any given time equally well adapted to the functions for which it is used: sometimes it is said to be *perfectly* adapted. Whether or not this is true, it is reasonable to assume that linguistic structure is very sensitive to the changing social and communicative needs of speakers. Furthermore, Weinreich, Labov and Herzog (1968) have claimed that linguistic variation (which can be a symptom of language change) is not only structured, but also functional, and that *it is the absence of variation that would be dysfunctional*.[4] In order to investigate the functions of language, however, we have to look at language in use, but as the functions of language in use are social and pragmatic, they are not readily accounted for within an exclusively system-based theory of language structure. We therefore have to look at *speakers* in addition to systems. Traditional speculation as to whether linguistic change is functional or not has, however, been based on the configuration of systems rather than on speaker-use of language.

Speculation about the functions of change has been common in the past: it has, for example, been suggested that there is a teleology, or overall purpose, in language change (for a discussion of this, see Lass, 1980), and even that change in language structures may follow a predestined path. This is plainly related to the idea of language as an independent 'growth' with a 'life' of its own. In this view of language, however, speakers would play little part in its development and could do very little about linguistic change, as the blind force of language in its purposive quest would overrule them (recall again the views of Müller, 1861). Related to these ideas in a general way is Sapir's (1921) notion of 'drift'. It is striking, as Prokosch (1939) points out, that related languages can undergo the same changes apparently independently: all the early Germanic languages, for example (except Gothic, records of which are too early), independently underwent the important change known as *front-mutation* or *i-umlaut*. It is as if the 'parent' language was programmed in such a way that the conditions were already present in it for the change to take place in all the 'daughter' languages.

It has also been suggested that language can make progress and improve in the course of time: for Henry Sweet (Henderson, 1971), the loss of grammatical gender in English constituted progress, as grammatical gender, according to him, is 'illogical'; Jespersen (1922) argued that modern languages of 'analytic' (weakly inflected) structure, such as English and Danish, have evolved to a higher stage than 'synthetic' (heavily inflected) languages, such as classical Latin, and are more efficient instruments of communication, mainly because they are thought to have a more transparent one-to-one relationship between meaning and form.[5] For example, an auxiliary verb phrase, such as English *I have said . . .* , is more transparent than the Latin equivalent *dixi* because person, tense and aspect in English are expressed in separate units, whereas in Latin they are all carried in the second syllable of *dixi* and cannot be unravelled from its surface form. Jespersen's judgement here depends, of course, on the assumption that transparency in language structure is a desirable thing. Clearly, however, if some other criterion were used (and such criteria as euphony, economy and elegance have also been used), completely different conclusions might be drawn, and Latin might then be held to be superior to English, as it often has been; therefore, it is safer to assume that differences in overall grammatical structure are neutral. They can all be used equally efficiently or inefficiently by the speakers of the languages concerned.

I have described these kinds of argument as speculative because it is impossible to test them empirically: they are based on value judgements, which are often ethnocentric or class-based, and in the wrong hands they can sometimes lead to quite damaging opinions. For example, if it is believed that the structure of one language is superior to that of another, it can then be suggested that this is due to the cognitive superiority of its speakers. In fact, there seems to be nothing inherent in the structural properties of language to suggest that change has a positive function within language structure.[6] Within these structural parts – phonology, grammar, lexical and semantic structure – it is quite impossible to demonstrate empirically that language *systems* have in-built tendencies towards progress or decay, that one language is more or less 'efficient' than another, or that there is a teleology in linguistic change. If change is functional, it must be speaker-functions that are involved.

In fact, if we focus exclusively on the internal properties of language, it is much easier to make a *prima facie* case for the argument that variation and change in language are *dysfunctional*, rather than functional. This is because dialect divergence and language change lead to difficulties in communication between speakers – a fact that is obvious to any fieldworker who studies a 'divergent' dialect, and to any analyst who transcribes the tape-recordings (they can be very difficult to understand); it is also familiar to anyone who tries to read an early English text. Therefore, if linguistic structure exists for the purpose of successful communication, why does language change? Why do languages diverge from one another in the course of time, and why are some dialects of a language partly or wholly incomprehensible to speakers of other dialects? The apparent paradox has of course been noticed by many, and it has been quite recently commented on by Francis (1983: 15–16):

> If the purpose of language is communication, it would seem that the more homogeneous the language, the more efficient the communication. Why, then, does the increasing variation resulting from differential change not make communication difficult, unreliable, and eventually impossible? If so, the propensity for language to change would ultimately lead to a breakdown in the principal function for which language exists.

It is interesting that Francis – as a dialectologist – seems to presuppose here that increasing divergence does *not* lead to breakdown of communication. One only has to look at the histories of related languages that were at one time dialects of the same language to realize, of course, that it *does* lead to breakdown. There is no need to disagree with Wyld (1936: 7): 'the process of differentiation is almost infinite, and the tendency of language is not, as it has sometimes been wrongly said, in the direction of uniformity, but of variety.' Language change can, and does, lead to breakdown of communication.

The belief that language change is dysfunctional is most clearly expressed in popular attitudes to language. These commonly conceive of languages as ideal and perfect structures, and of speakers as awkward creatures who violate these perfect structures by misusing and corrupting 'language': this is essentially a belief in the rape of languages by speakers. These attitudes are strongly expressed and highly resistant to rational examination. So strong is this intolerance of speaker-variation and change that in many countries academies have been set up to enforce a uniform 'correct' usage and to prevent uncontrolled divergence; indeed, in the biblical story of the Tower of Babel, language diversity is attributed to original sin. There are, of course, socio-political and economic reasons for these attitudes, which we have discussed elsewhere (J. Milroy and L. Milroy, 1985a), but they are powerful and deep-seated and they cannot be ignored.

In so far as these prescriptive agencies have a rational purpose, this purpose seems to be the maintenance of communicative efficiency in carrying information-bearing messages over long distances and periods of time. For conveying information in these ways, uniformity and standardization of language are highly valued, and it is usually in the written channel that the highest level of this kind of efficiency is achieved. Spoken language, as far as we can tell, continues to vary and change, and it is in spoken language, and not in writing, that structural (for example, phonological) change is implemented. Writing systems promote uniformity and suppress variation and change: it is typically in the day-to-day situational contexts of speaker-interaction that structural changes take place, and it is in these contexts that they have to be investigated. That is why Principle 1, which I put forward in chapter 1, should be borne in mind.

Popularly expressed attitudes to correctness and uniformity, therefore, do not square with what human beings actually do in conversational contexts. On the one hand they believe in uniformity, while on the other they promote diversity. Clearly, if speakers consistently carried their expressed beliefs into practice, the result would be a uniform and stable state of language – the world of the idealized native speaker in a perfectly homogeneous speech community – and not the diversity that exists in the real world. It seems, therefore, that in expressing adverse judgements on variation, speakers are subscribing to the notion that the main function of language *should be* the successful communication of information-bearing messages (as in the writing system), and there is plenty of evidence that from this point of view variation and change can indeed be dysfunctional. But there is also plenty of evidence that the successful communication of information-bearing messages is not the only function (or necessarily the main function) of language in use. To clarify the argument, I shall now consider some examples of communication difficulties that arise from language diversity.

2.3   Malfunctions of Language Diversity

Cross-dialectal miscomprehension was one of the interests that led to the setting-up of the Belfast research programme.[7] We were interested in the first place in how commonly differential linguistic structures could lead to miscomprehension, and more specifically whether 'non-standard' speakers actually have the easy access to standard English that is so often assumed. This has further theoretical implications – especially for the idea of the 'polylectal' or 'pan-lectal' grammar of English, which was a current interest in the 1970s. Within the projects, we collected many examples of cross-dialectal divergence and miscomprehension, of which the following is an example. Speaker A is a speaker of a Hiberno-English dialect, and B and C are 'standard' speakers:

(1)   A   How long are yous here?
     B   Oh, we're staying till next week.
        (silence of about 2 seconds)
     C   We've been here since Tuesday.
     A   Ah well, yous are here a while then.

The miscomprehension here is indicated by the period of silence after B's reply, and it arises from the clash between different linguistic systems. In certain constructions Hiberno-English dialects consistently use the *present* tense where standard English uses the present *perfect*. Thus, 'How long are yous here?' (in HibE) means *How long have you been here?*, whereas in SE (Standard English) the present tense form means (or at least implies) *How long are you going to stay here?* or *What is the total length of your stay?* Speaker B construes the HibE utterance according to the SE rules. An 'appropriate' response, however (one which would be immediately perceived as *relevant* to the question in this conversation), would in HibE refer to the past (for example, 'since Tuesday') and not to the future. While it is true that breakdowns occur for many reasons other than this, there is no doubt that breakdowns arising from the different structures of divergent dialects are quite common (see also Berdan, 1977; Trudgill, 1981), and that they are naturally perceived as inconvenient when they are noticed.

Sometimes, however, there is no period of silence or hesitation, as in (1), and the conversation proceeds apparently normally, even though there actually has been a misunderstanding. The hearer may continue to believe that the first speaker has said something quite different from what was intended, or the hearer may wait for the miscommunication to be 'repaired', or it may simply not seem to matter very much at the time. But we do have attested cases where the miscomprehension could be quite serious. In some Hiberno-English (and Scottish) dialects, the conjunction *whenever* is used almost equivalently to *when*. Thus, if someone says: 'Whenever my husband came in he beat me', we know from observing Ulster usage that the reference is to one occasion only: the speaker is *not* suggesting that her husband beat her *every time* that he came in. An outsider, however, is likely to interpret this to mean that the husband beat her many times. Consider also the following exchange:

(2)　A　Do you think he's going to die?
　　　B　I doubt so.

B, who is a speaker of Hiberno-English, does not mean that he believes that the person will *not* die; his meaning is the opposite. He is saying that he is afraid that the person *will* die (the utterance means approximately 'I'm afraid so'). In this case, I was Speaker A, and the usage was known to me as a widely distributed one in Scots and Irish dialects. If the interlocutors do not have access to the two different systems, however, there will be a miscomprehension. Thus, if a newscaster says 'Mr Major doubts that the economy will deteriorate', speakers of these dialects may interpret this to mean that he is afraid the economy *will* deteriorate, when the speaker actually means that he thinks that it *won't* deteriorate.

These cases of breakdown arise from deep-lying differences in the syntactic structures of the different dialects, which make the pan-dialectal grammar (Bailey, 1973) of English a dubious proposition.[8] The semantic distinctions carried in the Hiberno-English tense/

aspect system are structured totally differently from standard English (Harris, 1984; J. Milroy and L. Milroy, 1985a); thus, the miscommunication in example (1) is due to major differences in the abstract rule-systems of these dialects. Furthermore, all those involved in the miscommunications reported above are native speakers of English, but it appears that their 'native speaker intuitions' (or competences) do not extend to the rules of all relevant varieties. These examples also show, therefore, that our native speaker competence does not necessarily guarantee comprehension of varieties that are removed from us in time, space or social space. To put it simply – we do not have total comprehension of dialects divergent from our own.

The assumption that speakers of a language are (or should be) mutually comprehensible is rather basic in popular attitudes to language, and it also seems to underlie some professional linguistic approaches (for example, Smith and Wilson, 1981). Clearly, if there can be miscomprehensions arising from structural differences in the dimensions of spatial and social variation, it is likely that in the chronological dimension of change there will also be miscomprehensions. A change entering the language of a younger generation, for example, may well be miscomprehended by older generation speakers. However, the idea that mutual comprehensibility between generations is a *constraint* on possible changes is quite deep-rooted amongst historical linguists (see Lightfoot, 1979: 376, for a justification), and is often taken for granted. But it is dangerous to assume this too lightly: we cannot demonstrate that mutual comprehensibility between generations (or between groups of other kinds) is always a *necessary* factor in determining which linguistic changes are possible and which are impossible, and sociolinguistic investigations (from which most of the data reported in this book are derived) strongly suggest that it is not always primary. It may be that some innovative groups do not particularly wish to be comprehensible to others, or that rapid social change (for example, in the genesis of Pidgin/Creole languages) overrides the principle of mutual comprehensibility. The constraint proposed by Lightfoot is, it seems, a variant of the idea that heterogeneity is necessarily dysfunctional, and that mutual intelligibility is functional. It seems to me, however, that the question we should be asking is why linguistic changes that lead to miscomprehension (and divergence into mutually incomprehensible varieties) can happen at all. What is the motivation for such changes, and what is their function?

The examples discussed above concern variations in language structure that lead to comprehension difficulties, but they have also raised, in a much more general way, the question of what actually happens in conversational exchanges between speakers. In section 2.4, I shall be concerned with this latter point: I shall attempt to show that it is the multiple speaker-functions of language in use that make linguistic change possible and suggest that we must look at these speaker-functions if we are to make progress in understanding the nature of language change. This implies a modelling of the locus of linguistic change that differs from system-based models of the kind that we have discussed The language-internal presuppositions of these models have been projected on to the mental capacities of human beings, and linguistic change has thus been seen as consisting primarily of changes in the mental representations of the speaker in the form of rule-addition, rule-loss, and other rule-changes. But as we cannot directly observe mental representations (whether they are described as rules or in some other way, for example, as parameter-settings), suggestions of this kind are somewhat more speculative than matters that can be verified by observing speaker-interaction. In order to propose a more socially realistic account of change, there-fore, Labov has argued that the locus of change is not in the individual speaker, but in the group, or at least that we have to look for it in group behaviour. What is implied here is more specific than that: it is that linguistic change is located in speaker-*interaction* and is negotiated between speakers in the course of interaction, much as other aspects of discourse are negotiated between them. Bearing in mind this speaker/system distinction, therefore, I shall introduce the discussion of speaker-function in section 2.4 by first considering the way in which functional change has been handled in system-based historical linguistics.

2.4   The System-oriented Approach to Function

The system-oriented (as opposed to speaker-oriented) approach to functional change originates with Martinet (1955), whose arguments depend on the information-bearing function of language and the presumed need to preserve mutual intelligibility. I have commented briefly on this in chapter 1. Martinet proposes that in phonetic/

phonological change a phonetic opposition that is useful in maintaining meaning-bearing distinctions will, other things being equal, resist neutralization and loss of distinctiveness. Thus, for example, if the speakers of English had found it useful in communicating information to maintain the EModE phonetic distinction between words of the *meet, beet* class and words of the *meat, beat* class, they would, according to the theory, have been inclined to maintain it. The fact that they did not (in some dialects) requires a functional explanation, which in effect proposes that the distinction between the two phoneme classes was no longer useful in maintaining meaning-bearing distinctions, and this is generally argued in terms of *functional load* (see especially Samuels, 1972). It is suggested that one of the two categories had low functional load in distinguishing between words in ordinary usage; for example, the words in that class might not have been used very often, and when they were used, they were perhaps used in contexts where confusion with the other class was unlikely to occur (thus, as *meet* is a verb, whereas *meat* is a noun, it is unlikely that you will misunderstand *I meet him* as **I meat him*).

This type of functional argument can also be used to explain exceptions to 'regular' changes. For example, the idea of *homonymic clash* may be used to explain why certain items in early English did not undergo regular development: if they had, they would have become phonetically identical with other forms. Lass (1980) cites the item *shut*, which if it had developed regularly would have become identical with *shit*: according to the theory this was prevented by the functional need to keep the items distinct. However, it is easy to find counter-examples, where the need to prevent homonymy did not operate: for example, homonymy of *rush* ('hasten') with *rush* (a plant) has not been prevented. In some circumstances quite dramatic loss of distinctions can take place, and there are examples in the literature of wholesale merger of previously distinct classes of items: Labov, Yaeger and Steiner (1972) cite the reduction of five distinct vowel phonemes of ancient Greek to *one* (/i/) in modern Greek. Because of apparent counter-examples like these, Lass (1980: 75–80) points out that these functional arguments as applied to given cases are unsatisfactory. Social dialectologists are in little doubt that speakers will happily tolerate a great deal of phonemic merger, allophonic overlap and approximation, and homonymic clash.

None of this, however, detracts from Martinet's original insight, which recognizes the importance of speaker-function – in this case the information-bearing function: the apparent circularity in arguing about given instances is probably very largely due to the limitations of the historical database (which is incomplete and deprived of situational context), and to some reluctance to investigate what happens in the language of live speakers, where hypotheses such as functional load can be more fully tested. Historical linguists know that language is used to convey information, but they cannot specify very easily what additional social and pragmatic functions might have been involved in particular changes (which after all took place long ago in circumstances that we cannot fully investigate). Yet, although the information-bearing function is the one that comes most easily to mind, it is only *one* of the functions of language in use: other functions interact with it. Thus, in historical change, the need for mutual intelligibility over distances and the maintenance of meaning-bearing distinctions can be overridden by these other functions – by the identity-function, for example. This is suggested by the cross-dialectal miscomprehensions discussed above, by the pattern of multiple merger in Greek cited by Labov, Yaeger and Steiner (1972), and by many other instances.

In this connection, it is useful to recall the metaphor that I appealed to in chapter 1 – the idea that in viewing language as a system *où tout se tient* we are implicitly comparing it to a machine. The function of a machine is known beforehand: the function of an internal combustion engine is to propel a vehicle, and if it does not succeed in propelling the vehicle, we know that it has malfunctioned. If we believe that we know beforehand that the principal function of language in use is to communicate decontextualized information-bearing messages explicitly and unambiguously, then – pursuing the system-based metaphor – we shall have to view communicative breakdowns as malfunctions. Of course, in given situations, they may be perceived in this way, and if we put the argument on a more abstract and general plane, we shall then have to conclude that language change and variation are in general dysfunctional. But if this is so, why then do human languages vary and change?

We can draw only one conclusion, which is that variation and change must also be functional for speakers of languages: if this were not so, languages would be uniform and they would not change. Indeed, there is a case for claiming that if linguistic change were impossible, speakers could not function adequately in speech communities. But the functions of language in speech communities are multiple and are not limited to the information-bearing function. In social dialectology we attempt to explore the question of function by observing and analysing the language of ordinary speakers in conversational contexts. To return to the machine metaphor: we can take for granted the function of a machine, but we cannot take for granted the functions of language. Thus, as we do not know beforehand what all the functions of language in the speech community might be, we have to find out what they are and how they interact with one another by exploring the speech community. This is by far the single strongest justification for research in social dialectology of the kind that we and others have carried out.

2.5 Speaker Functions in Discourse and Conversation

What I intend to do here is to tackle the question of discourse functions in an introductory way, without venturing too far into the enormous literature on discourse and conversational analysis. We can start by noticing some of the binary distinctions between *types* of discourse that have been suggested. Ochs (1979) proposes that discourse can be divided into two broad types: *planned* and *unplanned*. Brown's (1982) distinction between *message-oriented* and *listener-oriented* speech is based explicitly on the *functions* of discourse in social settings. Message-oriented speech is characterized by explicitness and independence of situational context or shared knowledge between participants. According to Brown (p. 77), message-oriented speech is 'goal-directed. It matters . . . that the listener understands . . . and that he understands . . . correctly. The point of the utterance is . . . communication of a propositional or cognitive (information-bearing) message to the listener.' Listener-oriented speech, on the other hand, is characterized by inexplicitness and vagueness, with primary attention to the feelings and attitudes of conversational partners. As Brown comments: 'it is often the case that speakers in primarily listener-oriented dialogue don't seem to be talking about anything very much . . . we may judge it to be successful if the participants succeed in maintaining friendly relationships.'

Historical linguistic views of language function tend to assume without comment that *the* function of language is something like the message-oriented function – which is often described as *communica-*

tive – and not like the listener-oriented function (in which the meanings conveyed are social or context-dependent); they assume that communication between speakers is, or ought to be, explicit and context-independent in the interests of conveying cognitive propositions efficiently from speaker A to speaker B, in a context where the aim is to convey new information to someone who does not already know it. Let us consider, however, what this would actually mean in terms of the use of language in social contexts.

Clearly, it would allow the written medium, as the function of writing is to communicate messages outside the immediate interpersonal context, and, to be effective, it must be explicit. It would also allow certain kinds of speech event, such as reports or lectures, for much the same reasons. In conversational exchange,[9] however, such a view of language use would account for only those parts of conversations in which 'new' and explicit information is given and received; for example, the information that is passed in question–answer adjacency pairs of the kind:

(3)   A   Where were you on the night of 15 August?
      B   I was looking after Mother at the motel.

Such exchanges are, however, especially characteristic of, and frequent in, formal settings, such as classrooms, courtrooms and interviews of various kinds (including some sociolinguistic ones) and may indeed be required in such settings: they are not especially characteristic of conversation. The conversations that we collected and analysed in the inner-city Belfast projects (L. Milroy and J. Milroy, 1977), for example, could not have been adequately described in these terms. Speakers in most conversational contexts are not solely (or even mainly) concerned with passing decontextualized new information to one another, and the casual conversations that sociolinguists record are not mainly made up of question–answer adjacency pairs or elicitation–response sequences. On the contrary, much of our discourse is *unplanned* and *listener-oriented*, in which speakers 'don't seem to be talking about anything very much' and in which the primary goal seems to be the maintenance of 'friendly relationships' (Brown, 1982: 77). It can be assumed, therefore, that speakers in casual social contexts are not usually concerned with avoiding homonymic clash or with being especially clear and explicit:

they are satisfied if the conversation progresses successfully, and the success of the conversation is judged in social terms. If misunderstandings occur because of homonymic clash or for any other reason, they can be repaired if necessary: speakers appear to accept the results of vagueness and ambiguity on the assumption that 'intended' meanings will be clarified *if necessary* as the conversation proceeds.

Underlying this distinction between discourse functions there is another more general distinction. This is the stark contrast between what is desirable in the written medium (or context-independent speech-styles such as lectures) and what is desirable in, and characteristic of, speech-exchanges in social settings. It is very clear that much of the historical linguistic tradition has been based on assumptions derived from the functions of writing, rather than speech. However, such features as redundancy, vagueness and ambiguity, which are disfavoured in writing, are wholly characteristic of everyday speech. Furthermore, many of the features that are positively dysfunctional in context-independent language are actually functional and necessary in the conduct of successful conversation: lack of explicitness, hesitation, ambiguity, incompleteness and repetition are themselves very important aspects of how conversation is organized.

This has been clearly demonstrated by conversational analysts such as Schegloff (1979). Far from being random and disorganized, ambiguity and the other characteristics we have mentioned are systematic strategies of conversational interaction. They are used for monitoring the reactions of conversational partners and for clarifying and repairing the mistakes or misunderstandings that might have occurred in the interaction. In fact, one of the most important aspects of conversation is the very high value that is placed on *indirectness*: this is in obvious contrast to message-oriented styles, in which directness is valued and indirectness disvalued. Direct imperatives (demanding actions), for example, and direct interrogatives (demanding relevant responses, as in (3)) are quite rare in conversation. This is because exchanges in speech are social and personal: the high value placed on indirectness is a result of the speakers' concern for their own 'face' and that of their partners (Brown and Levinson, 1987): they are often much more concerned with being polite, that is, avoiding threats to 'face', than with passing information efficiently and economically. In spoken contexts, the directness that is so highly valued in information-bearing styles is perceived as threatening.

These remarks may be sufficient here to draw our attention to some of the functions of language in use apart from the message-oriented function, and they have some consequences for our ideas about how linguistic changes are implemented. Theories based exclusively on the message-oriented function of language must plainly be insufficient: it seems very unlikely that linguistic changes over time could have been implemented mainly in this function, that is, in formal styles such as lectures, or in formal settings such as courtrooms or classrooms, especially since this function values stability and resists change; for the most part, changes have been initiated in countless millions of casual (mainly unplanned, listener-oriented and context-dependent) encounters between speakers. It is in these casual exchanges (and not primarily in formal settings) that the sociolinguist looks for evidence of change in progress. It is the use of speech in these context-tied situations that actually allows linguistic change to be negotiated between speakers, and we need to emphasize this here, because linguistic *innovations* plainly belong to the class of phenomena that may be miscomprehended in context.

If we can accept that it is characteristic of conversation that some utterances will be miscomprehended, we can also presumably accept that it is the principles of conversational organization that permit *repair* of such miscomprehensions. Clearly, it is possible that in the course of a conversation innovations may be introduced and, as they may be unfamiliar to some participants, they may be miscomprehended; however, as we have seen, the principles of conversation allow for clarification of these miscomprehensions. For this reason, and for other contextual reasons, the principles of conversation permit linguistic changes to be negotiated between speakers and thus admitted into the language system: it is the conversational context that provides the conditions for change to be accommodated. Decontextualized discourse, on the other hand, does not in principle cater for these misunderstandings: it therefore resists ambiguity and vagueness, and in the present perspective it is hardly surprising that in its written forms especially it has also been observed to resist structural change.

2.6 Speaker-Functions: Marking Social Roles

The discussion so far has focused on the functions of discourse in conversational settings, and I shall continue to refer to these pragmatic aspects of language from time to time. However, there is another relevant aspect which is largely independent of the idea of discourse types, and which has been prominent in social dialectology since Labov's (1966) New York City study. This proposes that variation within the structural parts of language (such as phonological and morphological variation) is used by speakers to mark varying social roles. Social meanings – in the words of Blom and Gumperz (1972) – are carried in linguistic structures. Style-shifting and code-switching (switching from one language or dialect to another) are socially functional: they are related to changes in the situational contexts of speech events, to the social characteristics of the participants, and to the varying purposes of exchanges in speech. Furthermore, speakers normally attach great importance to this kind of variation and assign strong social values to what are essentially arbitrary differences. To exemplify this kind of function, I shall now briefly consider the question of style-shifting (which functions in essentially the same way as code-switching).

The fact that style-shifting is functional is rather neatly demonstrated in cases where the expected variation is, apparently, absent. We have discussed such a case in some detail elsewhere (J. Milroy and L. Milroy, 1985a: 123–5), and this example is a useful demonstration of Weinreich, Labov and Herzog's (1968) point – that the absence of variation is dysfunctional. According to Lavandera (1978), members of the Argentinian Italian community, who are bilingual speakers of Italian and the *cocoliche* dialect of Spanish, are perceived by monolinguals as deficient in their Spanish. However, there is actually nothing deficient about the structure of their Spanish (as Lavandera shows): what is lacking is the *stylistic* variation, sensitive to occasion of use (and other factors), that monolinguals observe. There is a lack of stylistic variability, not a deficiency in command of the 'core' structure of the language. The perceived absence of variation in this case demonstrates, of course, that stylistic variation is – for the monolinguals – functional; that is why they notice it. For *cocoliche* speakers, on the other hand, it is their bilingualism that is functional: their communicative competence is exhibited in their command of two languages, rather than in observing the stylistic variation inherent in one of them.

But it is also clear that speakers may have very strong feelings about particular regional or social dialects, even though in linguistic terms the differences between dialects are arbitrary. One of the first things I noticed in my early descriptions of Belfast vernacular was the strong 'stigma' associated with certain non-standard pronunciations. In a dynamic account of the phonology (J. Milroy, 1976a), I found it most convenient to think in terms of the avoidance of stigma rather than convergence towards a higher-class or standard form, but it was not clear why some non-standard forms were avoided and others favoured. Amongst younger inner-city speakers, it was clear that stigma was attached to certain forms of rural origin (such as palatalized /k/ and dental /t/), but not to others (the raising of /a/ before velars showed no recessive tendencies). Thus, it seems that communities can disfavour pronunciations that were formerly favoured; and despite the fact that sound-segments do not carry meaning in the ususal sense, this phenomenon seems to have something in common with the operation of taboo, which is so well attested in the vocabulary. It is also associated with 'face' and politeness.

These brief discussions of social dialect, style-shifting and conversational functions are sufficient, I think, to indicate that there is more to language in use than the communication of decontextualized information of a purely cognitive kind. It now seems appropriate to summarize the main points, as I have not been trying to argue merely that language in use has multiple functions – this is a view that will be readily accepted by any sociolinguist. I have been concerned with the limitations of what I have called system-based historical linguistics. By this I mean virtually any approach to historical linguistics (traditional or current) that is centred entirely, or almost entirely, on the properties of language as an abstract object, and that excludes the systematically observed behaviour of speakers of languages. These language-internal approaches have made immense progress in producing sophisticated 'grammars' and models of linguistic change, but they have not come very close to the actuation problem and the causes of change. Furthermore, as we have noticed above, when speaker-roles are referred to in system-based arguments, they tend to be referred to in a rather *ad hoc* and unsystematic way, usually on the assumption that the message-oriented function of discourse is the one that matters. We therefore need a theory of the embedding of language change in society, but we do not so far have a social theory of this kind that can rival the sophistication of system-based linguistic theory. Yet, it seems that we cannot develop such a theory if we remain wholly within the constraints of orthodox historical linguistics. In section 2.7, therefore, I shall conclude this chapter by commenting on a state of affairs that underlies some of the matters raised in this introduction, that is, the limited nature of the *database* of historical linguistics. By discussing this we can focus on the methodological interface between historical and social linguistics and go on in later chapters to suggest what would be involved in a socially-based theory of language change.

2.7   Limitations of Historical Inquiry

It is obvious that data preserved from the past are likely to be more limited in certain ways than data collected at the present day. Here we notice two major limitations. The first is that past states of language are attested in writing, rather than in speech. This has many consequences, of which the most general ones depend on the fact that written language tends to be message-oriented and is deprived of the social and situational contexts in which speech events occur. This is relevant, of course, to our discussion of function, above, and to other matters that will arise in later chapters: for example, interpreting written texts as evidence for pronunciation.

The second limitation is that historical data have been accidentally preserved and are therefore not equally representative of all aspects of the language of past states. Thus, whereas research into present-day states proceeds in a controlled way by collecting and analysing data for the specific purpose of drawing generalizations about language and about specified aspects of language, the researcher into past states must use materials which were not in the first place collected for this purpose. Some styles and varieties may therefore be over-represented in the data, while others are under-represented. For some periods of time there may be a great deal of surviving information: for other periods there may be very little or none at all. It is reasonable to say that the database of historical linguistics, as compared with that of sociolinguistics, is impoverished.

To the extent that historical linguistics is subject to these limitations, it is what Diaconis (1985) has called an 'uncomfortable' science. In this respect it is similar to some aspects of other sciences such as geophysics, macro-economics or astronomy, in which the scientist has relatively little control over the database. The astronomer, for example, does not have experimental control over the visits of Halley's Comet: thus, just as the astronomer does not have control over space, so the historical linguist does not have control over time; to be more specific, historical linguistics does not have *experimental* control of its database, and so it cannot always isolate the variables that may be involved in an explanation. It is quite appropriate here to mention the analogy of the blind men and the elephant, which has so often been mentioned before, or to use metaphors of the 'tip-of-the-iceberg' type, because it is very much a matter of proceeding from a base of very limited knowledge. Thus, whereas social dialectology can plausibly claim to be to some extent an experimental science (because it is possible to control some variables in the frame of the investigation), historical linguistics cannot. Sometimes the data may be so impoverished that decisions cannot be made as to what is the best description amongst a set of possible descriptions, or what is the best explanation amongst a set of possible explanations. The result is that interpretations of the surviving evidence are often strongly dependent on current theoretical assumptions (which may of course be dubious) and, more widely, on current ideological positions (which are even more dubious). Many examples of this difficulty can be cited:[10] here I shall refer only briefly to a rather general one.

One example of a difficult area for the historical investigator is the chronology of sound-changes in the history of a language: this can often be uncertain and controversial. As a result of the limitations we have noticed, and the imposition of certain theoretical orthodoxies on what is or is not possible in sound-change, there has been a strong tendency in historical descriptions to assign a date to a sound-change at what seems to be the time of its completion, and (until recently) for relatively little interest to be shown in the earlier stages of change. Indeed, sometimes it seems as if change in a whole phoneme class is believed to have taken place all at once with simultaneous actuation and completion – perhaps overnight at some date in the early seventeenth century. However, if we are to understand the nature of change, we want to know as much as possible about its actuation, implementation and diffusion; therefore, we want to explore the early stages if possible (I shall discuss this further in later chapters). But the limitations of historical databases often make this difficult. Because of these limitations, therefore, it seems that our understanding of the nature of linguistic change will ultimately depend, not mainly on historical data, but (recalling Principle 1) on our ability to observe it systematically at the present day in social contexts of use, because that is where we can most readily locate change in progress in a specifiable social context.

This in turn makes it possible to project backwards. By using the insights we are able to derive from the much richer data of present-day researches we should be able to understand more fully what happened in the history of the language, and I shall return to this in later chapters. However, the main point here is that in order to observe in a detailed way the contexts in which linguistic change takes place we need to focus on present-day data. Accordingly, in the following chapters, my aim is to build up a theoretical approach to the social origins of linguistic change by focusing on present-day data. In chapters 3 and 4, we focus on analysing and interpreting patterns of variation in the speech community.

3

Analysing Language in the Community: General Principles

3.0 Introduction

The purpose of the next two chapters is to consider how far the practical analysis of language use in live speech communities can contribute to our understanding of language change. I am concerned largely with laying a basis for this by first determining the general patterns of language variation and social variation in which changes in progress may then be discovered – in other words I am concerned with the embedding of language variation in society. My concern in the present chapter is mainly with *linguistic* patterns, which amounts to a description of the main methods and principles of social dialectology as we have tried to develop them, especially as they concern the analysis of what are usually called 'non-standard' varieties. In social dialectology we need to abstract from speaker-interaction and the social contexts of speech events as we observe them, to project the data on to the configurations of language systems (recall Principle 1). Analysis of purely linguistic variation is, however, an essential part of a study of language change, because language change is manifested as change in systems; therefore, in this chapter, I am mainly concerned with the principles of observing and analysing language variation in the community. In chapter 4 we shall consider the sociolinguistic interpretation of these patterns.

As the language system is the focus of our study here, we start with the idea of the linguistic *variable* (for example the vowel /a/ in such items as *cat, bad, have*), and our first task is to discover what the possible variants of a variable may be: subsequently, the quantitative distribution of linguistic variants may be demonstrated by reference to the familiar *speaker-variables* of social dialectology, such as age and sex of speaker. But the important point to remember is that we do not observe these *sociolinguistic* patterns directly: it is the speech of individuals in conversational settings that we observe and describe, and it is by analysing a large quantity of spoken language from many speakers that we can then demonstrate the patterns that emerge from our data. I shall be discussing the general principles of this kind of analysis, and I shall start with some remarks about the general context within which the Belfast research (1975–82) was designed – the context of historical linguistic description.

Here, we need to recall the very broad distinction that has been mentioned in chapter 2, between historical linguistic theory (and the theory of change) on the one hand, and historical linguistic description, on the other. Of course this is not an absolute distinction, as historical descriptions depend on some kind of theoretical orientation, and theory depends on systematic observation and description of linguistic forms (otherwise there is nothing to have a theory about). For practical purposes, however, we can accept this broad distinction here. But it is clear that the data collected in close investigations of live speech communities are much richer than the data preserved from early language states, and they are observable in a larger number of dimensions and at a much finer level of detail; thus, the patterns revealed in systematic investigations of live communities appear to the observer as much more variable and multidimensional than historical patterns (as these are usually reported). That is to say, the variation is not necessarily patterned in one single linguistic dimension (for example, it does not necessarily move in a single *phonetic* direction: it may diverge in two or more directions), nor does it necessarily display a unilinear or unidirectional pattern in terms of any independent 'social' variable: on the contrary, the patterns shown in relation to different social variables may conflict and interact in a variety of ways. In the Belfast research programme one of our aims was to use the complex patterns discovered in a live speech community to throw light on the kind of movements that might have taken place in linguistic change in the past.

In conventional historical description, three very prominent interrelated tendencies had been noticed. These are, first (as I have mentioned in chapter 1), a tendency to focus on patterns of change alone with little or no attention to *stable patterns* of language through time; second, a tendency to unidimensionality, that is, an inclination to think of the history of a language as the history of a single homogeneous variety and of sound-changes as proceeding in straight lines; and third, as noted in chapter 2, a tendency to impose theoretical and ideological orthodoxies on (sometimes rather sparse) data that might often be open to alternative kinds of interpretation. Of these orthodoxies, the ideological ones are perhaps the easiest to explain here, and they are relevant to what I have to say later, so let us consider here a very general point about the effects of ideology – the apparent contrast between typical models of ancient language states, on the one hand, and recent language states on the other.

It is noticeable that for the distant past of language orthodox models of change, such as the Indo-European family-tree model, are mainly models of *divergence* (in these models languages are envisaged, like galaxies, as moving away from one another at considerable speed), whereas for recent centuries models of language history are predominantly *convergent*. Specifically, the history of English since about 1550 is often presented as what Lass (1976: xi) has called a 'single-minded march' towards RP and modern standard English, with divergent developments either excluded or admitted only in so far as they throw light on 'standard' English. This is in clear contrast to the divergence model in Indo-European studies, and as a result of this contrast, the shape that emerges from historical language description (from ancient times to the present day) is not so much a pyramidal shape (with gradual convergence at the top) as a funnel shape (the kind that is used for pouring liquids), as in figure 3.1.

At about the year 1550 the pyramidal base of the funnel suddenly narrows and from that time proceeds in a straight and narrow path to the present day. That is to say, scholars have assumed that around 1550 the English language became much more convergent than it had been before even though there can be no direct evidence that *spoken* English did become more convergent. Following this type of model, conventional histories of English have customarily given considerable attention to phonological and morphological change and diversity in Indo-European, Germanic and Early English. At the Middle English stage, the description of divergence is still very salient (partly because the states attested in writing are unquestionably divergent states), but we also begin to notice attempts to launder the data retrospectively in such a way as to focus on those features that lead to modern

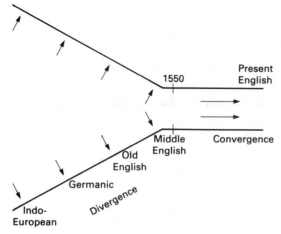

Figure 3.1 The divergence/convergence model, from Indo-European to the present day.

'standard' English and to ignore, reject or explain away those features that deviate from it. Examples are noted below and in chapter 5. Then, at around 1550, the story becomes exclusively about standard English. A model like this cannot be a sufficient basis for a convincing *explanation* of a recurrent phenomenon like linguistic change because *both* divergence and convergence can be present in language states at any time, or, perhaps, at all times. But what we have to notice here is that it cannot be right for mere historical *description* either: as there is no such thing as a uniform language or dialect (and standardization implies uniformity), and as sound-changes do not proceed in straight lines, this cannot possibly be an adequate conceptualization of English phonological history.

There are traditional influences at work here, and they are ideologically loaded. H. C. Wyld, for example, was a very great expert on the grossly divergent regional dialects of Middle English, but when it came to post-sixteenth-century English, he was quite insistent that the only object worthy of our study was Received Standard English. Such views have an ideology behind them (though not necessarily a conscious one), involving as they do a decision that the language of 'the Oxford Common Room and the Officers' mess' is an appropriate object of study, whereas that of 'illiterate peasants' is not (Wyld, 1927). From the point of view of standardization theory, this backward projection of Wyld's 'Received Standard' on to earlier states can be seen as an attempt to *historicize* the standard (literary) language – to create a past for it and determine a *canon*, in which canonical ('genuine') forms are established and from which unorthodox ('non-genuine' or 'corrupt') forms are rejected. This retrospective model has been influential and pervasive in historical description: since Wyld wrote there has been further important work on Early Modern Standard English and its history, notably that of Dobson (1955, 1968). Naturally, the ideological assumptions behind this unilinear model have led to dismissive attitudes to 'non-standard' dialects. In his account of EModE pronunciation, Dobson (1968: 551) dismisses 'vulgar' and 'dialectal' sources, and I shall comment further on this tendency in chapter 5. Even so, it's surprising to find the following comment in the work of a distinguished historical linguist: 'Nonstandard forms may be found among antisocial groups, such as criminals, or a rebellious younger generation, or among rustics' (Lehmann, 1962: 142). This has the effect of marginalizing non-standard vernaculars – appearing to present them as abnormal or pathological language states – when the majority of human beings throughout history must have used varieties that were, to a greater or lesser extent, non-standard. Thus, the imposition of these preconceptions on the object of study necessarily leads to a distorted view of the history of a language. As a language is variable at all times, the many different varieties can each be seen as having continuous histories, with influences passing to and fro between them, as represented in figure 3.2. If our ideological preconceptions incline us to an exclusive interest in standard English, we will produce what is in effect a history of literary English; this will exclude and neglect other historical patterns that are capable of enriching our description of the history of spoken English and, ultimately, of adding to our understanding of the general phenomenon of linguistic change.

Clearly, the difference here between traditional approaches (as exemplified by Wyld, Dobson and others) and sociolinguistic approaches is that, whereas the former project a uniform state (standard English) on to the past, the latter project linguistic *variability* on to the past. This backward projection is one of the things that has motivated my own work on present-day speech communities, and my interest in how the *authority* of the legitimized variety is promoted in linguistic scholarship (J. Milroy and L. Milroy, 1985a). I shall have more to say about it in later chapters.

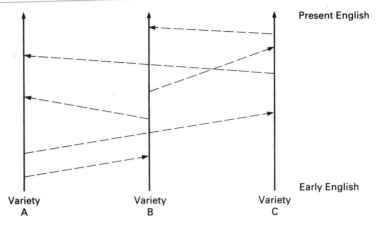

Figure 3.2 Simplified model of multidimensional change in the history of English. (The dotted lines represent influences passing from one variety to another.)

3.1 Shapes and Patterns

My purpose in the remainder of this chapter is to set out the main principles of exploring multidimensional language states in present-day communities, on the assumption that historical states of language must also have been multidimensional. A major contribution of Weinreich, Labov and Herzog (1968) and the quantitative paradigm has been to demonstrate that heterogeneity in the speech community can be shown to be have *patterns* in it. But we noticed in chapter 1 that linguists have often lived by metaphors – the biological metaphor in the nineteenth century and the machine metaphor today. If we speak of patterns and shapes in speech communities, we are again talking in metaphors, but this spatial metaphor is one that I have found congenial in speaking of linguistic history and the complexities of usage in live speech communities. The phonological system, for example, can be described as having a 'shape', but there is also a *sociolinguistic* shape of the speech community, involving society as well as language. If we can describe this (and the Brown and Gilman (1960) 'power and solidarity' model is suggestive as a beginning), we can use it to help to model the embedding of language in the community.

The perception of shape and pattern in apparently disorderly (but dynamic and mobile) things is usually mentioned with reference to visual perception, and it is commented on in the sciences and the arts alike: it is prominent, for example, in the notebooks of the poet Gerard Manley Hopkins (J. Milroy, 1977), in his careful descriptions of cloud formations, waterfalls and other dynamic phenomena, and much of the poet's imagery depends on a kind of 'observer's paradox' (rather different from the familiar Labov version), through which a dynamic phenomenon can nonetheless appear to have stable shapes and patterns within it and, conversely, a static phenomenon may appear to contain mobility. But it is also apparent in the perceptions of some scientists, especially in subjects that are, like historical linguistics, 'uncomfortable' sciences – meteorology and some aspects of astronomy, for example (see Diaconis, 1985; Gleick, 1988). At the most general level, therefore, it is convenient to think of the speech community as having a 'shape' and of language in the community as being capable of displaying patterns, much as we might think of these other dynamic phenomena as displaying shapes and patterns. To the extent that language is perpetually shifting and changing, it plainly resembles dynamic states such as weather and cloud formations more closely than it resembles static objects. In the case of language, however, the patterns are not immediately observable in the way that, say, cloud formations are: as we have noted above, they are observed in the configuration of the data after the analysis has been carried out. But as there must always be some kind of *observer-effect* in patterns revealed in this analytic way, the position of the observer, and the preconceptions that he or she brings to the act of observing, must be accounted for at every phase of the research.

Observation of historical states is affected by the limitations of the database, and we can liken this to a situation in which the object is viewed from a distance. When this is the case, some patterns will be obscured or invisible, and many details in the patterning will be unobservable. The present-day sociolinguist, however, who is observing and exploring a 'new' language situation is in a close-up position; he or she can observe the phenomena at successively finer levels of detail and thus reveal fine-grained patterns that are not accessible in historically attested states. But first let us stand back a little and, starting at the surface of the phenomenon, let us consider the most general 'shapes' and patterns that speech communities may exhibit.

At this superficial level, different kinds of speech community shape can be readily distinguished. For example, some states that can be easily identified are bilingual or multilingual, others can be viewed as bidialectal, and yet others as monodialectal (but still variable). Although the matter is much more complicated than this, with many subtle gradations within and between these different shapes, this rough classification is sufficient for our present purpose. The Belfast community is a broadly monodialectal one, but within this it can be described as a *divergent-dialect* community (Johnston, 1983). It is this typological point that I would like to consider now, bearing in mind the question of historical divergence and convergence that I referred to above.

From a static point of view, the term 'divergent-dialect situation' can be understood in two senses: first, Belfast dialect (for example) is observed to be divergent from other dialects and, particularly, from 'mainstream' norms of language, such as RP and standard English; second, the dialect exhibits a great deal of *internal* variation – much greater than is generally reported for these better-known varieties (this is approximately the phenomenon that Le Page (1975) calls *diffuseness*). Thus, it is not a uniform state (as standard English appears to be in handbook descriptions), but a highly variable state, with many complex patterns observable within it. As compared with handbook accounts of supposedly homogeneous varieties, therefore, it can be characterized as a 'normal' situation, as it is the *normal* state of language to be heterogeneous. But what is important here is that, just as present-day language states are normally heterogeneous, so historical language states must also have been heterogeneous in similar ways; hence, unilinear historical descriptions of single varieties (such as 'standard' English) cannot be adequate descriptions of the history of a language. In section 3.2, we shall briefly consider these two aspects of divergence: external and internal.

3.2 Describing Divergent Language States

As we do not have intuitive knowledge in detail about states of language that are divergent from us in time, space or social space, we cannot reliably project our own linguistic intuitions on to them. In order to describe them, therefore, we may be inclined to use as a reference point the linguistic norms of some well-described dialect such as 'standard English'. But this is not acceptable either, because there will then be a danger of projecting the norms of standard or 'mainstream' varieties on to the dialect (imposing them from above, as it were), and this will result in a distorted account of patterns observed *within* the community, which may bear no direct relation to these other varieties. We cannot assume that a divergent phonological system, for example, is structurally similar to or derivative from RP, or that lexical items belong to the same phonemic sets, or that the tense/aspect system is structured in the same way as that of standard English. In Belfast, for example, all these things are quite different. Nor are we likely to know beforehand the *sociolinguistic* functions of all the linguistic variants identified – whether they mark age, sex or contextual style differences, for example. Thus, the exploration of a present-day divergent state of language resembles the exploration of a historically attested state to the extent that we cannot successfully describe either of these in terms of an external (and usually superordinate) variety. That is to say, you cannot describe sixteenth-century English as if it were a variant of RP any more than you can do this for divergent present-day varieties.

Let us consider briefly what difference all this makes to our analysis and interpretation. Specifically, what interpretations of data would be available to us if we relied on 'mainstream' norms, and how would these differ from internally-based interpretations? Here, I shall look at some examples of internal linguistic variation in Belfast in (roughly) ascending order of generality in order to show how little we can rely on outside norms in preparing a *sociolinguistic* analysis. First, a particular instance: one of the many cases of 'hypercorrection' that were noticed.

In exploratory recordings (1975), the word *queue* occurred several times pronounced as [ku:] (without the [j] glide), by a middle-aged female in a careful style. There is no externally-based explanation for this, as there is no sign of [j]-deletion as a known process in the history of Ulster dialect, and it is not favoured by RP, which on the contrary *replaces* the [j] of [j]-deleting dialects (Trudgill, 1974; Wells, 1982). Nor is it found in the more 'standardized' forms of Ulster English. To understand what is happening here, we have to know that Ulster vernaculars have palatalization of initial [k] in certain prevocalic positions (as in [kjat, kja:r] 'cat, car'), and furthermore that this is recessive in inner-city Belfast. Figure 3.3 shows the recessive pattern:

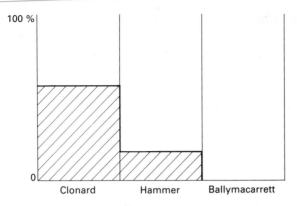

Figure 3.3 Recession of palatization in middle-aged males in *car, cat,* etc. (Clonard: 62%; Hammer: 14%; Ballymacarrett: 0% palatization.

palatalization is hardly present at all except in males over 40, and the area which has the most recent immigration from the country is the most conservative.

From this internal knowledge of Belfast English we can conclude that the speaker who says [kuː] for *queue* is using a careful style strategy to avoid the palatalized segment (see my comments on avoidance of stigma in chapter 2.6, above), which is a strongly regional marker and also a marker of older male speech. Therefore, we can say that the speaker's 'knowledge' includes the knowledge that /k/ is palatalized in the dialect. But we could not draw these conclusions if we relied on external norms, on general historical information as codified in historical textbooks, or on our own 'intuition'. We must, therefore, use such instances empirically to help to establish what the internal linguistic norms of the community actually are, and to do this is to be accountable to the data in quite a strong sense.[1] In fact, we made considerable use of hypercorrection phenomena of this kind in preparing our phonological analysis.

A second example concerns the pronunciation of /a/ before velar consonants in words of the type *rag, pack, bang*. In Belfast vernacular (henceforth BV) the vowel is front-raised as far as [ɛ] in this environment. However, there is also a substantial incidence of a *low* vowel with a prominent closing glide: approximately [aɪ]. This has the effect that such items as *back* can sound very similar to RP *bike*, and the outsider may easily miscomprehend 'I was on my *back*' as 'I was on my *bike*'. It is clear that the 'underlying' norm: ([ɛ]), is not the RP norm, even though the movement towards [aɪ] may be modelled on some external norm. However, as it results in near-homophony with RP *bike*, it seems that the constraints of the local system are much more powerful than any superordinate norm: whereas *back* can be [baɪk], *bike* is not normally [baɪk], but [beɪk]: there is a partial avoidance of homophony. Clearly, the explanation for such phenomena must be based on an analysis of the local vowel system, not that of RP.

My next examples are more generalized, and they concern the imposition of external RP stereotypes on the vowel phoneme /a/. One common local belief about Belfast English is that upper-middle-class people tend to front-raise /a/ (as in *bat*) towards the conservative RP value: [æ] (but we found little sign of this in any part of our research). However, inner-city speakers normally, and quite consistently, have [æ] and [ɛ] in items where the vowel precedes a *velar* consonant (as noted above), and I have sometimes been told that this is affected by RP. Our quantified investigations (for example, J. Milroy, 1984), however, have repeatedly demonstrated that the only environments that show a consistent front-raising pattern are these velar environments; thus, while it affects the whole phoneme /æ/ in conservative RP, it is confined to velar environments for most Belfast speakers. Clearly, if it were based on RP, there would be no reason why it should affect this environment and not other environments, and these internal facts about BV are quite sufficient to establish independence from RP. And this independence is further supported by the existence of the 'velar-raising' rules in other Ulster varieties: they are carefully described by Gregg (1964) for Larne, and by Patterson (1860) for nineteenth-century Belfast, and so in this case they are plainly of some antiquity.[2]

Also within the /a/ system, however, there is a high incidence of *back* varieties of /a/: in BV, this vowel is realized in certain following consonantal environments as a long, back vowel, which is in many contexts virtually identical to RP (as in RP *dance, bath*); on a superficial view we may therefore be tempted to believe that speakers are adopting this external norm. The consonant environments that encourage backing of /a/ are: (1) following voiceless fricatives (as in *grass, path*); (2) following voiced obstruents generally (as in *has, bad*), (3) nasals (as in *Sam, man*); and (4) /r/ (as in *car*); but backing does not occur before voiceless stops (as in *bat*), or nasals followed by a voiceless obstruent (as in *dance*). Of these environments, however, only the voiceless fricative and /r/ environments coincide with the backing environments of RP, so we are clearly dealing with a different /a/-backing rule. The difference from RP can be appreciated quite easily by reference to the pair *can, can't*: *can* has the long *back* vowel predicted by the single nasal environment, whereas *can't* has the short *front* vowel predicted by the nasal + voiceless obstruent environment (compare also *dance, ranch*, etc., which are short, front). This is the opposite of RP (where *can* is front and *can't* is back), so we plainly cannot explain this back /ɑ/ pattern by relating it directly to RP. There are many other examples that show the RP (and general southern British) rules as 'flip-flopped' in certain environments in Belfast: they are of historical interest, and we shall return to them in chapter 5. What is important here, however, is the fact that a description of these divergent configurations in the phonological system is an essential basis for subsequent quantitative analysis: the further away the variety is from mainstream norms, the more important this prior description becomes.

The above examples were noted prior to quantitative analysis, and were used, with other observations, as the basis of an internal phonological description on which all our subsequent work has been based. However, the general independence of the /a/ system from mainstream influence is supported even more conclusively by the broader community norms as they emerge from later quantitative analysis. We have demonstrated in various publications (for example, J. Milroy and L. Milroy, 1978) that in the inner city there is a change in progress moving from front values of /a/ towards back values, beginning to affect even those environments that were formerly always front (for example pre-voiceless stop environments, as in *map, that*). However, as we move out of the inner city the trend to backing is reversed, and the system swings back again to front realizations (J. Milroy, 1982b): it converges on front-vowel realizations to the extent that all items (except those with following /r/) including items such as *grass, path* (which are back-vowel items in *both* RP and inner-city vernacular) have the *front* vowel. Thus, if we project this information on to the socio-economic class dimension, the movements of /a/ show a zig-zag (or a split-level) pattern from front to back and then from back to front, as in figure 3.4. RP thus has no direct effect on the convergence pattern displayed by middle-class speakers: therefore, if we start with the RP norm and derive these speech community patterns from it, we can falsify the situation totally. In this case the main falsification would be that hundreds of thousands of inner-city

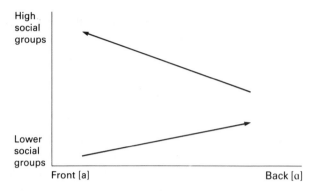

Figure 3.4   The zig-zag pattern in the community.

speakers who are not remotely interested in RP have 'borrowed' back
[ɑ] from RP. It might also appear from such an analysis that
working-class people are converging towards RP back [ɑ] in *grass,
path,* and middle-class people diverging from it, when in fact there is
no evidence that the usage of these speakers is influenced by RP in
any way at all.

To this extent, of course, a synchronically divergent language state
requires the same kind of treatment as a historically divergent state: in
neither case can it be assumed that the norms of some 'standard'
variety can be successfully projected on to it. In section 3.3 we turn to
the principles of exploring linguistic variation in present-day vernaculars.

3.3   Exploring Language in the Speech Community: Some General Principles

It is clear from the above examples (and from many others) that we
have to describe the speech community in depth and in its own terms.
That is to say, our conclusions about phonological structure must be
accountable to, and 'warranted' by, the data. If we do not do this, we
shall not find out very much about the social functions of variation in
the community or about the sources and motivations of change, and
our results will therefore be superficial. They may also be misleading.
For example, if we observe only public speakers in Belfast (news-
casters, reporters and the like), we will notice that some of them adopt

quasi-RP forms in their public styles. In the inner- and outer- city work in Belfast, however, these forms (for example, fronting, un-rounding and diphthongization of /o/ to /əʊ/, as in *home, stone*) did not occur at all in hundreds of hours of recording. Therefore, if we had taken our cue from these public styles, we would have produced a top-heavy account that would have been of only marginal importance to the social 'life' of the speech community. From this perspective, the success of Labov's work in New York City, which is based on more widely-known variables, suggests that New York City speech is much less divergent from mainstream American English than Belfast is from mainstream British English. To that extent, therefore, we are dealing here with a different kind of analytic task. It is also relevant to notice that Horvath and Sankoff (1987) in their Australian work found the social variables the most difficult to deal with and the linguistic variables 'well defined'. In these dialect-divergent studies (J. Milroy, 1981; Johnston, 1983; Newbrook, 1986), however, it is the *linguistic* analysis that is the greatest immediate challenge facing the investigator: if we do not investigate the internal linguistic structure of the speech community itself, the sociolinguistic interpretation of the data will be at best superficial, and, at worst, wrong.

In addition to this external divergence, however, communities like Belfast also exhibit massive *internal* linguistic divergence, and we must attempt to find out what are the internal social functions of this divergence. In New York City Labov was able to show important patterns of variation on the basis of only five linguistic variables; in contrast to this, Pellowe et al. (1972) identified in Tyneside (a divergent dialect community) no less than 303 linguistic variables that they considered worthy of study. In Belfast we assumed that the number of socially-patterned variables that we might uncover could well run into the hundreds. If we adopt here Le Page's distinction between *focusing* and *diffuseness* in language states, a community like Belfast is relatively diffuse (divergent within itself) in comparison with more homogeneous communities, but relatively focused when com-pared with communities in which there is extensive code-switching and code-mixing (such as the Caribbean communities studied by Le Page and Tabouret-Keller, 1985). But to suggest that a speech community is diffuse (or internally divergent) is not to imply that it is necessarily unpatterned or unstructured: on the contrary, our task is to find out how the variation is structured by demonstrating what the patterns in the community are like. However, our descriptive task will be more difficult, as it involves dealing with greater *complexity* of variation than would be the case in more focused communities, and it has to be carried out at a very fine-grained level. There are many different ways in which speakers may exploit, in varying social functions, the resources of variation that are available to them, and we do not necessarily know beforehand what these are, how they interact, or what the limitations on possible variants may be. However, as it is the 'normal' state of language to exhibit structured variation, I have suggested above that speech communities like Belfast can be regarded as 'normal' speech communities.

I mention this here because it has sometimes been thought that this type of community is abnormal or atypical. Romaine (1982b), for example, suggests that these may be atypical communities and, further, that such communities may exhibit two 'norms' within them (we shall return below to the question of internal norms). Similarly, Johnston (1983) describes the patterns discovered in his Edinburgh work as 'irregular'. But the Belfast and Edinburgh situations are abnormal and irregular only if it is assumed that the patterns revealed in the New York City study are the normal and regular ones, and that Labov's findings on the structure of that speech community are universally applicable. There is of course no reason why the patterns revealed in one pioneering study should be taken as definitive and exhaustive for all communities: it is an empirical matter to determine what kinds of pattern can be revealed in speech communities and hence to determine what the norms of particular speech communities may be. And this, of course, is in accordance with Principle 2, suggested in chapter 1.

The guidelines that we rely on here are parallel to those of 'exploratory' science, as described by Tukey (1977), Diaconis (1985) and others, and also to those of ethnographers who investigate the internal structures of non-mainstream societies. The papers in Cohen (1982), for example, describe research into geographically peripheral communities in the British Isles, such as Shetland, Tory Island and the Isle of Lewis. Their aim is to explore and describe the internal social systems that govern behaviour in these communities, and of course they gain access to these systems through studying overt behaviour in the communities. Being aware of the (external) divergence between these cultures and 'mainstream' culture, they are anxious to avoid imposing what they call 'crude mainstream stereotypes' on to the interpretation of these internal systems: they want to get access to what the patterns of behaviour mean internally and how these are perceived by in-group members. As the investigators are themselves out-group members, they cannot have reliable prior intuitions as to the social meanings conveyed and must investigate these by observation and analysis. This is very much the position of the observer of 'divergent' speech communities: the difference is that the linguist's ultimate goal is to draw generalizations, not about behaviour in general, but about language behaviour.

I have implied above that a major difference between more diffuse and more focused communities is relative complexity of variable linguistic structure: Cohen (1982) is very clear on the question of internal complexity. The 'voice' to the in-group is, according to him, more complex in structure than the 'voice' to the outside world, and the internal meanings and functions of variation in behaviour are not easily accessible to outsiders. This last point is a familiar one, which fits in well with the remarks on observing patterns that I have discussed above. In the Belfast research, we wished, like Cohen, to approach an explanation for 'the complex differentiation *within*' communities, by exploring and analysing in-group patterns and functions of differentiation; in the event, we showed that a great deal of variation has in-group functions that are not readily accessible to outsiders, and we shall review this in chapter 4.

In the analysis of linguistic variation, therefore, we were looking for fine details of variation – variation that shows internal patterning within the speech community, but which may have no social meaning for outsiders – and in the first application for funding it was specified that the research was intended to extend the quantitative methodology to a type of community that had not been studied in this way before. It was of course necessary to introduce modifications in method and procedure, which have sometimes been (wrongly) thought to be in opposition to Labov's work. These modifications are required because of the similarity of our task to the ethnographic tasks described in Cohen (1982). As these anthropologists chose to investigate geographically peripheral communities, so we chose in the first instance to investigate communities that are marginal in a different sense. As hundreds of thousands of speakers use Belfast vernacular, it is hardly marginal as a linguistic variety; but in the tradition of linguistic inquiry it *seems to be* marginal. Linguists have taken little notice of such communities in the past – their language is not part of the central 'canon' – and so such vernaculars are still largely peripheral to the general body of linguistic knowledge. We chose to investigate in the first place the speech of those who are not very likely to be directly affected by mainstream norms, and whose speech is of the type that had been least explored by descriptive linguists – the urban working class. The intention was to relate the linguistic variation revealed to social patterns within the communities themselves, avoiding prior assumptions about social norms that might seem to be imposed from outside. In this work we give full weight to the speaker/system distinction that has been introduced above, and hence to the general principle that *speakers* are ultimately responsible, not only for introducing and adopting linguistic changes, but also for *maintaining* diversity in language states. In section 3.4, I move on to an outline of the methods of the Belfast research.

3.4   The Belfast Research Programme: Principles and Methods

The empirical research in Belfast was carried out in two stages. The first stage was the inner-city project, 'Speech community and language variety in Belfast' (October 1975 – June 1977). The second stage (1979–82) consisted of two major projects: the outer-city speech community studies and a random-sample 'doorstep' survey. There were also a number of minor studies in connection with the main research programme.

As we have noticed above, the success of any social dialectological project in a dialect-divergent community depends crucially on adequate methods of analysing *linguistic* variation, and it is this analysis that takes most of the time. For methodological reasons, it is important to distinguish between this and the socially based *interpretation* of the results, because if the social factors involved are seen as the motivating principle for the selection and analysis of linguistic variables, the investigators may be accused of biased selectivity and circularity. Within the inner-city study, we *believed* that the language might show patterns of differentiation between older and younger speakers and between the sexes, but we did not *know* that it would, or if it did, what the precise differences would be. No one had investigated inner-city language in this way before, so for all we knew there might have been no significant differences at all, and we were told by at least one colleague – not very encouragingly – that 'Broad Belfast' dialect was all very much the same. But it is important to affirm the independence in principle of the linguistic and social analysis at this stage of the work, especially as this does not always seem to be recognized. Wardhaugh's (1986: 175–7) reference to the Belfast research, for example, appears to suggest that the whole thing was undertaken as an investigation of *social network* and the linguistic variables selected specifically for the purpose of demonstrating network patterns quantitatively.[3] If this had been so, however, it would have been a weakness: the strength of our arguments on social network (and other social aspects of the research) depends precisely on the fact that these socially-based criteria are not the motivating factors for our selection of linguistic variables.

The research consists of different methodological phases, which we can describe as *collection, classification, analysis* and *interpretation*. In practice they overlap: for example, while the inner-city data was still being collected, we were analysing the tape-recordings that had already been obtained. It is, however, useful to think of these phases as separate in principle. The analytic and interpretative phases are the most relevant to the subject-matter of this book. In this chapter, I am mainly concerned with analytic methods, and in succeeding chapters with interpretation; I shall confine my remarks about collection and classification to those points that affect the interpretation of the findings.

3.5   Collection and Classification of Data

The type of sampling used in the five community studies is *quota-sampling*, and our main concern is not to claim absolute representativeness for the whole city, but to guard ourselves against the accusation that our informants might be hand-picked from amongst friends and neighbours – or, worse, from our students. In this respect, therefore, our work conforms to the general principles of Labov's work and is not comparable with studies (experimental or otherwise) that are based on the language of, for example, RP-speaking or near RP-speaking persons from amongst the analyst's own university students.

For these reasons, access to the communities was obtained through suitable intermediaries, who were not used as informants. Thereafter, the fieldworkers were passed on from person to person within the communities; thus, the informant groups were self-recruited in that the speakers were not known to the investigators beforehand. In J. Milroy and L. Milroy (1977), we justified this method, somewhat retrospectively, in terms of the social network model (the fieldworker can be described as a second-order network contact), and it is useful methodologically to think of it in this way (indeed, many other investigators have successfully used the idea of social network as an explicit part of their fieldwork strategy). But the essential point here, whether or not we describe it in terms of the network model, is that we are concerned not with a superficial survey of the communities, but with obtaining depth of coverage. In the perspective of this book, the contrast with traditional dialectological method, and with data-gathering in orthodox historical linguistics, is clear and requires no further comment.

As for the fieldworker's position *vis-à-vis* informants, our concern is to *account for* this (this can be seen as an extension of the notion of *accountability to the data* into the fieldwork phase) and to use it as part of our method of data classification. We do not use Labov's concept of the *vernacular* – the language used by speakers when they are not being observed (which is described by Labov as the most 'regular' style) – and this is in accordance with Principle 1, suggested in chapter 1: language in use is always observed within a social context of some kind. The immediate reason for not using Labov's concept is that the vernacular must be an idealization – on a par with other idealizations such as dialect or speech community – and so as an idealization it must be inaccessible in practice (recall that you do not observe the language: you observe people talking). But if by any chance it were ever possible to locate this 'vernacular' in the usage of an informant, we would have no criteria for demonstrating that we had located it, any more than we could locate 'the dialect' in the speech of a single informant. We have used the term 'vernacular' in a different way: for us it is a 'primitive' term roughly synonymous with 'real language in use', and it is interpreted on a continuum of relative closeness to, or distance from, the idealized *norm*, or (in some cases) the idealized *standard language*. I shall have much more to say below about vernaculars, norms and standards, and that is one reason why I have to comment here.

Otherwise, the fieldwork strategy in large-scale quantitative studies must be broadly the same as that of Labov: we need to go as far as possible in obtaining *casual* styles from informants and to develop ways of distinguishing styles on a continuum from 'careful' to 'casual' style. But we do not claim that we have reached the 'vernacular', or the most casual of possible styles, for any informant (although some reports on our work have stated that we have): we merely claim that our data is rich and variable enough to enable us to classify styles on the stylistic continuum in an extremely well motivated way.

I have noted above that in both social and historical linguistics the position of the observer is crucial and is relevant to the interpretative phase in that the observer may affect the data in some way. It is consistent with this that we should use the role of the fieldworker in speech-exchanges as a means of classifying different speech-styles. We explained this during the course of the research (L. Milroy and J. Milroy, 1977). Briefly, when the fieldworker is actually *interviewing* the informant and thus controlling the exchange, the style is labelled 'interview style'. It is possible to distinguish this style from others in that the discourse turns in interview style are alternating and relatively brief; they follow a question–answer discourse structure, and they are often of roughly equal length. Here, the degree of control exerted by the fieldworker over the speech-exchange is the guiding principle, and the fieldworker's aim is to get away from interview style (that is, to *lose* control) as soon as possible. In our 1977 article, we use transcripts from our data in which: (1) the question–answer discourse structure is overridden; and (2) in which the fieldworker is not in control, but is a participant/observer. The differences in discourse structure are quite obvious (the reader is referred to L. Milroy's (1987) report of our field methods, where the same transcripts are used).

Much of what I have said here is relevant to the second methodological phase (*classification*), but it should also be noted that we do not make prior classification of social levels of language in the way that many other urban dialectologists do. Bertz (1975: 77), for example, in his study of Dublin, uses a prior classification into 'drei *Sozio-stilistischen Typen*': 'educated', 'general' and 'popular' Dublin English, and his informants are pre-classified in these groups. We are of course aware that educational levels may be important at some stage, but we do not pre-classify in this way because we do not assume beforehand that we *know* the sociolinguistic structure of the speech community: this is what we are trying to find out! Our classification is based solely on the speaker-variables of age, sex and area, and on contextual styles, and this is regarded as a procedure whereby we can establish the internal linguistic norms of the community. The classifications we use normally depend on fine-grained analysis of *language*, and I move on in section 3.6 to the analytic aspects of the work.

3.6   Analysis

Whereas for Horvath and Sankoff (as noted above) the linguistic variables are 'well defined', this is not so in a dialect-divergent community: in such a community few of the linguistic variables can be said to be defined at all. This difference seems to be partly a consequence of the relative homogeneity of Australian English on the one hand, and the heterogeneity of Belfast English on the other. But there is another reason why communities like Belfast are difficult to deal with, and this is that the phonology of such communities is not usually adequately described and codified beforehand, whereas more information of this kind is available for varieties closer to 'standard' English. The result of all this is that because of the divergence of Belfast English from other varieties and the internal divergence within it, we do not know beforehand what is the correct lexical input to any phonological variable, we do not necessarily know what the variants of the variable are, and we may not be at all certain about what precisely might count as a variable. Therefore, if we are to find out what linguistic variation means to in-group members and how it functions in the community, much more prior observation and analysis is needed than would be required for better described varieties.[4]

In order to locate the variables that might be worthy of study, and to define the variants of the variables, a broad description of the phonological system has to be prepared beforehand. A 'practical phonological' description of Belfast was prepared in March 1975 and updated while the research was in progress (J. Milroy, 1976a, b). The main points arising from this are that: (1) the vowel system is totally different from mainstream British English in terms of vowel-length, vowel-height, diphthongization and other properties (for example, vowel-length is not usually contrastive, as it is alleged to be in RP, and so most vowel-phonemes, such as /e/, as in *gate, save*, are realized as *considerably* longer or shorter allophones according to consonantal environment); (2) allophones of phonemes can overlap phonetically with allophones of other phonemes in a manner that is not permitted by classical phoneme theory (Bloomfield, 1933); (3) lexical items do not necessarily belong to the same vowel phoneme classes as they do in RP and SBE (for example, whereas *good* and *food* have different vowels in most SBE, they have the same vowel in Ulster English); and (4) many sets of lexical items exhibit vowel alternations, in that the vowels in these items are realizations of two different phonemes. More detailed accounts of Ulster phonology are now available in J. Milroy (1981) and Harris (1985), and we shall return to aspects of phonological variation at various points in this book. Here, I want to discuss the principles on which variables are selected for quantitative analysis.

As there is probably a large number of variables that might be socially interesting, it is necessary to select a representative sub-sample of different types of variable in a well-motivated way, and to specify the range of potential linguistic variation that lexical items in these sets may undergo. The second point is crucial for the reason that if we include in the set items that cannot undergo the variation in question, or items that undergo different patterns of linguistic variation, the quantitative results will be false. A final point that has to be borne in mind is that in order to make generalizations based on the type of quantitative analysis pioneered by Labov, a large number of tokens must be analysed (usually thousands); however, it happens that some variables that are quite salient in the community occur relatively rarely, and so we cannot make reliable quantitative statements about these covering the range of speaker variables, even though they may be involved in linguistic change and may be important for historical projections on to earlier English. It is for this reason that for the central part of the projects we selected representative variables that occur frequently and can therefore be quantified in terms of the full range of speaker-variables.

The main variables for the inner-city research (most of which were reported in J. Milroy and L. Milroy, 1978) were therefore selected on the general principle that a large number of tokens must be identifi-able in the data, and it is clear that this stark necessity must override any other consideration. Within this general constraint, however, we attempted to find representative variables that belonged to two broadly-defined types (the second of which can be subdivided) that we describe in terms of their linguistic (and not their social) characteristics. These are: (1) variable sets in which the lexical items are very numerous and are distributed throughout all or most of the range of a phonemic class (we can call these 'large-set variables'), and (2) variables that are restricted to a small class of lexical items (small-set variables). Within this second class, there are two sub-types. The first type (2a) is phonologically defined and includes variables such as (th), which concerns deletion of (ð) intervocalically in a small defined set of lexical items of the type *mother, gather, together.* If enough tokens occur, this type is the easiest one to deal with, and usually exhibits very sharp patterns of social divergence according to age and sex of speaker in studies such as ours. The second type (2b) consists of lexical sets, the membership of which cannot be reliably predicted on phonological grounds alone, and this type is additional to the types of variable that were studied by Labov (1966) in New York City (these were types 1 and 2a). We do not know for certain what the total membership of any such set is, how many items belong to it, or the extent to which speakers vary in assigning items to the set. These are open-ended sets, and they can be called sets of *phono-lexical alternants.* Realizations of the vowels in the relevant items belong to two different phonemes; these alternants (like type 2a variants) are usually extremely socially salient in the community, but for obvious reasons it can be difficult to deal with them quantitatively. Of these, the set that I selected for careful examination within the main projects is the (*pull*) set, which deals with alternation between [u] and [ʌ] in a set of lexical items such as *pull, put, foot, shook.* I shall return to the (*pull*) set as an example of phono-lexical alternation, largely because such alternation appears to be typical of dialect-divergent communities, and is extremely important in the arguments that I shall develop in later chapters on phonological change and on the effects of strong and weak social ties in communities. But the (*pull*) set is only one of many: the others, although often salient, are usually unsuitable for quantification throughout the range of speaker variables because of the low numbers of tokens attested (many examples are listed in J. Milroy, 1981).

This is not a watertight classification, and it is not exhaustive.[5] It is procedural only: we used it in Belfast as a guideline to help us to select variables that would represent broader and narrower patterns of lexical coverage. However, the quantitative methods of the 1960s and 1970s had successfully dealt with large-set vowel-variables (type 1), quantifying them through the whole range (or most of it) in a single unilinear dimension of phonetic variation (such as raising or backing). In the dialect-divergent community we found this problematic, and we located only two vowel variables that could be reliably quantified in this way. These are the two categorically short vowel phonemes /ʌ/, as in *cut, dull* (quantified as a binary counting rounded v non-rounded realizations) and /ɪ/, as in *hit, fill* (counting front v centralized realizations). The difficulty in finding such variables is in itself a measure of how internally divergent BV actually is, and it is striking that the variables that show the sharpest patterns of social variation are subsets within the larger sets. For consonant phonemes, quantification throughout the phonemic range is of course impossible, since the potential for variation in consonants differs according to the position of the segment within the word or morpheme, but it is the difficulty with vowel variables that is most significant here. In other studies, investigators have often been able to assume that they know the lexical input to commonly occurring vowel variables such as (e) and (a) and also that all the lexical items counted have the much the same potential for variation (that is, the direction of variation will be consistent throughout). In Belfast (and in divergent dialect situations generally) the matter is much more complicated.

In purely linguistic terms, there are two reasons for this difference between Belfast and certain other studies. The first arises from the fact that most BV vowels are long or short according to following consonantal environment. The length difference is much greater than allophonic length differences in RP and is easily audible. But the long and short allophones are also qualitatively quite different. The low and mid vowels, such as /ɛ/ (as in *set, bed*), are short before voiceless stops and before any sonorant + voiceless obstruent (for example, in *set, went*), but long elsewhere (for example, in *mess, bed, men*). They are also short in certain conditions in disyllables and polysyllables. But for /ɛ/, the short variant can be a low vowel ([a, æ]) and the long variant is a mid vowel that is easily heard to be qualitatively distinct. The pattern, which is more fully described in J. Milroy (1981) and Harris (1985), is shown in table 3.1.

This speaker shows a very regular pattern with certain environments categorically low and others categorically mid. The result of all

Table 3.1   MC Senior (53) 'formal' style

| Monosyllables | | | All disyllables/polysyllables | |
Low	Mid	Mid	Low	
went (4)	left (5)	—	electric	
get	men (2)		heavy	centre
set	then (4)		textile	Wednesday
met	well (3)		very (8)	fellows
next	them		terrible (3)	definition
	less (5)		Devlin (2)	fun-
			reckon	damentals
			twenty	yourself
			genera-	fundamental
			tions	myself
			general (2)	Grenville
				intellectual

this is that there are two subsets of /ɛ/ with very different potentials
for variation. Our figures for short (ɛ) in figures 3.5 and 3.6 show a
pattern of variation between low and mid realizations with the mid
realizations beginning to occur in environments that were formerly
categorically low, and with females leading in this change. The long
allophone of /ɛ/, however, cannot be low, but varies between mid and
higher-than-mid realizations and can develop a centring glide. In the
simple type of quantification that we used, it is clear that we would
need to quantify the long-vowel environments separately from the
short-vowel ones, as the potential for variation is different in each
case. We can regard (ɛ) as representative in two ways: it is representative of our method of analysis, but it also represents a pattern of
linguistic change that is valid for all the mid and low vowels: /a/,/ɛ/,
and /ɔ/. Where there is change in progress at the moment, we have
found that it is manifested in all these vowels as a pattern of
lengthening (or 'tensing') of previously short vowels.

The second reason for this relative complexity is that, as we have
already noticed, given lexical items do not necessarily belong to the
same sets as in 'standard' English. Thus, because of the divergent
history of the dialect, there can be subsets within larger classes (such
as (ɛ)) which do not vary in the same way as other items in the set. In

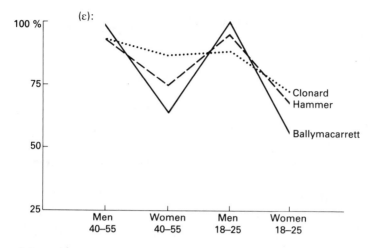

Figure 3.5 Percentage low vowel in variable monosyllables and prefixed and inflected disyllables.

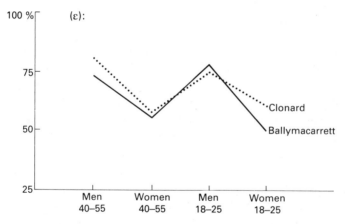

Figure 3.6 Percentage low vowel in all other disyllables. The Hammer figures (which have been excluded) correspond closely to those of the Clonard.

the (ε) set, for example, some short-vowel items (including *get, never, ever, yes*) that should exhibit variation between [ε] and [a] also have an alternant in [ɪ]. Thus, occurrences in [ɪ] have to be excluded from the main quantification, and the (*get*) subset, provided that we can accurately specify its membership, can in principle be quantified separately as a set of *lexical alternants* of the (*pull*) type (2b). It is in fact very common to find subsets like this within larger classes, and when we quantify them they usually show sharp patterns of social differentiation. But, as we have noticed above, we often cannot quantify these subsets meaningfully throughout the range of speaker-groups and styles because occurrences of the relevant variants are relatively rare. Yet, it often happens that these variables are socially salient and important for historical projection on to earlier states of language.

Therefore, as it takes a considerable amount of time to scan the tapes looking for rarely occurring variants, we have selected one particular variable of this kind, which we call *meat/mate*, and have studied this quantitatively outside the main projects in a different way. The variation here concerns the incidence of [e]-type pronunciations in words of the type *meat, leave, peace, easy, seize*, and more particularly the question whether the [e] variants of this class are merged with the class of *mate, save, lace, daze*, or not. We are not primarily concerned here with the distribution of this variable through the range of speaker-groups and styles, mainly because this is quite evident from our tape-recordings before we start, and without formal quantification. The [e] variant is exclusively a casual style variant, which does not occur at all in more formal styles and is unobtainable in word-list elicitations. It is also much less common in female speech than in male; therefore, our quantification is based on male speech alone. And this selectivity is of course justified by my immediate aim, which is phonological rather than sociolinguistic – to discover whether we can reasonably speak of a *meat/mate* merger in Belfast English. Clearly a number of factors that have to do with the history of English (chiefly the reported merger of *meat/mate* in the sixteenth century), with patterns of language maintenance, and with phonological theory and description, have also motivated the choice of this variable, and we shall return to these in chapter 5. However, the main reason for mentioning it in this methodological discussion is to show how subtle and fine-grained our analysis must be if we are to give an adequate account of the function of language variation in close-tie communities. The paradox here is that this variable is very difficult to access and would not be accessed at all if our field methods and analytic methods were inadequate; yet, the variation has strong social meaning within the community. Indeed, our quantified results suggest that the [e]-type vowel of the *meat* and *mate* classes may have been maintained as separate since Middle English, functioning as a social marker, without merger, but with close approximation and overlap (J. Milroy and Harris, 1980; but see further chapter 5).

The discussion so far has focused on the sociolinguistics of dialect-divergence and the methods that can be used in order to establish in-group norms of language use that are not previously part of the knowledge of the investigator. In the discussion I have taken the necessity of quantification for granted (although it sometimes happens in such communities that some patterns of variation are obvious without formal quantification). Before we proceed in chapter 4 to discuss the interpretative phase of social dialectological research, however, it seems to be appropriate to add a few further remarks on the use of quantitative methods.

3.7   Excursus: On the Uses of Quantification

We noted in chapter 1 that when we observe language in use, what we actually observe is the speech of individuals in conversational sett- ings – we do not directly observe overall *patterns* of use in the sociolinguistic dimension. Thus, if – as an outside observer – you listen to 'core' vernacular Belfast speech, it will actually sound all much the same to you: you will not easily observe without systematic analysis many of the differences that exist and you will not usually be able to tell how far these co-vary with social factors, such as age, sex and area. This is because the differences are in general not categor- ical: the 'dialect' is a property of the community, and every native speaker has roughly the same kind of access to it and roughly the same knowledge about it. But the speakers that you are observing 'know' how to use the resources of variation available to them, and they use them for many purposes, including the marking of varying social roles and functions. Thus, the incidence of particular variants differs according to these roles and functions. This is why a very fine-grained analysis is needed, and why we will not get very far in synthesizing our findings in relation to large databases like this if we do not use quantification: as these differences are not categorical, we usually will not be able to demonstrate them convincingly unless we quantify.

Quantification is usually taken for granted in social dialectology, but it is not used in some other branches of sociolinguistics (for example, those researches that follow Gumperz's model), and there can be disputes about whether or not it should be used in given instances. We shall briefly consider some criticisms from within sociolinguistics below. But questions have also been raised about it in non-social areas of linguistics, and these are often attached to reservations about the theoretical nature of sociolinguistics as a discipline. Chomsky (1975) expressed the view that sociolinguistics is a harmless activity like butterfly-collecting, but that it is not 'theoretical'. Although this was some time ago, similar dismissals have continued to surface in the work of those who adopt Chomsky's theoretical position. A recent example is Smith (1989), who thinks that Labov's work is not theoretical because it does not address 'any linguistic issue'. It is surprising that remarks of this kind from influential linguists are still appearing, and that is why some comments are needed here, not only on quantification, but also on the relation between 'method' and 'theory'.

Smith says that quantitative methods are inappropriate to linguistic inquiries and cites as a warning Labov's work in New York City, which he represents thus: 'The classic example of a quantificational linguistic study is provided by Labov's investigation of the determinants (age, class and casualness) of New Yorkers' pronunciation of /r/, pre-consonantally and finally, in words like "fourth" and "floor"' (1989: 180–1). Apparently, this refers not to the Lower East Side survey, but to Labov's preparatory department store survey (Labov, 1966; 1972b). This of course was not the main part of the work, but a pilot study used to test and refine some hypotheses about the wider sociolinguistic situation, which was then investigated more fully over a much longer period of time. But the whole study was set up within a much more general theoretical orientation: the theory of linguistic change; it was not merely an attempt to demonstrate age, class and style differences, as Smith implies. So this account seems to be based on a misunderstanding of what Labov's work has been about. But other commentators have also had something to say about the use of quantification in linguistics. Lass (1980), for example, has pointed out that stochastic (probabilistic) laws are not predictive, and has seemed to suggest that the quantitative paradigm is theoretically uninteresting for this reason. There have also been criticisms using similar lines of argument from within sociolinguistics (Romaine, 1981, 1984b; Cameron, 1990).

But there is nothing to argue about here, as the act of quantifying is not intended to be predictive, explanatory or theoretical: it is a methodological tool that is used by those who wish to make accountable statements about the distribution of linguistic forms in real speech communities in cases where this is not evident without quantification. In many situations, you will not be able to demonstrate beyond reasonable doubt what the linguistic patterns in the community are – what speaker-knowledge of those patterns is like and which of the patterns show that linguistic changes are in progress – unless you quantify. And you certainly will not be able to demonstrate these things by relying on your own introspections! What must be understood, therefore, is that there is a difference between the act of quantifying data and the substantive claims made by the investigator after the patterns have been established by quantification. These claims (for example, that such-and-such a change is in progress) are not in themselves *quantitative* claims: they are substantive and are independent of the quantitative method. If the claims were made simply on the basis of introspection without systematic observation in the community, they would be of precisely the same order (except that they would be unaccountable and probably much less reliable). So I have treated quantification here as methodological: it is part of the analytic phase of social dialectology, and it is parallel in this way to the use of quantification and statistics in certain other sciences.

Both within sociolinguistics and outside of it there have been discussions that appear to attack quantitative method for making claims about causation and correlation. Romaine (1981, 1984b) and Cameron (1990), for example, specifically cite our Belfast research as an example of the 'correlational fallacy'. Clearly, this kind of work would not be undertaken unless it was thought possible that causal relationships between variables might exist, just as a medical researcher might hypothesize a causal relationship between cigarette smoking and lung cancer, or as a historical linguist might hypothesize that a contributory cause of palatalization of [k] is an adjacent front vowel. It is natural to look for causative factors, and we have treated causality much as it is treated in experimental research generally (see Plutchik, 1974: 174–87). But we do not generally fall into the trap of believing that a statistical correlation between two variables demonstrates that one is *the* cause of the other; it is assumed that the actuation of language change is multi-causal,[6] and we have frequently demonstrated that the speaker-variables interact with one another (that is, that no speaker-variable all by itself can 'explain' a given configuration of language).

However, the misunderstanding about quantitative method can be quite serious and can also get tied up with problems about statistical significance testing. Smith, for example, further points out that Labov did not use 'tests of statistical significance, so his interpretation of the figures is anyway suspect'. It is surprising that an anti-quantitative linguist should advocate confirmatory statistical testing, but it is very important to understand that the proposition put forward here is simply wrong. If Labov's interpretations were suspect (and of course they are not), this would not arise from the fact that he failed to test for significance. There was no reason for him to do so because the claims that he wished to make were quite simple (they did not involve complex interactions of different speaker variables), and because in his analysis the same patterns were repeated for every variable studied, tending in the same direction in every case in terms of both class and style (*several* classes and *several* styles). Thus, the results are very impressive: there is obviously a regular pattern in them, and as they are accountable to observed data, they are much more persuasive than categorical statements about language that are made on the basis of introspection alone. The same applies to the examples that I discuss in chapter 4: some of these show gross differences between social groups on the basis of hundreds or even thousands of tokens, which would not be apparent without quantification. Where there are dramatic differences of incidence for different groups, where the social pattern investigated is simplex (for example, class difference only), and where the differences virtually always tend in the same direction, it is often unnecessary to test for significance, because the patterns revealed are so clear that no one could believe they are the results of pure chance. In fact, since social dialectology is an exploratory science, many important patterns of variation are adequately demonstrated by *exploratory* statistical techniques, which are designed to reveal patterns in the data rather than test for significance (Tukey, 1977; Diaconis, 1985). The graphs and diagrams of the quantitative paradigm are, in effect, examples of this.

Where there are numerous relevant variables, however, confirmatory statistical testing will help to give us confidence in our results, and it is up to the analyst to decide in a given case whether these methods are needed. In sociolinguistics they are normally used in cases where several different independent variables (such as sex, age and network) may be interacting, and therefore possibly cancelling out the effects of one another. I explained this (J. Milroy, 1982b: 43) in relation to the simplification pattern in short /a/ (see chapter 4.5 for the findings of this study), which we measured by using a three-way analysis of variance. To simplify: it might happen that there is no significant difference in terms of one social variable (such as class), but that this statistic conceals other differences or similarities within the results in terms of other social variables (such as age or sex). Thus, it could turn out that a difference is best accounted for not by the first social variable that you quantify (for example, social class), but by a second or third one (for example, sex of speaker).

Since we carried out these studies, much more sophisticated computational programs have been developed for the social sciences. There have also been considerable advances in 'variable rule' methodology, with the development of GOLDVARB (Sankoff, 1986), and the journal *Language Variation and Change* has been founded, with an editorial policy that concentrates on quantitative methods of linguistic analysis. Properly used, it seems to me that quantitative methods can only lead to advances in our subject. As for my own research, there are some areas of it in which quantification has not been used because in these areas it was not necessary or appropriate for the purpose I had in mind (see for example the discussions in chapter 5). In the social dialectology carried out in Belfast, however, quantification was necessary: if it had been possible to do the work without quantifying, we would have done it that way!

3.8 Conclusions

The purpose of this chapter has been to outline the main principles of analysing language in the community, and I have paid particular attention to exploring dialect-divergence. In such situations we typically do not know beforehand what all the linguistic variants involved actually are, so we must use very careful and accountable methods of selection and analysis. But in previously unexplored speech communities, we do not have reliable *social* intuitions either.

That is to say, we do not know how these patterns of variation function within the community: we do not know what social meanings the variation carries for in-group members. To explore the situation, therefore, and establish the relation of linguistic variables to speaker variables, we normally require quantitative methods, which in some cases may involve sophisticated statistical techniques. But as quantitative method is not a primary interest of this book, I shall move on in chapter 4 to the interpretative phase of this kind of research.

4

Interpreting Variation in the Speech Community

4.0 Introduction: Investigating Community Norms

Up to now, we have been mainly concerned with analysis of data. In this chapter the emphasis is on the interpretative phase of the work. What does this linguistic variation mean, and what contribution can our analysis of variable states of language make to understanding variation and change in language generally?

We have approached this task by focusing on the question of linguistic *norms*, and it is relevant to recall here Principle 2 (chapter 1). In the lay person's view, and in the view of some professional linguists, the norms of language are associated with notions of standardization and 'correctness' or with hierarchical dimensions of social structure (or all of these), and they are usually felt to be *institutional*: that is, they are thought of as being prescribed by authority through the writing system, the educational system and other agencies (for a relevant discussion, see J. Milroy and L. Milroy, 1985a). There is no doubt that factors like these are important in what we may call the social 'life' of language, and they are implicated in many aspects of linguistic variation and change. To understand them properly, however, we need to relate them to wider social structures, and we shall consider this aspect of sociolinguistics in chapter 7. However, these institutional norms do not tell anything like the whole story, and this is particularly true if we focus on *spoken language* in casual conversation and on phonetic and phonological variation: as we noticed in chapter 3, the norms of a superordinate variety cannot be projected on to the norms of a speech community without distorting our description. But more generally, if we use superordinate norms as our main reference point, we cannot explain why, despite superordinate pressures towards uniformity, varieties of English and other languages can still remain so astonishingly divergent from one another and so variable within themselves. It must be the case that the norms of these variable states are agreed on by *internal* consensus in the communities concerned.

These divergent states are often subjectively perceived as having distinctive characteristics that mark them out as discrete varieties: people can recognize regional varieties such as 'Birmingham' English, 'Yorkshire' English and so on, and they often have a fairly clear idea of how such varieties are distinguished from one another. If this is so, these varieties must incorporate within themselves sets of recurrent and distinctive *norms*, through which they can be characterized, but which do not usually coincide with the norms of the standard language. This chapter is about determining the norms of usage that characterize real speech communities and about the relevance of this to determining the direction of change within the communities. The kind of norms we are concerned with here are sometimes called *community norms* in order to distinguish them from the superordinate norms that I have mentioned, and I shall suggest below that a major difference between superordinate and community norms is that, whereas 'standard' norms are uniform, community norms are sometimes more aptly described as *variable* norms.

Underlying all this there is a more general question that impinges very directly on the explanation for linguistic changes. This is the second principle for the social modelling of change that I discussed in chapter 1. As I pointed out there, it seems to be impossible to give a full *description* of a linguistic variety (whether it is 'standard' English, or a dialect, or a style or register) without making decisions about what the 'norms' of the variety are, that is, without making decisions about what the *speakers* agree on as structures that are appropriate for that variety.

To take a simple example: suppose we are comparing two dialects, one of which has the vowel /eɪ/ (in words of the type *gate, place*) where the other has /aɪ/. In an intra-linguistic description, we will simply state this difference as a structural linguistic fact (and do the same for the other differences we notice) and that will be the end of it: dialect A has one structure, and dialect B has another. But this difference is also a *social* fact: people are normally aware of differences of this kind, and they often attach the utmost importance to them. We can easily understand this if we assume that dialect A is 'standard SBE', and dialect B is 'Cockney'.[1] However, in an objective language-based description, one variant is just as 'good' or 'efficient' as the other. But, as we noticed in chapter 1, it is a social fact in a much more deep-lying sense, because these dialects are the possessions of their *speakers*. The occurrence of /aɪ/ in one dialect and /eɪ/ in the other is a result of the *agreement* within each community on a *consensus norm* of usage within that community, and the difference cannot be explained without some reference to this fact. There would be little point in having these different norms (which are arbitrary in linguistic terms) if they did not carry social meaning, distinguishing between one community and another and carrying a sense of community identity for speakers.

The same general point applies also to patterns of linguistic change, and is most evidently relevant in the case of *sound*-change. Suppose that in the course of time the vowel /aː/ in a particular language becomes open /ɔː/, as it did in Southern Middle English in words of the type *home, stone* (OE *hām, stān*). No purely internal linguistic explanation can account for the fact that the change happened in this way in some dialects and in different ways in others. Nor can it explain why indeed the change should have happened at all: why did the speakers not simply retain /aː/? Again, this change, like synchronic variation between dialects, is a social, as well as a linguistic, fact. It came about through changes of agreement amongst speakers over the course of time involving greater and greater consensus on open /ɔː/ as the appropriate realization, and it is not fully explainable in purely linguistic terms. But just as speakers attach great importance to *variation* in the structural parts of language, so they must also attach great importance to *change*: if they did not, then there would be no reason why changes like this one should be accepted in speech communities.

But there is still more to be said about linguistic norms. Although some of these community norms that we have mentioned above may be recognized by outsiders as regional or social markers, many others are better described as internal: they mark social differences *inside* the community. These internal norms are the special property of the community itself, and they are not evident to the outside observer; therefore, to find out what they are, we must investigate the communities in depth and at a fine-grained level of detail. The three small inner-city communities that we studied in this way would have been assumed by traditional scholars to be homogeneous in language, and the fine-grained but systematic variation I am referring to here would not have been thought possible. We were principally interested in how linguistic norms that are highly divergent from 'mainstream' English are *maintained* in communities of this kind. As social class is irrelevant in this case (there is little, if any, difference in social class amongst our inner-city informants), the social groupings we used to approach the sociolinguistic structure of the community were the uncontroversial ones of age, sex and area, and *social network* was adopted as an additional speaker variable during the course of the research. We used this in conjunction with the other variables to assist in exploring internal community norms of language.

4.1 Social Network

We have used *social network* in two ways within the research: first, as a quantitative speaker variable and, second, as an interpretative category, and its use in the projects arises from our interest in exploring these community norms. As an interpretative category, it has important advantages over other social models that we might wish to use. The fundamental one in an investigation of this kind is that we do not need to accept any prior assumption about how society at large is organized or structured, and so in our interpretation we do not need to import any presuppositions from theories of social class and social structure or taxonomies of class or status, which may of course be controversial. We need only accept the fact that individuals have social contacts with other individuals, because social network is about individuals and the relationships that can be contracted between them, and not primarily based on pre-defined group structures. To that extent it does not matter in principle whether the individuals are described in a particular society as 'upper class', 'middle class' or 'lower class', or whether the society is rural or urban: it is a universal that all individuals in all societies have contacts with other individuals (even the exceptional case – say, a hermit – has occasional societal contacts or has had them in the past, and 'isolates' are special cases). The advantage over stratificational social class (as in Labov, 1966) as a principal variable is the universality of the network concept: whereas stratificational social class theory cannot be universally applicable to all historical states, to bilingual situations, or to language- (that is, speaker-) contact situations (and all of these are relevant in historical description), all speakers at all times have had ties of some kind – weak or strong – with other speakers. Thus, unlike social class, social network does not require us to project *at the initial stage* a fully-fledged theory of social structure on to the linguistic data. We can therefore view social network, or some similar model of relationships between individual speakers, as the basis of a strictly *sociolinguistic* theory.

Furthermore, the idea of network impinges fairly closely on the notion of sociolinguistic *functions*, as we have presented this in chapter 2, because it is a fundamental postulate of network analysis that individuals create personal communities that provide them with a meaningful framework for solving the problems of their day-to-day existence (Mitchell 1986: 74). So the network relationships contracted between individuals are functional, just as linguistic variation is also functional (L. Milroy, 1987, discusses examples in which social network relationships are important enough to be viewed as survival mechanisms). There are other conceptual similarities between network analysis and linguistic analysis.

One of these is the fact that the social networks of individuals are, like language itself, open-ended and changing, and they cannot be precisely delimited for this reason. Furthermore, social network is conceptually at a more generalized level than are definable groupings, such as church or political organizations or street gangs (and the model may in principle embrace these within it). Thus, a person may be conscious of, for example, family and friendship relationships, or membership of institutional groups, but he/she is not fully aware at any point of the multiple web of (mainly informal) relationships that constitute a 'social network'. As it is conceptually so different from the idea of the 'peer-group' used by Labov (1972a) and Cheshire (1982), it is relatively difficult to operationalize social network as a quantitative speaker variable.

In order to adapt the idea for use in an monolingual urban situation, we have adopted for practical purposes certain procedures from ethnographic work, for example, the idea of measuring the intensity of network contacts; on the basis of this we can identify *clusters* of individuals within which the network links are relatively strong. Thus, for us, the idea of varying strength of network links is the nearest we can get to understanding the notion of a *speech community*. I shall return to, and elaborate on, these points. Here, the main issue arising is that, following Bott (1971), strong network ties can also be seen as *norm-enforcement mechanisms*. In this way, social network gives us a model for demonstrating how states of language are *maintained* through normative consensus within the communities, leaving external influences out of the argument at this stage.

4.2   Variable Norms in the Speech Community

An important general finding of the inner-city research is that in most of the linguistic variables quantified, there is a contextual style difference for all twelve groups of speakers, and there is also a sex-based difference. We have reported on the stylistic pattern quite fully in a number of places (for example, J. Milroy, 1981; L. Milroy, 1987), and I will not go into detail on it here. Although in some instances the sex/style differences are very slight, they are quite consistent in that they usually tend in the same direction, much as Labov (1966: 7) found for social class and style: 'Native New Yorkers differ in their usage in terms of absolute values of the variables, but the shifts between contrasting styles follow the same pattern in almost every case.' The conclusion we are entitled to draw from these findings is that, in general, female usage tends towards the more 'careful' end of the stylistic continuum and male usage towards the more 'casual', and it seemed at this stage of our research that we had some justification for the claim that in linguistic variation, sex-differentiation is prior to class differentiation and need not be interpreted as subsidiary to class (as it normally has been). Figure 4.1 is an example of clear sex differentiation in all three inner-city areas.

Notice, however, that although we may have views on the social class distribution of [ð] deletion (it can be readily observed to be less common in middle-class Belfast English), social class is at this stage an external category. We are interested here in finding out what the norms are *within* a single social stratum and how they function for the speakers: at this point in our work we have no justification for relating this pattern to social class differences. Figure 4.1 shows only a difference according to sex of speaker, but as this is quite consistent

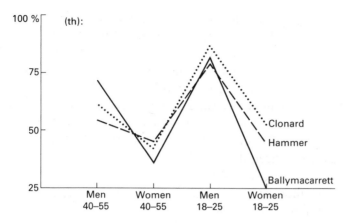

Figure 4.1   Deletion of medial [ð] in words of the type *mother, together.*

between generations, it has another quality: it is also a *stable* variable. It is this stability, and not any externally imposed category, that gives us the important clue to how the sociolinguistic patterns are maintained in speech communities. The norms of the community include stable differences between the sexes, with females tending towards careful style variants and males towards casual style (thus, when males are speaking in relatively formal settings, they will use a higher proportion of 'casual' variants than females will). But the most general conclusion that we draw from this kind of pattern is that the norms of a speech community are not necessarily uniform within that community, with every group agreeing on a single appropriate realization. We can therefore interpret our findings as evidence that what the community agrees on in this case is a pattern of stable differentiation over two generations between male and female usage.[2]

It seems, therefore, that *focused* patterns in real speech communities are not patterns in which all groups speak in the same way, but patterns of relatively stable differentiation within the community. In Belfast, however, we found that the three inner-city communities differed in the degree of focusing they exhibited. The community that showed the most stable and consistent patterns of gender-differentiation was the East Belfast Ballymacarrett community. It was immediately hypothesized that the relative degrees of focusing and diffuseness might be related to different degrees of social stability in the communities. In Ballymacarrett, there was less unemployment, traditional gender roles were more clearly differentiated, the population was resident in traditional streets of terraced houses, and for the most part it had been established there for generations. In the other communities, unemployment was rife, traditional gender roles were less clearly differentiated (with many women working while the men were unemployed), and there had been population movement. Additionally, the Hammer community was in the process of housing redevelopment, and many in-group members had moved out of the immediate area. Figure 4.2 shows the flattening-out effect – an effect that was also noticed (but usually to a lesser extent than this) in other variables: there is sharp differentiation in one community, but much less in the others. In fact almost all the variables quantified display the sharply differentiated pattern most clearly in Ballymacarrett.

What this suggests is that if there ever were a completely stable community which was totally insulated from the outside world, there would be stable differentiation within it – and gender-difference might often be one aspect of this. Stable differentiation is the normal state of affairs, and the existence of this variation is one of the things that makes linguistic change possible, in that the different variants can be latched on to by different groups and for different social functions: thus, the patterns of consensus can change in the course of time. Conversely, a community in which large-scale quantification reveals blurred and uncertain patterns of differentiation is likely to be relatively unstable and, in Le Page's terms, diffuse.

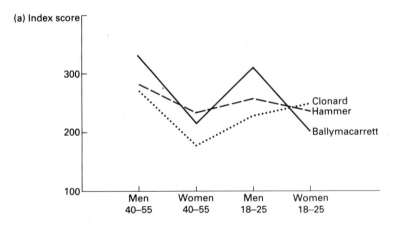

Figure 4.2 'Flattening-out' effect in gender variation in the Hammer as against Ballymacarrett.

The manner in which we used the social network variable has been fully described elsewhere (L. Milroy, 1987), and I shall limit my comments here to the question of focusing, stability and norm-enforcement. Ballymacarrett was the only one of the three areas in which there was a clear and consistent correspondence between the strength of a person's network structure and his or her use of vernacular (or casual) variants. It was this kind of evidence that led us to use the social network model in a systematic way: as Ballymacarrett is the most stable and well-established of the communities, we can conclude that the social conditions there are favourable to the emergence of a close-knit network structure of the kind often found in low-status communities (Young and Wilmott, 1962), and there is ample ethnographic evidence that a close-knit structure of this kind is capable of imposing normative consensus on its members. In other words, relatively close socializing patterns have the effect of maintaining traditional norms, including stable patterns of internal differentiation, and resisting change from outside. What we have tried to show here is that in this respect linguistic behaviour conforms to the same principles as the other patterns of social behaviour that have been studied by anthropologists.

But we have also noted that gender-differentiation in language is sharper in Ballymacarrett than in the other communities. Here, male network patterns prove to be more close-knit (as measured by a network strength score: NSS) than female networks, whereas this contrast is not so marked in the Hammer and is cancelled and partly reversed in the Clonard (one of the highest-scoring groups for NSS in West Belfast is the young *female* group in the Clonard, and this largely accounts for the Clonard score in Table 4.1). In fact, Ballymacarrett is the only area in which the gender difference in NSS is *statistically* significant. This is clear in Table 4.1.

Table 4.1 Mean network scores (maximum 5)

	Male	*Female*
Ballymacarrett	3.9583	1.3333
Hammer	2.1250	1.8750
Clonard	2.7500	2.8750

Thus, as we have noted above, agreement on norms (as consequence of close-knit and stable social patterns) results not in uniformity of usage within a community, but on agreement on a pattern of stable differentiation. In a relatively focused community such as Ballymacarrett, therefore, we observe much greater regularity in the patterning of the variable elements than we do in less focused communities, and we may further suggest that the variants used in such a focused community develop a clear and consistent pattern in their social functions. That is to say, it is more generally agreed here than elsewhere that preference for back realizations of /a/, for example, indicate close personal ties, casualness of conversational type, and/or male identity, and that other realizations indicate greater social distance and/or female identity. The less focused the community is, the less clear will be the relationship of specific linguistic variants to their various social functions. These points are of the greatest importance in developing a social model for the study of linguistic change, and there is much more to say about relative degrees of network strength as they affect patterns of change: I shall, therefore, refer back frequently to these findings.

As our work has sometimes been interpreted as conflicting with that of Labov, it should be noted here that the above characterization of the speech community is fundamentally of the same type as his and can be seen as derivative from his insights. Older characterizations of 'speech community', such as that of Wyld (1927: 47), assume that everybody speaking a 'dialect' speaks in the same way: these scholars would therefore have believed that inner-city Belfast is homogeneous and would simply not have expected to find the enormous diversity that actually does exist, so they probably would not have bothered to investigate it. Labov's (1966) definition, like ours, is based on agreement on norms of variation within the community rather than on the absolute values of the linguistic forms themselves. We can regard his clear statement as a hypothesis that can be empirically tested (and not a 'tenuous abstraction', as Lass, 1980: 121, views it), and our own investigation (as reported so far) as empirical testing of his claim. The difference that emerges is that whereas Labov's statement is based on speaker-agreement within the dimension of social class (and hence derivative from the 'shared value' hypothesis of stratificational class theory, on which see chapter 7), the characterization that I have built up thus far is based on the variables of age, sex, area and network, within a single social class, and without reliance on a prior model or theory of social class. It is this, and not any dispute about the existence of variable norms, that leads in practice to a number of differences in our treatment of 'speech community' and to some differences in our model of linguistic change.

It follows from what has been said so far that, as stable norms can be observed through analysis of linguistic patterns, change in progress will show up as violations of the expected 'normal' patterns. More generally, as linguistic stability consists in agreement on patterns of variation and on the social functions of the variants, linguistic change will appear as changes in agreement: as older patterns of agreement recede, so new patterns of agreement will emerge, and in the interim stage there may be some apparent randomness (or lack of agreement, or conflicting patterns) in the distribution of variants. Linguistic change, therefore, is *change in agreement on norms of usage*, and what we observe in our quantified data is difference in the *quantitative incidence* of certain variants in particular social groupings. This typically appears as a gradual pattern: therefore, from a sociolinguistic point of view, sound-change is most definitely a gradual process.

This view of what is meant by sound-change is very different from the traditional view, because it is speaker-based and not system-based. Let us explain this briefly. A language-centred description typically suggests that speech-sounds are objects that can actually change ([a] can 'become' [o], and so forth), when this is not what happens at all. Old English [aː], for example, did not actually 'become' open [ɔː] in Southern Middle English (as in OE *hām* > ME *hom(e)*). What happened was that *speakers* gradually and variably began to use open [ɔː] in environments where [aː] had formerly been used: the process was one of substitution rather than change *sensu stricto*.

For all these reasons, we have treated sound-change as something rather wider in scope than a simple unilinear process in a purely phonetic/phonological dimension. It is accepted that change in this unilinear aspect will indeed appear in our quantified findings – as a crossover pattern which violates the pattern of stable norms (as in Labov's classic example of class/style overlap for post-vocalic /r/ in New York City), and I shall discuss examples of this in later chapters. However, it is characteristic of quantified patterns that they can conceal what lies behind them and so they can be interpreted much more deeply than in this unilinear way. In the remainder of this chapter, therefore, I am concerned with the wider patterns of consensus and conflict in speaker-evaluation of the linguistic variants that we have studied, and I shall relate these to the concept of strong and weak ties in communities. I shall start by considering in section 4.3 some variables which are characteristic of Belfast English, but which seem to function at a somewhat higher level of generality than those that we have mentioned so far – as identity markers for the community as a whole rather than for internal differentiation within it.

4.3   Variables as Markers: the Identity Function

As we have seen, linguistic variables may be markers of certain fine-grained social functions within the community,[3] which can be broadly considered to be identity functions, and which may appear as age, sex or areal differences, for example. However, it may happen that particular variables selected for analysis turn out to be especially markers of one of these functions rather than another: one variable may be chiefly a close-tie network marker and another a marker of gender-differentiation. It is for this reason that in our quantitative analysis we have treated speaker variables as independent of one another. In fact, a particular variable may have more than one function, but it is only by a close analysis that treats speaker variables as independent that we will be able to determine whether this is so. I shall discuss an extended example of this in sections 4.6 and 4.7. Here, I have another purpose: I want to draw attention to the fact that different variables may be used by the community to mark functions of higher and lower levels of generality. For example, some variables (or variants of them) may be markers of gender-difference in the close communities, whereas others may not show fine-grained internal differentiation, but may be best interpreted as variables that mark Belfast vernacular *as a whole* as different from other varieties. These are not so much part of the 'inner voice': in Cohen's (1982) terms, they are perhaps more readily interpreted as the 'voice to the outside world'.

It is clear that some variables in English do function in a very general way: for example, variation between the alveolar and velar nasal in the present participle ending (ing) is universal and can be said to mark the whole English-speaking world as a single speech community. More narrowly, but still at a high level of generality, some variables may function as identity markers for whole status groups or for larger regions than merely an inner-city community. In British English, examples of this are [h]-dropping and glottalling, which are regionally widespread and usually marked for social status or style. As these broader functions are of importance in a theory of language change, I shall discuss them briefly here.

Some of Labov's New York City variables are of this broader type, and the larger number used by Trudgill (1974) are mixed in this way: some of them (such as [h]-dropping and (ing)) are common to many varieties, whereas others have social meaning only, or mainly, for Norwich and Norfolk speakers. As our inner-city work was mainly focused on very fine-grained differentiation, we have so far paid less attention to these more generalized markers in Belfast English, and in some cases we have not published the quantitative findings that arose from studying these. One such variable that has a wide distribution is the lateral consonant (L). In a number of dialects in northern England and peripherally in southern Scotland (J. Milroy, 1982c) there is a high incidence of noticeably 'clear' (palatal) variants of /l/, chiefly in pre-vocalic syllable-initial position, but also in other positions. As for Irish English, commentators routinely state that clear [l] is 'ubiquitous'.[4] For Belfast, however, this is certainly not so. It is characteristic of the inner-city vernacular that a noticeably clear (palatal) [l] is pre-vocalic but that a noticeably dark (velar) [l] is post-vocalic. But what is of interest here is that there is no difference between the three inner-city areas in the use of initial clear [l]. It is firmly established, and when there is a tendency to 'darkening' of initial [l], the conditions that apply are linguistic and not social: relatively 'dark' [l] occurs mainly before relatively retracted vowels. Thus, the clear [l] in initial pre-vocalic position is a broad regional marker, and we conclude from this relative invariance that it is not undergoing change. The Belfast *contrast* between clear and dark [l], however, is not characteristic of all Irish English or of all Ulster English. It is a feature of Belfast and surrounding areas and marks the speaker as a native of this region. However, at a more fine-grained level, there *are* differences in the incidence of the *dark* [l] variant (but not initial clear [l]) in the inner city according to age, sex and area. The findings for initial (L) are given in figure 4.3: as the total possible score is 200 (for maximum incidence of dark [l]), these scores show a very marked preference for clear [l] in initial position for all groups with no

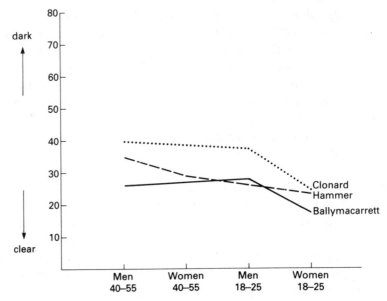

Figure 4.3 Average index scores by area for (L) in initial positions (maximum score: 200).

significant differences, and only a tendency for the young females to increase in their clear [l] usage (Owens, 1977).

At a somewhat less general level, however, there are also variables that function as markers of BV (as against more general Ulster or Irish varieties) and that do not vary significantly within the inner city in social terms. An example of this is variation between low and mid-front realizations of /a/ before velar consonants in words of the type *rag, pack, bang*, which show only slight differences in terms of age and sex within inner-city Belfast. However, the front-raised realization is easily perceived to be a very salient marker of vernacular speech in Belfast: as an identity marker, therefore, it marks nativeness to Belfast and adjacent areas, and it seems to be very firmly established. It contrasts in this way both with middle-class speech and with many of the dialect regions of south, mid and west Ulster.

I have discussed these matters briefly here because the broad distinction I have drawn is relevant to describing the 'shape' of the speech community and locating patterns of change within it. The markers that are characteristic of a variety perform social functions at lower and higher levels of generality. In the main parts of the Belfast projects we were more concerned with these lower levels of generality, because the findings have consequences for the notion of 'speech community'. As we have noted, if there were ever such a thing as a variety that was completely insulated and unaffected by external influence, these findings suggest very strongly that it would not be uniform and that there would still be variable community norms within it. But in reality there is no such thing as a wholly insulated variety: however strong the links may be that bind a population together, there will always be *some* consciousness of external norms, and this will have two kinds of effect on in-group behaviour. First, there will be resistance to external influence, and this will manifest itself as consensus norms within the dialect that affirm solidary behaviour. The agreement throughout the inner city on the (*bag*) variable can, for example, be interpreted in this way. Second, the external influence will in some cases actually be success- ful, and we may therefore be able to demonstrate how the new forms penetrate the solidary community. This implies that we need to take conflict into account here as well as changes in consensus.

I shall return in chapters 6 and 7 to consider these points more fully in the context of a model of weak and strong ties. In the remainder of this chapter, I want to use the solidarity model suggested by 'social network' to help to interpret patterns of variation in Belfast, referring to the inner-city and outer-city community studies and to our random sample 'doorstep' survey.

4.4   Investigating Patterns in the Inner City

In this section and the following ones I am concerned with the 'shape' of the Belfast speech community as a whole, and in particular with a kind of patterning that is not directly accessible by the classic methods of Labov (1966). These methods typically use a hierarchical model of society and measure linguistic variation in a single phonetic dimen- sion (such as, vowel-height) against a unilinear social dimension (in most cases socio-economic class). The result of this is that linguistic variation and change can appear to be unidimensional. For example, within a particular phoneme class, social groups can appear to be differentiated by greater or lesser preference for one particular phonetic realization of a single sound-segment. In this respect, these methods fit in well with traditional views of sound-change also, for these too are frequently unilinear (vowel A 'becomes' vowel B in the course of time). What these methods do not directly tell us is how wide or narrow the range of internal linguistic variation is *within* each social group, and how much the groups differ in the range of variants used. It may, for example, happen that social group A uses only two variants of a variable, whereas social group B uses three or four, and this type of difference may well be of just as much interest as an absolute difference in phonetic realization.

In fact, these differences in extent of variability within groups are sociolinguistically very important. It was clear from a very early stage of our Belfast work that to describe the inner-city phonology was a more complicated task than to describe 'middle-class' phonology, because there appeared to be much more variability within inner-city language than in higher status language. In this dimension, therefore, the speech community can be envisaged as being shaped like a pyramid, with greater variability at the lower end and greater convergence (or relative uniformity) at the upper end. It seems to be worth inquiring why this should be so, and what generalizations about sociolinguistic variation and change we can draw from this fact.

To approach this question, we bear in mind the principle that variability in language is socially functional. We also bear in mind the principles enunciated by Cohen (1982: 8) of ethnographic work on small solidary communities, which I have referred to in section 4.2 and which distinguish between the 'voice to the outside world' and the 'much more complicated' voice of the community 'to its own members'. According to this view in-group variation (in social affairs generally) is not only functional within communities, but also subtle and complicated, and difficult for outsiders to access. We are interested here in understanding the functional pressures that maintain these complex patterns of variation.

For our present purposes, there are two main senses in which the inner-city phonology can be said to be complicated: first, there is a much higher degree of 'low-level' allophonic variation in the inner-city than in outer areas, resulting in a wide range of variation and frequent overlap between phonemes; yet, this variation can be shown to be rule-governed; second, there is a high incidence of what I have called phono-lexical alternation (as measured in variables of type 2b) in the inner-city, which is much reduced in outer-city communities. In chapter 3, we noticed that lexical alternants (of the *pull* type) are highly salient in the community, and it has been shown in various studies (such as J. Milroy, 1981) that these alternants encode values of greater and lesser solidarity. In what follows my main purposes are: (1) to demonstrate the patterns of simplification that can be traced by comparing our inner-city data with that of the city-wide random sample 'doorstep' survey and the outer-city community studies; and (2) to consider how far a theory of strong and weak ties can account for the maintenance of complex patterns and the development of simpler ones. My first example concerns allophonic complexity. I shall use here the data on short /a/, but similar conclusions hold true of other vowels (for greater detail, see J. Milroy, 1976a, 1981; Harris, 1985).

The Belfast /a/ system varies considerably in terms of length, height, backness, rounding and diphthongization, and shows variation to a degree not attested in standard accounts of English phonology: if we include pre-velar items (as in table 4.2), the range (in place of articulation) is from mid-front to low-mid back. Table 4.2 is a simplified representation of the range of /a/, in terms of following consonantal environments. It is simplified in many ways: it ignores patterns of length and diphthongization and excludes tokens of post-velar environments in which front-raising occurs (chiefly among older speakers). Yet, it is still sufficiently detailed to make our main points.

Table 4.2   Range of realizations for /a/ in inner-city Belfast

ɛ	æ	a	a	ɔ
bag	back	back	grass	bad
bang	flash	bag	bad	man
		flash	man	can
		chap	pal	hand
		hat	hand	
		can't	can	
		ant		
		aunt		
		dance		

The pattern displayed here incorporates variation, but notice that the distribution of variants is rule-governed. The pre-velar vowel can vary between mid-front and low-front, but it cannot undergo backing.

Short vowels before voiceless stops (or sonorant + voiceless obstruent) are also front, but non-velar items cannot undergo front-raising. Before fricatives (except palatal fricatives) and voiced consonants generally, a long back vowel is favoured, with labial and nasal environments most inclined to display the rounded back vowel. In short, the heterogeneity in the system is orderly: it can, in principle, be described in terms of variable rules. Similarly, it can be described phonologically in terms of a set of sub-scales, in which the potential for lowering and backing will vary in degree for different subsets.

We had much evidence during fieldwork that these complicated rules are maintained by community pressures: for example, when a young East Belfast informant applied a strategy of front-raising (similar to RP) to the item *chap* (on a word-list), he was loudly mocked by his companions, who perceived his pronunciation as an attempt at RP (which for them is an effeminate stereotype). The item can be realized with a fully low front vowel, and a strategy of *backing* (but not of front-raising) can also be used in this social group.

To return to the main point about allophonic complexity: it is obvious, even from the simplified displays in the table, that these complex patterns are not easily learnable for outsiders, even though they are regular. How, for example, could an outsider know that normative consensus in the speech community does not permit backing in velar environments or fronting in most other environments, or that sonorants followed by voiceless obstruents predict a front vowel? It seems that these patterns are maintained by insider knowledge depending on the extent to which speakers belong to relatively close-knit groups. To the extent that these close-knit social relations are weakened, we may expect that these linguistic complexities will be reduced. In section 4.5 I shall adduce evidence from the outer city that suggests that this view is correct.

A second sense in which the inner-city phonology may be said to be complex is in the incidence of lexical items that have two alternative vowel pronunciations quite distinct phonetically and phonemically from each other. There are many such sets, and most of them (such as the *meet/meat* alternation) are highly salient. They are discussed in chapter 5 and by J. Milroy (1980, 1981); J. Milroy and Harris (1980); Harris (1985).

As exemplification of this, we have usually used the (*pull*) set. These items can be realized with a low-mid back short vowel (unrounded or slightly rounded), alternating with a high central to front rounded short vowel. In one realization they rhyme with *cut, dull*, and in the other with *good, pool* (both of which have short [u] in Scots and Ulster English). The set has deep historical roots and consists mainly of ME /u/ items with initial labials (such as *pull, bush, full*), and certain ME /o:/ items (such as *shook, foot*). Since 1860, as far as we can tell, three items that were formerly alternants have been reclassified as categorical [u] items (Patterson, 1860); thus, the speed of transfer has been very slow, and the set as a whole has been quite resistant to change. As we noticed in chapter 3, the full membership of this limited set is not predictable by environmental phonological rules: for example, whereas *shook, look* belong to it, *cook, book* do not. The items *wood, wool, hood* and probably *soot* used to belong to it, but do not now (Patterson, 1860). Yet, although *wood* no longer alternates, the homophonous item *would* does alternate. Furthermore, if *hood* could belong to the set, there seems to be no reason why *good* should not also have belonged to it; yet, as far as we know, it never did. Nevertheless, inner-city speakers know that some /u/ items can alternate and that others cannot. Thus, although some environmental phonological factors (such as initial labials) are involved in defining the set, speaker-knowledge of which items can alternate must depend largely on memorizing the items singly. It seems that the best explanation for the survival of this kind of insider knowledge is that the knowledge is reinforced by frequent close contact with other speakers, and this is best accessed by a theory of network ties, which when they are strong function as norm-enforcement mechanisms.

Furthermore, as we might expect, these alternations are functional. The existence of these sets provides an important sociolinguistic resource for inner-city speakers, and their survival must surely depend on this. First, in a broad sense, the 'in-group' variant: [ʌ], can be held to affirm group identity. More importantly, I think, the alternative choices can encode messages of social nearness or social distance – or, if you like, degrees of social distance. The in-group form encodes messages of intimacy and closeness, and, like the T pronoun (Brown and Gilman, 1960), can actually be *required* amongst close friends in casual circumstances: its strong affective meanings, however, are not easily accessible to outsiders. The other alternant is the out-group form, and this of course is used in interactions with those who have relatively weak ties with the speaker, or in situational contexts in which social distance is present. Again, we have evidence from fieldwork about the functions of these alternants: one man of 27 commented that during his years away from Northern Ireland, he had stopped using what I have called the in-group alternants of the (*pull*) set. The most obvious explanation for this is that during his years away from home, he would develop a large number of relatively weak ties: in such circumstances, the in-group alternant would cease to have any function for him and so could be abandoned. This functional explanation seems to be more satisfactory than, and logically prior to, one based on *prestige*: as it happens, this individual's activities away from home had not been upwardly mobile.

If weak-tie situations can exist even in the inner-city communities themselves (L. Milroy (1987: 131) discusses the case of Hannah McK from the Clonard area who has a density/multiplexity score of 0), it is to be expected that within the wider social structure of a city, social distance between groups will develop even more. In such circumstances, the norm-enforcement mechanisms that maintain the complex structure of inner-city variation (and other patterns of language use) will be weakened, and simplification is likely. In section 4.5 I shall use some of the findings of the doorstep survey and the outer-city community studies to inquire further into this.

4.5   Linguistic Patterns in the Wider Speech Community

The traditional view of urban dialect was that it is not 'dialect' at all. This term was reserved for the rural dialects, which had been legitimized by nineteenth-century investigations, and which were believed to be 'genuine' in a way that urban dialects are not. The latter were widely regarded as corrupt and impure (see for example the views on Cockney cited in note 1, above). This attitude to urban dialect seems to have been given further impetus by the view of Wyld (1927) that urban English can be described as the 'Modified Standard' of 'city vulgarians'. This implies that it can be characterized as an unsuccessful, or partly successful, effort by urban dwellers to achieve competence in 'standard' English (which for Wyld is the English of the upper and upper-middle classes). Our work in Belfast, however, and that of colleagues in other cities, makes it clear that this cannot be convincingly demonstrated. The language of urban people, to the extent that it is 'modified', is modified *vernacular*: it cannot be adequately explained in terms of modifications to the 'standard' (in which many speakers show no interest at all). It is easier to understand it as an attempt to move away from something already characteristic of the community than as an attempt to move towards some outside idealization (compare my comments on avoidance of stigma in Chapter 2.6, above). In this section, I am concerned with the modifications to the inner-city vernacular that can be observed in outer-city language.

In our second project, we selected our two outer-city areas rather carefully. We wanted them to represent a section of the community that was quite close in the social hierarchy to the inner-city population, and in the event many speakers in the samples had inner-city social and family contacts. The intention here was to test our theory by making things difficult for ourselves: it would have been much easier to select upper-middle class communities and to demonstrate gross differences between them and the inner city. This, however, would have been to trivialize: the results would be of little interest. But the speakers in Andersonstown and Braniel are strong Belfast speakers: an outsider would be unlikely to notice much difference between their speech and that of the Clonard and Ballymacarrett. In order to show that there are differences in language, therefore, we have to listen to many hours of tape-recorded speech, select variables that we believe may pattern in some way, and quantify. The most salient difference between these outer-city informants and the inner-city ones is not linguistic, but social, and of course we knew this. As for the doorstep survey, this was carried out in order to generalize about the speech of the city as a whole, and in this way to be able to describe modifications to the vernacular that might be of general import. Here, I shall first consider some results of the doorstep survey.

I have elsewhere shown (J. Milroy, 1982b) that the range of variation in (a) is greatly reduced in speakers outside the inner city. Table 4.3, which is from the doorstep survey of speakers throughout the city, shows total convergence on a low front vowel for /a/, and table 4.4 demonstrates another interesting point. In it the two front-raised items (*castle, dabble*) appear to be randomly front-raised rather than governed by any systematic rule. The vernacular rules predict that *dabble* will be subject to backing – certainly not front-raising – and it is unlikely that this speaker is following the highly recessive rule for front-raising after velars in the item *castle* (this has been largely abandoned by younger low-status speakers). Table 4.5,

Table 4.3   /a/ range for a middle-class Belfast speaker: word-list style
(random sample survey).

	ɛ	æ	a	ä	a	ɔ
bag			+			
back			+			
cap			+			
map			+			
passage			+			
cab			+			
grass			+			
bad			+			
man			+			
castle			+			
dabble			+			
passing			+			

Index score of convergence on [a]: 0 (max. convergence)
Range score: 0 (min. range)

Table 4.4   /a/ range for a middle-class Belfast speaker: word-list style
(random sample survey).

	ɛ	æ	a	ä	ɑ	ɔ
bag			+			
back			+			
cap			+			
map			+			
passage			+			
cab			+			
grass			+			
bad			+			
man			+			
castle		+				
dabble		+				
passing			+			

Range score: 1

Table 4.5   Range of variation in /a/ showing simplification pattern by status group and gender

Average range scores (maximum 5):		
Lower group (LWC–MWC)	2.83	
Upper group (UWC–MC)	1.97	
No. of speakers with range of 1 or less:		
Lower group	1	(4 per cent)
Upper group	11	(31 per cent)
No. of males and females with range of 1 or less:		
Males	3	(10 per cent)
Females	9	(30 per cent)
No. of speakers with range of 3 or more:		
Lower group	16	(66.7 per cent)
Upper group	10	(27.7 per cent)

based on the output of 60 speakers, shows that the reduction in range for this vowel throughout the city is clear and consistent (statistically, the pattern is very highly significant). Furthermore, it is sex-graded: females are *significantly* more likely to simplify than males. Although it is impossible in a doorstep survey to estimate network strengths for individuals, it is extremely likely that varying network strengths are also implicated in the simplification pattern. The more dense and multiplex the ties, the more likely it is that complexity will be maintained.

In the doorstep survey, two further variables were fully quantified, and others less closely examined. The pattern for (ɛ) (as in *went, bed*) proved to be virtually identical to that for (a). Superficially, the results for the lexical alternant class of (*pull*) were much the same also. The lower-status group figures were again very much higher than those for the upper group (2.17 as against 0.91, out of a possible 4.00): this means that lower group speakers, on average, use the vernacular alternant for *two* or more of the four lexical items, *even in word-list style* – a surprising finding in terms of Labov's predictions on contextual style. Word-list style is a careful style in his terms (but as we have shown in a number of publications, Labov's predictions about the stylistic continuum did not work in this divergent-dialect community in the way that they had worked in New York City). The figures for males and females are also consistent with our findings for (a) and (ε): females lead in the move away from traditional vernacular forms, and this in the long term tends to reduce allophony and simplify alternations. Thus, it may well be worth considering the possibility that sex-differentiation in language contributes to simplification patterns and hence to the establishment of supra-local norms. We now turn to the findings of the two outer-city community studies, which also show a pattern of reduction of allophony.

The social characteristics of the two outer-city communities differ quite considerably from those of the inner city. They are upper-working to lower-middle class. The people were not necessarily born and brought up in the same neighbourhood; many are upwardly mobile (unlike the inner-city people). Above all, very few of them meet more than one of the criteria used in the inner-city for measuring network strength, and the essential reason for this is that their network ties are not mainly territorial. The inner-city indicators were based largely on territorial assumptions, for example that people might have close relatives living in the same street or the next street, and that people would work in the same places as some of their close neighbours (L. Milroy 1987: 141–2). This was seldom true in the outer city. Those people whose families had moved out from the inner areas still retained some ties with relatives in the inner city, but clearly such ties are by definition weaker in quality than ties with immediate neighbours, and they were dismissed as relatively weak in our inner-city network analysis. In other cases, people had no inner-city ties, and ties with neighbours tended to be uniplex and open-ended, rather than multiplex and dense. Sometimes people did not even know their neighbours. Thus, although these outer-city neighbourhoods do not to a casual observer differ much from the inner city in language, they do exhibit clear social differences. In our project this meant that measures of network strength that we used in the inner city could not be readily operationalized for these speakers. In this respect, therefore, the outer-city studies lay the basis for the arguments about weak ties put forward in J. Milroy and L. Milroy (1985b) and further discussed in later chapters.

In such conditions, one important prediction is that the weakening of norm-enforcement mechanisms will bring about a reduction in the everyday functional value of the use of in-group linguistic variants. Thus, we are prepared to find that the simplification pattern apparent in the findings of the doorstep survey may also apply to the outer-city neighbourhoods. In addition, the breakdown of inner-city consensus may lead to patterns of usage that are less predictable by linguistic rule or by sociolinguistic pattern. Thus, some apparently random variation, or some lack of agreement on norms of usage (as in table 4.5) may be encountered.

It had been noticed in the inner city that many vowel variables could be described in terms of sub-scales according to following consonantal environments (as in table 4.5); we attempted, therefore, to operationalize this perception by distinguishing following environments roughly based on the sonority scales discussed by Taylor (1973) and others adapted to an 'allophonic length' dialect (J. Milroy, 1976a). They were as follows:

T = voiceless stop (incl. affricate) or sonorant + voiceless obstruent
TS = environment described in T + a following syllable in same morpheme
D = voiceless fricative or any voiced consonant not immediately followed by a voiceless segment
DS = environment described in D + a following syllable in same morpheme

These categories were used in the quantification of (a), (ɔ) and (ɛ) (as in *cap, stop, bet*) in the outer city (a modified version is used in sections 4.6 and 4.7), and a particular aim of the method was to distinguish between variation in quality and variation in length. Hence, in the range diagrams (tables 4.6 and 4.7), tokens are listed in columns showing length as well as place of articulation. It is immediately

Table 4.6 /ɔ/ in Andersonstown

ä	ɑ	ɑ	ɑː	ɔ	ɔː
T got (2)			T shop		
DS Polytech					
T shop				DS probably	D job (3)
T pot	DS concentrated				D of
	DS vodka				D God
				TS bottom	

Table 4.7   /ɛ/ in Andersonstown

ä	ɛ	ɛː	ɛ̣	ɛ̣ː	eː
	T set-up (2)		DS specials	D	
	T lent		T went	red	
	T went (2)			D tell	
	DS specials (3)			D ten	
	DS remember				
	TS twenty				

obvious here that, for (ɔ), the extreme left-hand column is empty, and that, for (ɛ), both the extreme left- and extreme right-hand columns are empty. In the inner city, however (see the Clonard figures in table 4.8), not only is the full range exploited, but the empty left-hand columns (for environment T in the inner city) are in the order of 100 per cent (that is, categorical) for virtually all the males (young and old) in the sample. This compares with quantities close to zero in the outer city, for most speakers. Similarly, the range from low to high-mid (in the case of (ɛ)) is reduced to a much narrower range in table 4.7. In this connection, Gunn (1982) reports that for (a) also the range in Andersonstown is reduced to variation between [æ] and [a] (the latter sometimes slightly retracted), but he adds that this is particularly the case for young speakers; older people frequently retain the vernacular rules of the inner city. Thus, these findings support the findings of the random sample, in which, as we have seen, the range of realizations is reduced in 'upper group' speakers.

There is also some indication that the appearance of particular items in particular columns is less easily shown as rule-governed than it is in the inner city. It is rather surprising to find, in table 4.6, that the item *shop* appears with a low back slightly rounded *long* vowel, and the rounded vowel in the disyllable/polysyllables *probably, bottom* is also rather surprising. These trends might of course represent the beginning of a change in progress, but if this is so, it is not yet established as a pattern that we can show by our methods as regular, and so we cannot demonstrate that it is a change. But from this, and from table 4.8, it is reasonable to conclude that the situation is in this respect less *focused* than in the inner city. The agreement on norms that we noticed in the inner city seems here to have been weakened.

Table 4.8 measures in broad terms low as against non-low realizations of (ɔ) in the two outer-city areas as against the inner-city Clonard area. Although this table ignores backness, roundness and other phonetic categories, it also shows us something of interest. The rule constraining low *v* non-low realizations is much closer to being categorical in the low-status inner-city area than in the outer city; indeed, for the T and TS environments, it is categorical. As we have noted above, it is qualitatively a near-front unrounded vowel categorically for most male inner-city speakers, but table 4.8 shows that, regardless of fronting, it is still always a low vowel in Catholic West Belfast. This finding may be interpreted as supporting the view expressed above that the inner-city vernacular, although it shows more complex patterns, is more amenable to description in terms of linguistic *rules* than outer-city speech. We can add that it may be the effects of network strength that maintain this relative consistency.

The general picture that emerges from these patterns of variation is one in which simplification patterns and loss of regularity and consistency are related to the weakening of network strength and the development of patterns of weak ties. There may well be other patterns of simplification besides these, and one of these seems to be the merger of classes that were previously distinct. The gradual loss of alternating classes, such as (*pull*) is also related to merger patterns, as the end result of this long historical process is loss of a distinction which at the moment is still *socially* functional. In the present perspective, I would propose that resistance to merger, lexical

Table 4.8

	Andersonstown		Braniel		Clonard	
/ɔ/–	(+ low) 81 (– low) 19	/–T	(+ low) 64 (– low) 36	/–T	[+ low] (100%)	/–T /–TS
	(+ low) 74 (– low) 26	/–TS	(+ low) 74 (– low) 26	/–TS		
	(– low) 86 (+ low) 14	/–D	(– low) 93 (+ low) 7	/–D	(– low) 87 (+ low) 13	/–D /–DS
	(+ low) 80 (– low) 20	/–DS	(+ low) 51 (– low) 49	/–DS	(+ low) 91 (– low) 9	

transfer and restructuring is promoted by the existence of strong network ties, and that types of change that result in simplification are encouraged by weakening of ties. Complex patterns, which (as we have argued) are functional, are maintained by the norm-enforcement function of dense and multiplex networks. For those whose ties are uniplex and (relatively) open-ended, these patterns are no longer functional and it is for this reason, and not primarily because of speakers' desire for 'prestige', that they disappear.

The purpose of our discussion so far has been to demonstrate that there are important patterns of change that are not readily captured in a paradigm that measures a unilinear scale of phonetic variation against a unilinear scale of socio-economic class. I have also avoided using the concept of prestige in the discussion because it appears that the patterns can be interpreted without reference to prestige. If we argue, nevertheless, that prestige models can still account for the trend to simplification and uniformity that we have revealed, we have to explain in this case *why* simplification should carry prestige. The trend to uniformity (not always necessarily simplification) that is often found in so-called prestige accents (such as RP) would seem itself to be related to functional factors. As Jakobson perceived long ago, those varieties that have supra-local functions and that tend to develop in the direction of koines display simpler phonemic systems than varieties that have purely local functions (for an excellent discussion of simplification and complexity in a range of language situations, see Andersen, 1986). It may well be that, in varieties that have supra-local functions, a high degree of complexity (at any level) is indeed dysfunctional.

In the social status dimension, of course, the network model is also explanatory, as different status levels in society are normally charac-terized by different degrees of network density and multiplexity (we shall discuss this more fully in chapter 7). At the lowest and highest levels, network density and multiplexity is normally high: it is chiefly in the middle ranges of society that social and geographical mobility lead to the development of large numbers of relatively weak ties: individuals at these levels have more uniplex and diffuse ties. At these levels, the complex variation which encodes rich social meanings to insiders simply becomes progressively more and more redundant: it is no longer functional for these mobile people.

Finally, in the dimension of sex-differentiation, it would appear from our studies of (a), (ε) and the (*pull*) alternant (in addition to many similar cases in the inner city) that females lead in the development of supra-local norms (including those that involve systemic simplification). This perception seems to come closer to providing an explanation for sex-differentiation in language than explanations based on prestige. In the following sections, we look more generally at patterns of change in two Hiberno-English vowels.

4.6   Reviewing Evidence for Change in Progress in Two Hiberno-English Vowels

In this section and the next I am concerned with tracking linguistic change in the vowels /a/ and /ɛ/ in Belfast English, relating these changes both to historical/ geographical background and to network structure. First, it is important to recall that in BV (as compared with textbook descriptions of standard English) many vowels have a startlingly wide range of realizations (see the range for /a/ in table 4.2). This results in overlapping: thus, some realizations of /ɛ/ are like /a/, and vice versa, and this applies particularly to the short vowel environments (following voiceless stop, following sonorant + voiceless obstruent). For some groups of inner-city male speakers vowels in words of the type *wet, went,* are very consistently realized as [a, æ], and this often seems to be merged with /a/, as in *sat, want.* First, we review the regional and social range of realizations of /ɛ/.

Figure 4.4 shows the result of a quantitative analysis of /ɛ/ realizations in two Belfast outer-city communities (Andersonstown and Braniel) and a smaller town (Lurgan) situated 17 miles southwest of Belfast. The symbol T indicates a following voiceless stop or sonorant + voiceless stop cluster; CS indicates that the vowel is in the stressed syllable of a polysyllabic word (this environment tends to favour short realizations); D indicates following fricative or voiced consonant (excluding /r/). Notice that the lowest short realization, [a], is not favoured, but that in Lurgan short and low realizations in short environments (T, CS) are more favoured than elsewhere (see also below), and that long realizations [æː, ɛː] in these short environments are rarer in Lurgan. The inner-city figures (Ballymacarrett, Clonard, Hammer) in table 4.9 clearly show some contrasts with the outer-city figures. Before voiceless stops, a low short realization ([a], [æ]) is categorical for many male speakers, while the

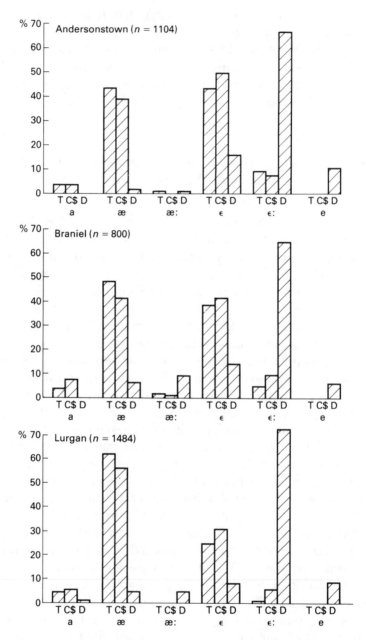

Figure 4.4   Percentage distribution of /ɛ/ (*bed*, *bet*) variants by following environment in outer-city Belfast (Andersonstown, the Braniel) and Lurgan. (Adapted from Harris, 1985)

Table 4.9   Percentage low realizations of /ɛ/ in typically 'short' phonetic contexts in three inner-city Belfast communities, Ballymacarrett (B), the Clonard (C) and the Hammer (H)

	Men 40–55	Women 40–55	Men 18–25	Women 18–25
T B	100	68	100	56
C	97	81	84	73
H	97	75	98	67
CS B	73	56	78	50
C	81	67	75	60
H	76	68	76	52

women more often prefer higher and often lengthened realizations. Thus, for typically low vowel environments, as in *wet, went*, females often have [wɛːt, wɛːnt] for 'vernacular' [wat, want]. In this respect the inner-city female pattern is similar to that found generally in outer-city communities.

These variable data give us a basis for examining processes of change, since they suggest initially that either the higher or lower variants are innovatory, or – more properly – that the direction of change is either raising or lowering of /ɛ/.

In fact, an examinations of historical documentation (real-time evidence) suggests that the direction of change is towards raising. Moreover, it appears that mid realizations are gradually appearing in environments (such as pre-voiceless stop) where low realizations were once the norm. It also appears that as the low variants are replaced by higher ones, the relevant vowels are lengthened and sometimes diphthongized: thus, as the rules are applied, conservative variants such as [rant, rænt]: 'rent', are replaced by [rɛ·nt] (raising and lengthening) and [rɛ·ənt] (diphthongization). The options open to speakers for the realization of /ɛ/ before voiceless stop or before consonant + voiceless stop may be described as follows:

1   Choose either *mid* or *low*;
2   If *low*, realize as *short*;
3   If *mid*, realize as *long*;
4   If *mid-long*, realize as monophthong or diphthong.

This is of course an idealized and simplified account, and the aim of listing such options is descriptive only. Nor is there any implied claim that all individual speakers have the same rules or rule-order – far from it. Accepting this as a broad description of the current state, we now examine some real-time data in order to confirm the direction of change.

Patterson gives a list of five words of the /ɛ/ class, which were then (1860) pronounced in Belfast with low realizations: *wren, wrestle, wretch, grenadier, desk*. These few examples are enough to show that the low realization was then more widespread than today: *wren* and *desk* do not satisfy the voiceless stop or sonorant + voiceless stop condition in monosyllables, and are now categorical [ɛ:] or [ɛ·ə] environments. Even the disyllable *wrestle* is unlikely to appear with [a], as the rule for raising and lengthening before [-s] now almost always overrides the tendency to lower and shorten in disyllables and polysyllables. Items like *wretch* and *grenadier* are now variable. Staples (1898) and Williams (1903) additionally give quite detailed descriptions of the vowel in the city, which allow us to infer that low variants had a much wider distribution then than they do today. The complete list taken from those early writers allows us to see that the low vowel appeared in environments where it would not appear now – for example, before voiceless fricatives and voiced stops. The distribution in present-day Belfast is quite different, as is shown by table 4.9 and figure 3.3. In conservative working-class speech, low variants are maintained in 'short' environments, very much as in the nineteenth century: but low realizations have been almost entirely replaced in long environments by mid realizations of /ɛ/. More 'prestigious' and less conservative speakers are less likely to use 'low' realizations, even in short environments.

It is evident that over the last hundred years or so mid realizations have been spreading at the expense of low realizations. Mid /ɛ/ has now almost totally replaced low /ɛ/ in 'long' contexts (pre-voiced stop, pre-sonorant + voiced stop, and pre-fricative). Low-status inner-city speakers (males) sometimes still have categorically low realizations in short environments, but in the more progressive outer-city housing estates the vowel is now categorically mid for some speakers. Interestingly, the distribution of variants in Lurgan is more similar to that of the inner-city areas than that of the outer areas (a pattern that applies also to other vowel and consonant variables). This relatively rapid linguistic change in Belfast has accompanied its rise in population from about 120,000 in 1860 to nearly half a million in the early years of this century, and Belfast may be taken as an exemplar of linguistic change in fast-growing communities (while rural towns and villages adhere to older patterns). The characteristic network structures of these different types of community are also relevant to the manner in which change may come about, in so far as urban growth tends at first to weaken strong pre-existing rural networks.

We may supplement our observations on /ɛ/ by considering evidence from present-day Ulster dialects. These are divided into two distinct types. Ulster Scots dialects are found in east Ulster in a belt extending from around Coleraine in the north, through most of County Antrim and much of County Down (which is south of Belfast – see figure 4.5). Most of Ulster to the west of this belt is English-based or mixed Scots-English. Present-day Belfast dialect is often described as an intrusion of this Mid-Ulster type into the Scottish eastern belt. Now, the long mid variants of /ɛ/ are overwhelmingly associated with present-day Ulster Scots dialects (Gregg, 1972) and are characteristic of modern central Scots dialects generally. Traditional Mid-Ulster English, on the other hand, is characterized by lower realizations in all environments. The pattern of distribution in these dialects is remarkably similar to that of nineteenth-century Belfast vernacular as described in Patterson, Staples and Williams. We may infer that this pattern is a residue of some earlier English vowel pattern that has not been well identified or described by historical linguists. There is sixteenth-century orthographic evidence, which we shall further discuss in chapter 5, that suggests some distribution of low vowel realizations for /ɛ/ in London English of the period: it seems possible that this pattern of lowering of historic short vowels has been overtaken in recent standard English and Central Scots by a pattern of raising and (in the latter case) lengthening. The Mid-Ulster dialects may therefore have preserved to a great extent an older general English vowel pattern, and they may help us to project knowledge of the present on the past.

The historical and geographical evidence then both suggest that the low realizations of /ɛ/ (conservative English in background) are giving way in a linguistically ordered way to the long mid realizations characteristic of present-day Scots. It is clear that this change is highly evaluated in Belfast in terms of social class hierarchy and status, as it is the more prestigious groups that tend to adopt it and the more 'advanced' (generally female and younger) group who introduce

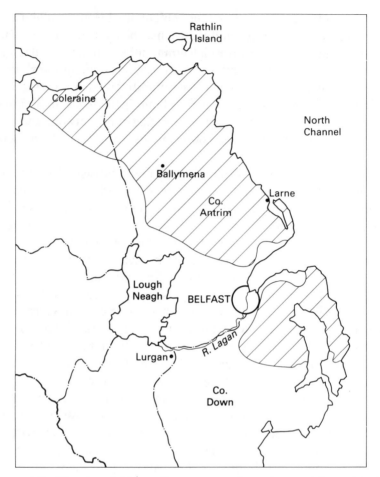

Figure 4.5 The 'core' Ulster Scots areas of north-east Ulster (shaded areas). (Adapted from Gregg, 1972)

it to the conservative inner-city communities (which are characterized by dense and multiplex network ties that tend to resist innovation and maintain conservative forms). The tension between innovative and conservative social mechanisms gives rise to a identifiable pattern of gradual diffusion, which may be represented as a historical shift from an older English-type pattern towards a pattern characteristic of modern Scots. As we have implied, the manner in which the change proceeds is conditioned by both social and phonological factors. We now turn to a description of change in /a/, with which the /ɛ/ system can be compared.

As indicated in table 4.2, the range of realizations of /a/ in present-day Belfast vernacular is considerable – from [ę] through [a] and [ɑ] to back raised and rounded [ɔ]. Again, as for /ɛ/, patterns of lengthening and diphthongization are present, with long vowels being associated mainly with back realizations and with the higher front realizations before voiced velars (see table 4.2). In what follows, we are concerned only with backing and retraction, and we therefore largely exclude the pre-velar environments (in which backing is not found).

Table 4.2 also shows that back realizations are favoured by following fricatives, non-velar voiced stops and non-velar nasals. Nasals favour backing particularly strongly. Middle-class urban speakers, as we have seen, tend to narrow the extreme range described above. The widest range is found mainly in the speech of inner-city male speakers. Furthermore, it is the males of Ballymacarrett (East Belfast) who use the backed variants most and who show evidence of spreading the backed realizations into voiceless stop environments (as in *that*, *wrap*), where short, front variants are expected. If there is evidence of change in progress towards backed varaints of /a/, it will therefore be male speakers who are leading it, rather than the females who lead the change towards raised /ɛ/.

Historical documentation suggests that /a/ backing is a recent trend. Patterson does not comment on /a/ backing at all. On the contrary, his remarks suggest that the Ulster tendency was towards fronting and raising and that the most salient Belfast feature was fronting and raising in velar environments (1860: 15).

> In some places [presumably in the north of Ireland: JM] the short sound of *e* is improperly substituted for *a*, in almost every word in which it occurs; in Belfast, however, this error is almost exclusively confined to those words in which *a* is preceded by *c* or *g*, or followed by the sound of *k*, hard *g* or *ng*.

A very few of Patterson's spellings may indicate that /a/ backing and rounding had been observed sporadically in -*r* and -*l* environments: he has *form* for 'farm' and *canaul* for 'canal'. However, examples of this kind are so few that they indicate only a slight tendency (possibly confined to some pre-sonorant environments), which is not enough for /a/ backing to be discussed as a stereotype. The item *car* appears in Patterson as 'care', in which the now highly recessive rule for fronting and raising after velars is clear. Items like *hand, band*, in which [ɔ] is now stereotypically expected, are given simply as *han, ban*, etc. Frequently, however, items that now have low and/or back vowels, are given with [ɛ]: these include *rether* for 'rather' (a rural Scots residue), *e* for *a* in single nasal environments in polysyllables such as *exemine, Jenuary* and in nasal cluster environments such as *demsel, exemple, Entrim* ('Antrim'), *slent, bendy* ('bandy'), *brench*.

Whereas Patterson's account indicates a system generally inclined towards front-vowel realizations, Staples (1898), writing nearly 40 years later, reports a 'low back wide' vowel before non-velar nasals, for example in *man, hand, land*. Since Patterson's time – /r/ environments have become categorically back realizations. Otherwise, the figures on present-day variations strongly suggest that since then it is nasal environments that have subsequently led the change, closely followed by fricative and voiced stop environments.

Thus, although raising and lengthening of /ɛ/ and backing of /a/ are both changes associated with modern Central Scots, the former is at present led in Belfast by females and the latter by males. It is clear from patterns of stylistic variation that (as we might already have inferred) the two changes have different social evaluations. As table 4.10 indicates, the backing of /a/ tends to be resisted by speakers in careful 'interview' style (whereas raising of /ɛ/ is *more* likely in careful

Table 4.10 Incidence of retraction and backing of /a/ by age, sex and conversational style in two Belfast communities, calculated by an index score ranging from 0 (minimum) to 4 (maximum). IS, interview style; SS, spontaneous style.

| | East Belfast (Ballymacarrett) | | | |
	Men (40–55)	*Women (40–55)*	*Men (18–25)*	*Women (18–25)*
IS	3.03	1.75	2.89	1.89
SS	3.58	2.58	3.43	2.10

| | West Belfast (Clonard) | | | |
	Men (40–55)	*Women (40–55)*	*Men (18–25)*	*Women (18–25)*
IS	2.79	1.77	2.36	2.36
SS	2.79	1.85	2.33	2.61

styles). Thus, men seem to be principally associated with a change that speakers do not consciously evaluate highly, while women are associated with one adopted by speakers in their more carefully monitored styles. We shall return to the table 4.10 pattern in chapter 6.

Our real time evidence confirms that the movement in /a/ is phonetically from front to back. This means that sporadic front-raising (found mainly in West Belfast) in such words as *flat, trap* ([flɛt, trɛp]) must be seen as residues and not as innovations. The fronting and raising rule in Belfast vernacular is virtually confined to velar environments and cannot apply to such words as *bad, hand, stab* (which are front in RP). The diachronic evidence shows that, for a century or more, the trend has been towards retraction and backing.

The evidence also indicates that the rule for backing diffuses geographically from East to West Belfast (see table 4.10). Scores for /a/ backing are higher for East Belfast males than for any other groups studied, and the range of environments in which backing operates is extended to voiceless stops amongst younger East Belfast males. It appears to be inner East Belfast (Ballymacarrett) that provides the model for working-class speech in the city (L. Milroy, (1980), 1987); this is represented by the (relatively) fully employed Protestant population of East Belfast.

Both /a/ backing and /ɛ/ raising are relatively recent phenomena in Belfast (but see below), and both are associated with a background in Scots. Patterson's account of Belfast shows characteristics of conservative rural Scots lexical distribution, much of which appears to have been residual and is now obliterated by restructuring. However, lengthening and raising of /ɛ/ and /a/-backing are modern Scots. Gregg's (1972) account of Ulster Scots gives overwhelmingly back realizations of /a/ and describes /ɛ/ as often long in realization (contrast the very short low realizations in conservative Belfast vernacular, such as [stap, dʒat] for *step, jet*). Similarly, /a/ backing seems to be a very general modern Scots feature (Lass, 1976). East Belfast adjoins the Ulster-Scots region of North Down (where backing is strong), whereas West Belfast points south-west down the Lagan Valley, the speech of which is Mid-Ulster with less Scots influence; furthermore, immigration to West Belfast is recent and is largely from a Mid- and West-Ulster non-Scots hinterland. Present day quantitative studies in Lurgan, a small country town south-west of Belfast in the Lagan Valley, confirm the existence of an /a/ system with little backing (front vowels have been noted in that area even before [r] and finally), which is quite similar to Patterson's (1860) account of Belfast in this respect (Pitts, 1982).

4.7   Social Network Structure and Speaker Innovation: an Analysis of /a/ and /ɛ/

In addition to the variables of age, sex and status, a further social variable associated with a speaker's *degree of integration* into his close-knit community appears to affect the probability of his being linguistically innovative with respect to choice of vowel variants. This variable is *social network*.

A major point emerging from our analysis of language/network relationships is that the variable network needs to be considered in relation to the variable *sex of speaker*. Indeed, as Gumperz has remarked (1982: 71), the network variable is in general closely associated with many others, including generation cohort, geographical location, and social status. Thus, our next task here it to pick out briefly the relevant parts of our analysis of the social distribution of innovatory realizations of /a/ and /ɛ/, as identified in section 4.6.

First of all, realizations of /a/ and /ɛ/ are strongly affected by the variable *sex of speaker*. Thus, although incoming variants of both vowels appear to have originated in the same hinterland Scots dialect, each has assumed a diametrically opposed *social* value in its new urban setting.

Raised variants of /ɛ/ are, in the low-status inner city, associated particularly with women and with careful speech styles. They are also associated generally with outer-city speech, and data collected by survey methods confirm that the higher the status of the speaker, the more likely he is to use raised variants (see J. Milroy et al., 1983). Different levels of use according to sex of speaker are particularly evident in Ballymacarrett, where it appears to be *younger female* speakers who are most strongly associated with the incoming raised variants.

The incoming variants of /a/ show an almost perfectly converse pattern of social distribution. High levels of backing are associated with males (particularly Ballymacarrett males, although levels in other inner-city areas are still quite high) and with casual styles appropriate to interaction between areas. The most extremely backed variants do not appear at all in outer-city speech. Interestingly, the sex-differentiation pattern across the three inner-city areas is not as consistent for /a/ as it is for /ɛ/; there is some indication that the young Clonard women are increasing their use of back realizations when compared with other female groups (see table 4.10). They also use these variants *more* than their male counterparts, although they follow the expected sex-differentiation patterns with respect to other phonological variables (see chapter 6 for a discussion of the Clonard pattern).

In summary, then, it appears that incoming variants of /a/ are associated with core Belfast vernacular, while incoming variants of /ɛ/ are associated with careful higher-status speech.

If we look at the relationship between speaker-choice of variant and individual network structure, the picture becomes even more complicated. With respect to both vowels, choice of variant shows a correlation with personal network structure in some subsections of the inner-city communities; but the details of this correlation are quite different for each vowel.

The vowel /a/ is particularly sensitive to variation according to the network structure of the speaker; but women appear to correlate their choice of variant more closely with their personal network structure than do men. This means that among women a relatively large amount of /a/ backing is more likely to be associated with a high level of integration into the network than is the case among men – a relationship analysed by Spearman's Rank Order Correlation (L. Milroy, 1987: 155). Although, as we have noted, women are much less likely than men to select back variants of /a/, this generally lower level of use does not prevent individual women from varying their realization of /a/, within the female norms, according to their social network structure. Thus, the *degree of fit* between phonological choice and network structure may be seen as an issue quite separate from the *absolute level of use* of a particular range of variants. We may thus argue that /a/ functions for women as a network marker to a greater extent than it does for men; by this we mean that there is for them a higher correlation between choice of variant and network structure, a tendency to select relatively backed variants being associated with higher levels of integration into the community.

When we look at the relationship between choice of /ɛ/ realization and individual social network structure, we find a pattern emerging converse to the one described for /a/; recall also that the incoming variants of the two vowels showed an almost converse distribution with regard to status, sex of speaker and speech styles.

Most importantly, there appears to be no tendency at all for women to use /ɛ/ as a network marker in the sense described above; but there is a significant correlation between network scores of male speakers (particularly young male speakers) and choice of /ɛ/ realization. A tendency to select relatively low (conservative) variants is associated with a relatively high level of integration into the community.

This complex relationship between network structure, sex of speaker and language use is summarized in table 4.11. However, our interest here is in a generalization which we are now able to make concerning on the one hand the relationship between language and network structure, and on the other the social identity of the innovating group. In the case of both /ɛ/ and /a/ it is the persons for whom the vowel has less significance as a network marker who seem to be leading the linguistic change. It is as if absence of this language/network relationship (a relationship that fulfils a cohesive social function) enables a particular social group to adopt the role of linguistic innovators. This appears to be the case regardless of whether the innovation is evaluated by the wider urban community as being of high or of low status. For although it is clear that /ɛ/ raising is diffusing on a much broader social front than /a/ backing, the generalization still seems to hold true that it is those persons in the inner city for whom the vowel functions less clearly as a network marker who are the principal innovators in their own communities.

Table 4.11   Contrasting patterns of distribution of two vowels involved in change, according to sex of speaker, relative frequency of innovatory variants and level of correlation with network strength.

	Change led by	*High correlation with network strength*
/a/	Males	Females
/ɛ/	Females	Males

It is important to note that even though back variants of /a/ are strongly emblematic of vernacular speech, they are nevertheless spreading to higher-status groups in the wider community. But this diffusion is being implemented in a manner very different from that affecting /ε/. We have noted that [ε] raising is characteristic both of low-status female speech and more generally of higher-status speech. The diffusion of [ε] raising on this wide social front is confirmed both by linguistic survey data and by more detailed outer-city community studies.

We noticed in section 4.4 that, by way of contrast, higher-status Belfast speakers avoid both extreme front *and* extreme back realizations, as they converge around cardinal vowel 4 in the middle of the phonetic range. However, a very interesting group of young, male, middle-class speakers can be identified in the sample of speakers studied in the survey. They also show the characteristic middle-class tendency to converge around a limited phonetic area, with relatively little conditioned variation. However, phonetically, the point at which they converge is further back than that characteristic of older middle-class speakers.

It appears, therefore, that the mechanism of diffusion associated with each of the vowels is different. Raised variants of /ε/ are apparently spreading in a linguistically ordered way, with 'long' environments affected first. For many outer-city and middle-class speakers, a raised vowel is already categorical in all environments. Although back variants of /a/ appear to be diffusing historically and laterally (through the low-status inner-city communities) in a linguistically order manner parallel to the processes affecting /ε/, the mechanism of diffusion upwards (socially) through the community is quite different. What seems to be involved here is a 'drift' phonetically to the back of the characteristic middle-class realization.

The data presented here suggest that social network structure is implicated in processes of linguistic change in at least two ways. First, a strong close-knit network may be seen to function as a conservative force, resisting pressures to change from outside the network. Those speakers whose ties are weakest are those who approximate least closely to vernacular norms, and are most exposed to pressures for change originating from outside the network.

Second, a detailed sociolinguistic analysis of [ε] raising and [a] backing – processes which have a common dialectal point of origin but have taken on very different social values in their new urban context – suggests that the *vernacular* speakers associated most strongly with the innovation are in each case those for whom the vowel functions least prominently as a network marker. It is as if a strong relationship between the network structure of a given group and choice of phonetic realization of a particular vowel disqualifies that group from fulfilling the role of innovators with respect to that vowel. Conversely, it may be the case that dissolution of the language/network relationship with respect to a group of speakers is a necessary condition for that group to fulfil the role of linguistic innovators.

4.8   Concluding Comments

We shall return to the question of linguistic innovation in chapter 6. In this chapter we have been concerned with interpreting patterns of variation in speech communities with reference to the norms that can be shown to exist at varying levels of abstraction and generality. We have also been concerned with locating patterns of change in relation to the social variables of sex and network, in particular.

In this discussion, however, we have found it necessary to turn to 'real-time' evidence (Patterson, 1860; Staples, 1898) in order to help us to locate the direction of change. It is this time-depth that will interest us in chapter 5, in which we turn to evidence for vernacular variation in earlier English.

5

On the Time-depth of Variability in English

5.0 Introduction

My purpose in this chapter is to extend the scope of the argumentation developed in chapter 4 by projecting a variationist view on to past states of language change and variation. The variationist account developed so far is built on the axiom that language is variable at all times. The potential for change is therefore always present in variation, and may appear as a progressively greater or lesser favouring by the speech community of particular linguistic variants from among the variants that are available in the community at some particular time: to that extent change can be said to consist of change in community norms. In this chapter I shall be concerned with the description and interpretation of past states of language, bearing in mind that these were variable states, and with 'the use of the present to explain the past'.

However, although I am proposing a variationist view of language change, I have to deal with this in a context where the dominant tendency has been to focus on uniform states (Weinreich, Labov and Herzog, 1968). In practice, the kind of uniform state that historical scholars have had in mind has frequently been the uniform *standard* language; for this reason it is appropriate to start with some comments on the tendency to envisage the history of English as a unilinear history of the standard language.

5.1 The Consequences of Standardization: 1
Projecting Backwards

We noted in chapter 2 that traditional accounts of language history from around 1550 have tended to be unidimensional and convergent. We also noted, in chapter 3, that it can be misleading to apply the norms of mainstream and centralized varieties to the description of divergent language states. Thus, just as it is dangerous to superimpose standard-based analyses on a present-day vernacular, so it must be at least equally dangerous to do this in dealing with past states, which are of course also divergent. Indeed, the limitations of historical databases (noted in chapter 2) would seem to make it considerably more dangerous.

Despite this, standard-based interpretations have been used so frequently in diachronic description that they have greatly affected the conceptualization of language history that we inherit from older generations of scholars. These scholars tended – seemingly without giving much thought to the matter – to accept the standard ideology and the doctrine of uniformity that is associated with it; indeed, as we have noticed in chapter 3, they were also influenced by ideological positions which they believed to be 'common sense'. To H. C. Wyld, for example – surely the best historian of English – it probably seemed to be common sense to believe that RP was the most important accent of Modern English, and that a historical account of English pronunciation should therefore be, in effect, a history of RP.

But only in certain areas of historical linguistic research is it appropriate to use standardization and 'the standard language' as our main reference point and focus of interest, and sound-change is not one of these areas. It is justified to use the standard language in this way if our primary interest is in those developments that themselves largely depend on the standard ideology (J. Milroy and L. Milroy, 1985a), for example, elaboration of vocabulary and certain developments in clausal syntax, because literacy – and hence standardization – are plainly involved in these, and their role can be investigated. Indeed it is possible that we do not understand these things very well *unless* standardization is taken into account. But it is a different story when we focus on phonological change. As Dr Johnson observed: 'sounds are too volatile and subtile for legal restraints'

(Bolton, 1966: 152), and the history of English phonology is not a history of the standard at all, but a history of vernaculars. Thus, the most general consequence of concentrating on standard English here is that a multidimensional history of phonology is made to appear as unidimensional – it becomes 'a single-minded march' towards RP and standard English (Lass, 1976, xi).

This unidimensionality is imposed on history by a backward projection of present-day standard phonology on to the past, and according to the theory of language standardization that we have tentatively advanced elsewhere (J. Milroy and L. Milroy, 1985a), it can be seen as an attempt to *historicize* the standard language – to create a past for it and determine a *canon*, in which canonical forms are argued for and unorthodox forms rejected. This in itself is part of the process of *legitimization* of the standard language, in which the accepted norms are determined, not primarily by consensus amongst speakers, but by legislation. But the tendency to project backwards in a single (standard-based) dimension can be seen in the work of many scholars, and it has two consequences that are of interest here.

The first of these consequences relates to our knowledge of the structural *forms* of language in older stages of English. The linguistic forms that are recorded in handbook accounts of change are, for the most part, those that lead to present RP, and not usually those that lead to other modern accents of English; as we shall notice below, the latter forms are often explicitly rejected from the historical account. Furthermore, when dates are suggested for changes in these forms, they are usually given, without comment, as the dates at which the changes took place in this standard variety or its unilinear precursor, and not the dates at which they might have taken place in some other variety. Despite this, however, they are then usually cited as the dates at which the changes took place 'in English'. Let us consider a simple example.

In many historical accounts, it is stated that late ME [a] developed into [æ] in the early seventeenth century (it does not matter here what date is cited; what is important is simply that a relatively exact date *is* cited). However, it appears that this change must relate to certain dialects of Southern British English at that date, and not necessarily to other dialects. After the given date, the same change may well have diffused to other dialects that were not affected at first, and Labov's well-known work (for example, 1980) on short /a/ in the northern United States suggests that this EModE change is still in progress there today. So – strictly speaking – it is not correct to say that it 'happened' in the seventeenth century and to leave it at that. This caution is all the more necessary when we realize that there are varieties in which this change has not yet taken place, more than three centuries later, and that there are yet other varieties in which different changes have taken place. Lowland Scots and Ulster Scots dialects, for example, have had backing of [a], and we have to work out from residues that in some ancestral forms of these, there may also have been front-raising (Lass, 1976; J. Milroy, 1981; and see chapter 4.6 and 4.7, above, and section 5.7, below).

Thus, in general, it seems that backward projection on to historical states of language has tended to be based on present-day standard English and SBE, rather than other dialects, and as in the examples cited from Dobson (below) there has been a tendency to think of a phonemic set (such as short /a/) as being invariant or nearly invariant within itself. But what is important here is that where allophonic variation in a phoneme class is discussed in the main handbooks and histories, this is usually variation that leads to a present-day characteristic of the standard variety. Typically, the changes discussed include such examples as the lengthening and backing process that led to 'broad' [a] in the RP class of *dance, path* and the rounding after [w] that led in mainstream accents to present-day *wasp, swan* (many British English dialects do not have either the 'broad' [a] or rounding after [w]). The moral of all this, of course, is that, as language is variable at all times, there is something unsatisfactory about applying a unilinear and uniform-state style of interpretation to an account of language history. This seems to suggest that EModE was consciously directing itself towards modern RP – in a state of 'becoming' RP, so to speak.

The second consequence of this unilinearity is that the *idea* of the standard is projected backwards on to states of language and society in which that idea may not have existed, or – if it did exist – may have been different in important ways from the idea of the standard as it exists today. We can demonstrate this backward projection of the idea of the standard by referring to the influential work of E. J. Dobson on EModE pronunciation.

Dobson (1955, 1968) continues the tradition of his predecessor, Wyld, in focusing very closely on the history of 'standard' English. It is pronunciation that Dobson is interested in, and the EModE phonological standard is referred to very frequently in terms that suggest that such an entity had some real existence at that time. Sometimes there are several references to the standard on one page, for example: 'ME *a* had become [æ] in . . . less careful Standard English in the late sixteenth century . . . In the sixteenth and seventeenth centuries there were two pronunciations of ME *a* in use in Standard English' (1968 II: 548). These comments do not seem to be based primarily on the notion of standardization as a *process* (J. Milroy and L. Milroy, 1985a) that might have been beginning to have an effect about this time: they present the standard language as a coherent entity – a *variety*, like any other variety. But they do make sociolinguistic assumptions: in context it is clear that they also assume the early development of a socially *elite* variety, and we can see from the first sentence of the quotation that 'carefulness' is probably also involved. But, although these concepts (standardness, eliteness, carefulness) are of different orders (and we shall return to these distinctions), Dobson does not apparently see any reason to keep them separate.

What is more interesting here, however, is the method of reasoning by which Dobson reaches his conclusions on how EModE pronunciation is to be codified and legitimized as part of the canon. It is wise to bear in mind that similar reasoning has been used by many others – so much so that much of our supposed 'knowledge' of the history of English phonology is filtered through this kind of reasoning. Essentially, any attested forms that can be characterized as 'vulgar' or 'dialectal' are rejected, much as the apocryphal books of the Bible are rejected. For example, Dobson notes that one source (Thomas Pery) 'shows the vulgar raising of ME *a* to [e]'. This, according to Dobson, is not surprising because Pery's speech 'was clearly Cockney . . . The evidence of such a writer does not relate to educated StE' (1968 II: 551). On the same page, evidence from the Paston Letters is rejected as 'dialectal', and the *Diary of Henry Machyn* is rejected on the grounds that Machyn was a Yorkshireman. Dobson seems to be quite sure of this, but Machyn was almost certainly a Londoner, and his *Diary* is one of the most valuable primary sources for the study of EModE London pronunciation. But as he was not an *upper-class* Londoner, we can guess that his testimony would have been rejected in any case.

Perhaps the most startling piece of reasoning occurs in Dobson's long argument against accepting early 'occasional spelling' evidence for raising of [a, æ] to [ɛ]. It goes as follows (1968 II: 549):

> The most important objection, and it alone is a decisive one, must be that no Englishman could conceivably use *e* as a means of representing [æ]. It may seem natural to a foreign scholar [presumably Zachrisson: JM] to suppose that the sound [æ] . . . might be spelt *e*; but it is little short of incredible that native English-speaking scholars [presumably Wyld: JM] should have accepted this view. No English-speaking child learning to spell . . . would write *ket* for [kæt]; the distinction between [æ] and [e] is an absolute one for him (since otherwise he could not distinguish, for example, *man* from *men*) . . .

But clearly this is *not* decisive, as no evidence is given to prove the negative – that English speakers do *not* 'confuse' [ɛ] with [æ, a]. In fact, native speakers *do* overlap here; they *do* have differential phonological rules controlling the distribution of /a/ and /ɛ/, and they *do* make spelling mistakes involving *a* and *e*. Furthermore, it is likely that the allophonic distribution of these sounds in EModE was quite different from the RP distribution today, and that the doctrine of (retrospective) phonemic purity (as displayed in the remark about *man* and *men*) is therefore inappropriate (supporting examples from the Belfast projects are cited in chapter 4.6 and below). Moreover, it is also certain that English-speaking scholars do not have reliable retrospective intuitions about EModE pronunciation any more than they have reliable intuitions about divergent states at the present day. There is no reason to think that their intuitions about /a/ are necessarily better than those of foreign scholars. So this elaborate argument has no reliable foundation: in short, it is wrong.

But it is of great interest, because it demonstrates a familiar mode of argumentation that has been more widely used in historical descriptions and that can be found in many places, and I shall comment on a similar case in ME below. The reasoning is not aimed at supporting a positive argument: it is negative and adversarial, and aimed at rejecting the arguments of other scholars and at excluding evidence that cannot easily be accommodated into a unilinear historical canon. The underlying idea is simply that some forms are 'genuine' and some are not. Ultimately, it does not matter very much what arguments are used to reject evidence: the point is that all possible *post hoc* arguments must be marshalled to defend one's position against other scholars: the more arguments that can be used, the better. In this case the immediate position defended (*contra* the work of Wyld and Zachrisson) is that orthoepic evidence is better than other evidence, such as 'occasional spellings' (Wyld, 1936), but the underlying assumption (which is more relevant here) is that it is possible to write a continuous unilinear history of 'standard' English pronunciation.

It is certainly true that some of the processes associated with standardization (on which see Haugen, 1972; Leith, 1980; J. Milroy and L. Milroy, 1985a) were well under way around 1600 (elaboration of function, use of a supra-regional writing system), but it looks as if some of them were still at the stage of being localized developments associated with the establishment of consensus on local norms, and this applies particularly to pronunciation, which is the level of language that is least uniform. In the phonetic/phonological dimension, I do not think we should speak too readily of Early Modern 'Standard' English. Perhaps I can make this clear by distinguishing tentatively between the notion of *prestige* and the notion of *standard language*.

5.2 Prestige Norms and Standard Norms

A standard variety or form is not conceptually the same thing as a prestige variety or form (on prestige, see J. Milroy, 1989): the main linguistic symptom of standardization is invariance. Standardization comes about for functional reasons, and its effect is to make a language serviceable for communicating decontextualized information-bearing messages over long distances and periods of time. In this respect its functions differ greatly from those of vernaculars (recall our discussion of functions in chapter 2). It is imposed through its use in administrative functions by those who have political power. Once it spreads into other functions, it acquires what we usually call 'prestige', in the sense that those who wish to advance in life consider it to be in their interests to use standard-like forms. Prestige, however, is a different concept altogether, as it can be subjectively attached by speakers to forms and varieties which are very distant from, and in conflict with, the codified norms of the standard. In recent years, Arab linguists (Abdel Jawad, 1987; Alahdal, 1989) have found it difficult to reconcile the concepts of 'standard' and 'prestige', because rural norms that are identical to standard Arabic are shown to be dispreferred in favour of urban 'non-standard' forms.

Our own work and that of Trudgill (1986a) has tended towards very similar conclusions. In this context, the well-known late sixteenth-century comments about the best English being spoken in the London area should be understood for what they are, and not necessarily as a sign of *standardized* pronunciation. They arise from a consciousness of the development of a stable (but variable) vernacular norm in London, knowledge that its norms differ from those of other varieties, and a belief in the superiority of London norms over those of other regions. What we are dealing with here is sociolinguistic: the development of supra-local regional and social attitudes to language. What we are *not* dealing with is a fully-fledged 'standard' pronunciation that can then be most usefully described in terms of a unilinear history since that time. If we do think in this unilinear way, we will be inclined to dismiss or devalue evidence that is important for our understanding of language history, just as some of our predecessors have done.

In order to understand the history of so-called standard English pronunciation, therefore, we need to assume – paradoxically – that there is no such thing. Standardization is not primarily about *varieties* of language, but about processes. Therefore, it must be treated as a process with an underlying socio-political motivation, which attempts to promote uniformity and suppress variability for reasons that are considered functional. Similarly, the standard can be regarded as the ultimate in the development of a supra-local norm of language. If we take this point of view, it seems that we will gain a better understanding of the history of what is usually called standard English, because we will be able to separate out those issues that *primarily* involve the development of standard (prescriptive or codified) norms from those that do not. The history of pronunciation is one of those issues that do not primarily involve standardization, because it is about the history of speech in face-to-face interaction and because standardization has always had less effect on pronunciation than on other linguistic levels. The history of standard pronunciations is not therefore something that we can usefully chart in a unilinear temporal continuum, as though co-existing varieties had no role except to 'feed' the standard 'variety' from time to time. This is an over-simplification – and a distortion – of language history.

Bearing these points in mind, the remainder of this chapter consists chiefly of a discussion of backward projection of variability, including case-studies from my own research. I shall start by considering the effects of the standard ideology on analyses of Middle English and go on to review aspects of variation in Middle English.

5.3 The Consequences of Standardization: 2
Variation in Middle English

One of the advantages of studying Middle English is that its written forms are highly variable. Before that time – in late Old English – the West Saxon literary standard was well established, and afterwards – from around 1550 – most printed documents appear in a (relatively) standardized form. The diversity of Early ME, however, is so great that – apart from the so-called AB Language – no two substantial literary documents are in exactly the same 'dialect'. If we compare two twelfth-century texts, such as the Peterborough continuation of the *Anglo-Saxon Chronicle* (East Midland) and Layamon's *Brut* (South-west Midland), we could not be blamed for believing that they are in different languages. The differences between them are of the same order as the differences between modern Dutch and standard German: the *Brut* retains the OE case-inflexions and grammatical gender, whereas the Peterborough *Chronicle*, even though it is an earlier document, has lost most of these. But not only is there considerable divergence *between* different texts, there is also normally great variability (particularly in spelling and inflexional forms) *within* the texts. Thus, ME language states, being so variable, should in principle be suited to the same kind of analysis that we use in present-day social dialectology, and by using variationist methods we should be able to explore at least some of the constraints on variation that might have existed in ME. In a present-day community, these constraints can be observed in spoken language: in ME we must locate these constraints initially through the writing system.

We can briefly demonstrate this point by comparing a modern case with a medieval case. Suppose we show that in a present-day vernacular there is structured variation in verb-forms of the type *he does/he do* (see Cheshire, 1982, for a relevant study), with one form perhaps being preferred in formal styles and the other in casual styles: we may also – by comparing the speech of different social groups and age-groups – show that one form is progressing at the expense of the other. As it happens, ME texts also frequently exhibit variation in verbal inflexions. Suppose, for example, a text (such as the *Bestiary*: thirteenth century, East Anglia) exhibits 3rd singular verb-form variation in *–es, –eþ* (such as *standes, standeþ*) and syncopated forms (such as *stant*): this may indicate that the text is composite and has been copied by scribes from different dialect areas (for discussions of these scribal questions, see especially McIntosh, Samuels and Benskin, 1986; Laing, 1989; McIntosh and Wakelin, 1989). But it could also be the case that all three forms (or perhaps two of them) were current in the underlying dialect of the scribe (or of the author), or – more properly – of the speech community to which he belonged. Indeed, as the writing system was not standardized, it is likely that variation of this kind would enter more readily into the texts than it would today, and that it may therefore be possible by comparing texts to trace the pattern by which one variant recedes and another spreads. However, we have to bear in mind that, because of the complexity of scribal histories and the fact that the provenance (date and place of writing) of the text is not usually divulged, the medievalist faces a number of difficulties that the present-day dialectologist does not face (for discussion see McIntosh, Samuels and Benskin, 1986 I; J. Milroy, forthcoming), but if these can be solved, the general similarity that I have suggested here is still valid.

Variability in ME, however, has sometimes been perceived as an obstacle rather than a resource, and as a result information that might be of some value to the historian has been rejected from the canon. It is interesting that although no one suggests that there actually was a 'standard English' in Early ME times, the doctrine of uniformity has nevertheless been applied to ME. In editorial and descriptive commentary, there are many comments about chaotic or 'lawless' spellings (for example, Sisam, 1915: xxxvii) and even editorial judgements to the effect that a given scribe could not have been a native English speaker, so variable is his spelling (Hall, 1920 II: 637). This last judgement (although it is commonly made) is speculative, of course, as the scribe is normally anonymous, but it is analogous to rejecting live speakers from a random sample on the grounds that they do not speak as we think they ought to speak, or rejecting attested spoken forms on the grounds that they are not what we would expect in some particular location. However, judgements of this kind can effectively block further investigation of variable constraints in the texts in question: they can be dismissed as 'corrupt' or 'unreliable' specimens of language. One way in which variation of this kind is discounted is to claim that the scribe was Anglo-Norman, or that the spellings are Anglo-Norman and therefore not valid evidence for the history of English.

The Anglo-Norman argument goes back to Skeat (1897), who specified particular features of spelling as Anglo-Norman. These are discussed by J. Milroy (1983), and it is noticeable that many of these features, such as *w* for *wh* (in words of the type *what, which*), have reflexes in later English pronunciation. The comments above by Sisam (1915) and Hall (1920) arise directly from Skeats's views, and, although these comments were made a long time ago, it would be a mistake to think that the Anglo-Norman argument has now been abandoned. Clark (1990) has recently referred to the 'myth' of the Anglo-Norman scribe and has collected a large number of comments from early in the century up until very recently from the work of distinguished scholars, in which attested forms are typically said to be 'Anglo-Norman' and therefore rejected. As a result of this 'myth', however, the very fact of variable spelling in an Early Middle English document becomes *in itself* a reason for concluding that the scribe was Anglo-Norman and therefore that his spelling can be corrected by editors and ignored by historical commentators and dialectologists. Even the work of scribes writing centuries after the Conquest has been dismissed in this way, seemingly mainly because it is *variable*, and not because we can (usually) know whether the scribe was a first-language speaker of Anglo-Norman, or whether it would have been relevant if he had been.

Leaving aside this argument, however, we must also recognize that scholars have sometimes been more generally influenced by the notion that written language *should be* uniform, even in a period in which it plainly was *not* uniform, and they sometimes appear to chide the scribes for spelling variably. Scragg (1974: 26), for example, comments that 'the existence of regional orthographies, and their confusion in the copying of texts resulted in a very lax attitude to spelling in most scribes.' In the context, this 'very lax attitude' seems to be measured against circumstances (such as late Old English or the present day) in which there is a uniform standard of spelling: thus, what this really means is that in Early ME there was no uniform standard, and indeed Scragg adds that these scribes had 'no conception of a spelling standard'. But he further comments – much more dubiously – that they used 'variant forms at will'. However, if the scribes really had used variants 'at will', we would actually be unable to read the texts, as there would be no system in the spelling; but there must always be *some* order in any spelling system that we can read, even if it is a variable system. Therefore, the scribes did not spell 'at will', but according to variable (and historically mixed) conventions. It is our task to attempt to specify the constraints on spelling under which they were working, always admitting that even after we have done this, there may well be residues of apparent randomness that we cannot explain.

5.4 Orderly Variation in Spelling

The existence of variable orthographies is an advantage to the ME dialectologist in exactly the same way that the existence of spoken variation is an advantage in present-day research. Although the scribes no doubt made 'errors', it should be possible to investigate variable texts *in extenso* to determine the extent to which variation in spelling (or indeed in other linguistic dimensions) is in fact orderly, and whether this variation can help us to work out what might have been happening in spoken English at the time. As an example, let us briefly consider some aspects of spelling in *Havelok the Dane*.

The *Havelok* text (Bodleian MS Laud Misc 108) is one of those sources that has been traditionally thought to be the work of an Anglo-Norman scribe (Sisam, 1915) on the grounds that the spelling is highly variable in the respects specified by Skeat and indeed in some other respects also. However, although it doubtless contains some forms that are simply 'errors', it also exhibits the kind of orderly variation that could be captured within a variable rule framework, but in spelling variation rather than phonology. The scribe does not have a free hand with spelling variation: there are constraints on the variants he uses. OE post-vocalic /ht, xt/, for example – in words of the type *riht, niht*, 'PresE 'right, night' – can be represented in the spelling of *Havelok* by *st, ht, th, cht, cth*, but *not* by, for example *gt, ght*, or by random and unpredictable forms such as *tc* or *m*. The variation is constrained in much the same way as present-day *phonological* variation in speech communities is observed to be constrained. For example, we can specify the constraints on /a/ before velars in inner-city Belfast by stating that it can be realized as a mid-front, low mid-front, or low-front vowel, but not as a low-back vowel. Thus, just as present-day phonological variation can be used as a clue to change in progress, so it may be possible here to use orthographic variation in the same way.

The spelling variants for OE (ht) overlap with spelling variants for other forms (from different sources in OE), just as phonological variants in present-day studies are found to overlap. Thus, if we take the realization *th*, we find that this can be used word-finally, not only for (ht), but also for (t) and (th). The result of this is that a spelling like *with* can realize three separate classes: OE *wiht* ('wight, person'), OE *wiþ* ('with'), and OE *hwit* ('white'), and this of course applies to other items of these types. To formalize this: the following (OE) classes can appear with final *th*:

1   Final (post-vocalic) dental fricatives:/θ, ð/, for example *with* (OE *wiþ*, PresE *with*);
2   Final (post-vocalic) dental stop: /t/, for example *with* (OE *hwit*, PresE *white*);
3   Final /ht, xt/: for example, *with* (OE *wiht*, PresE *wight*).

The *potential* realizations of these three classes are, however, different: (ht) items can also appear with *st*, *cht*, etc. (such as *wicht*): the other two classes cannot; (th) items can also appear with final *þ,ð* (such as *wiþ*): the other two classes cannot; (t) items can appear with final single *t* (such as *wit*, *whit*): the other two classes cannot. Thus, 'with, wight' cannot appear as *wit*, whereas 'white' can. To this extent, therefore, the variation is constrained, and not random. Applying the principle that change in progress is manifested in variation, let us consider its possible implications for spoken variation in ME.

The study of (ht) in *Havelok* is of course relevant to the date at which the velar fricative [x] before [t] (in *right*, *might*, etc.) was lost in English. The *prima facie* conclusion to be drawn is that in the variable phonology of the 'underlying' (East Midland/East Anglian) speech community, loss of the fricative and merger of *wight*, *white*, or close approximation and overlap, had already taken place. It is also possible that in this variable phonology there was some tendency to merge final/θ/with/t/. If developments of this kind were not in some sense in progress, then there would have been less likelihood of the scribe observing precisely *this* pattern of orderly spelling variation, because, given the variable state of the orthographic conventions known to him, he could have chosen to vary in other ways. Of course, it is quite another matter to go on to argue from this very limited piece of evidence that loss of the fricative in /xt/ was embedded in the English language as a whole as a completed sound-change at this early date. Yet, if we take this together with the fact that many other forms characteristic of modern English spread in these centuries from the East Midlands and the North, we can advance the hypothesis that this change was in progress in the East Midlands around 1300, and look for further evidence to support or refute this. If, however, we insist that the scribes were simply careless or poorly acquainted with English, we shall be inclined (as many scholars have been) to reject the evidence and date this sound-change much later – at a time when it was actually *completed* in 'standard' English. This, of course, will not bring us anywhere near the *origin* of the change. Furthermore, bearing in mind the reservations about changes in different varieties that I expressed in section 5.2 above, the early date suggested here for the loss of the velar fricative does not affect the fact that there are dialects of English (in Lowland Scotland) which have not yet lost the fricative.

Loss of the velar fricative is a change that was finally adopted in near-standard vernaculars and formal styles. ME sources, however, also contain variation that may be relevant to *non-standard* varieties and casual styles of speech; hence, there may be considerable time-depth to these variables also. In Section 5.5, therefore, we consider some non-standard examples.

5.5 The Time-depth of Present-day Non-standard Variants

A number of present-day non-standard and casual speech forms appear to be indicated by some features of variable ME spelling. Some of these are recognized as regional and have been studied as such (for example in Wakelin and Barry, 1968, a study of the voicing of initial fricatives in South-west England): others are more wide-spread in English. One of these is 'final stop deletion' (loss of /t, d/, and sometimes other stops, in final clusters in words such as *mist, mend*). This is today very common in many varieties of English (Guy, 1980; Romaine, 1984a), but not common in careful styles of RP (hence its exclusion from many accounts which claim to be accounts of 'English'). The maps of the *Linguistic Atlas of Late Medieval English*

(McIntosh, Samuels and Benskin, 1986) show a distribution of final consonant loss also in medieval *written* English, and I have noted a number of examples in *Havelok* and other texts. Thus, the phenomenon may have been part of variability in English for many centuries – more common perhaps in some dialects than in others, receding at some periods and progressing at others. Yet, it plays little part in standard accounts of the history of English before about 1600, and in ME stop-deleted forms (such as *bes, lan*: 'best, land') are amongst the forms that are typically corrected by textual editors as errors.

There are other features that may have much earlier origins than is generally believed. These include: 1) the (casual style) *-in'* ending on present participles (Houston, 1987; Labov, 1989); 2) certain widespread socially or regionally marked alternations in modern English, such as 'stopping' of dental fricatives in, for example *thick, that*, and [h]-dropping. I shall now consider in some detail this last phenomenon – variable loss of [h] in stressed syllables initially before vowels.

I selected this particular variable as a case-study for a number of reasons. The chief one is that it is a very salient stereotype popularly characterized as non-standard or 'vulgar', and is extremely widespread in England and Wales. The map (figure 5.1) shows that [h] is preserved in rural dialects only in the extreme north-east, and in parts of East Anglia and the West Country; but, if anything, the map probably understates the extent of [h]-loss. Most large urban areas south of the River Tees have considerable [h]-loss in vernacular speech, and this includes even Norwich in East Anglia – an area shown by the map as, at least partly, [h]-ful. As Trudgill (1974) has shown (see figure 5.2), [h]-loss in Norwich is socially stratified, with lower-class speakers tending strongly to loss of [h], despite the fact that surrounding rural dialects tend to preserve [h]. In general, [h]-loss is well established in urban vernaculars in England and Wales; thus, a majority of the population of the country have (categorical or variable) loss of [h].

However, it is also well known that social stereotyping of [h]-loss does not apply in Scotland, Ireland, North America and colonial Englishes generally, for the reason that [h] is stable in stressed syllables in these varieties (although [h]-loss *is* found in English-based Creoles). In this sense, the English-speaking world can be divided into two broad speech-communities: one in which [h]-dropping is widespread and has social significance, and one in which it is so rare (if it happens at all) that it is socially irrelevant.

Figure 5.1   *h*-pronouncing areas of England. (Adapted from Orton et al. 1963–9)

Although scholars have noticed instability in initial *h* spellings in early English, the traditional view is that there is little reliable evidence for '[h]-dropping' in English much before the end of the eighteenth century, and earlier instability in spelling is usually dismissed as unreliable in handbook accounts. One reason given for the alleged lateness of the phenomenon is its apparent absence from colonial English (Wyld, 1927: 220). From a variationist point of view, however, this is not necessarily conclusive, as language is variable at all times; thus, it could be the case that modern [h]-ful and [h]-less varieties are each equally derived from varieties in which [h]-loss was

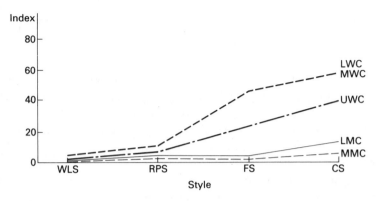

Figure 5.2 Variable (h) by class and style in Norwich (LWC/MWC/ UWC = lower/middle/upper working class; LMC/MMC = lower/middle middle class; WLS = word-list style; RPS = reading-passage style; FS = formal (conversational) style; CS = casual (conversational) style). (Adapted from Trudgill, 1974)

variable – not categorically absent or categorically present. In any case, colonial forms of English may have undergone change in (h); for example, there is evidence that, although Australasian English is [h]-ful now, it *used to* have [h]-dropping (Trudgill, 1986a: 138–9). The evidence of variable spelling in ME seems to point to an early origin, and if the arguments for this can be sustained, they have a clear relevance to understanding historical patterns of variation.

In modern times [h]-dropping – like -*in'* for (ing) – is extremely widespread and well established: as we have noted above, it is not confined to a particular region (as voicing of initial fricatives is, for example). In fact, most people in England and Wales drop their [h]s to a greater or lesser extent. Therefore, if the origin of the phenomenon is as recent as the late eighteenth century, it is difficult to explain how it could have become so geographically widespread in so short a time: it was already highly salient and overtly stigmatized by the latter half of the nineteenth century (for some citations see Phillipps, 1984, 136–9). Consider the following comment by the linguistic scholar Oliphant (1873: 226), made in the context of objecting to 'Americanisms':

> I ought in all fairness to acknowledge that no American fault comes up to the revolting habit . . . of dropping or wrongly inserting the letter *h*. Those whom we call 'self-made men' are much given to this hideous

> barbarism . . . Few things will the English youth find in after-life more
> profitable than the right use of the aforesaid letter.

Whatever we may think of Oliphant's views, we have to assume there would be little point in attacks on [h]-dropping by the educated elite unless it was highly salient and widespread, and it is reasonable to assume for these reasons that it probably has quite a long history in the language. The late eighteenth-century evidence adduced by Wyld and others is therefore likely to indicate the date at which it had become stigmatized as a 'vulgarism', rather than its date of origin. By that time – and not necessarily before – [h]-loss was recognized as an identifying characteristic of certain salient social groupings.

The most important reason for questioning the traditional view, however, is that variation in initial *h* usage is a very common pattern in ME texts. Whereas we have discussed orderly variation in spelling (above) by looking at distribution within a single text, the evidence for early [h]-loss depends on spelling variation across a number of texts. Many Early ME sources exhibit variable use of the letter *h* in syllable-initial positions before vowels (that is, in such words as *hate*, *hopper*). Sometimes it is omitted where it is historically expected to be present, and sometimes it is added where it is not expected.

This pattern of variation is widespread in Early ME, and the maps of the *Linguistic Atlas of Late Medieval English* also show a distribution at later periods. It has been very widely noted by careful editors such as Hall (1920), and (although the atlas map shows some West Midland distribution) it seems in the early part of the period to be most common in texts originating in the East Midlands, East Anglia and the South. It is quite common in southern texts of *c.*1200, such as *Poema Morale* and *The Owl and the Nightingale*, and in early East Midland/East Anglian texts such as *Genesis and Exodus, King Horn, Havelok*. It is found in the Otho text of Layamon's *Brut*, but not in the Caligula text, which is certainly south-*west* Midland. It is not characteristic of early texts known to be West Midland, such as those of the Katherine Group. The geographical distribution of relevant texts from *c.* 1190–1320 is from Lincolnshire or Norfolk (in the north) to the southern counties, but the instability seems to be greatest in the East Midlands. Certain later texts, mostly of a non-literary kind, display the same phenomenon. It is found in Kristensson's (1967) northern onomastic sources in the period 1290–1350 (he notes that it may be 'Anglo-Norman'), and Wyld

(1927, 1936) documents a number of later examples, from sources that include the *Norfolk Gilds* (late fourteenth century), The *Paston Letters* (fifteenth century), and the mid-sixteenth-century *Diary of Henry Machyn* (for a fuller discussion, see J. Milroy, 1983: 48–9). In my own investigations of many of these texts, I have noted additional examples. The following selective lists are from the thirteenth-century *Genesis and Exodus* (Morris, 1873), which is believed to originate in East Anglia. They include examples additional to those given by Wyld. List A documents omission of *h*, and list B addition of 'unhistorical' *h*:

List A   *a, adde, adden, as, aue, auede, aued, auen, aue* (parts of the verb 'have': lines 239, 240, 1251, 1505, 1760, 2388, 2425, 2720, and very commonly – considerably more so than forms with *h*; *algen, aligen*, ('hallow'): 258, 918: *ail* ('hail'): 3066, 3183; *ate* ('hate'): 373, 3638; *alt* (< infin 'hold'): 924; *atteð*('is called' < OE *hatan*): 813; *e* ('he, they'): 2341, 2708, 4094; *egest* ('highest'): 143, 1224; *eld* ('held'): 2999; *elles* ('of hell'): 4157; *ere* ('of them' < OE *heora*): 2855, 3773; *eðen* ('hence'): 2188; *eui* ('heavy'): 2559; *is* ('his'): 482, etc.; *opperes* ('hoppers', that is, 'locusts'): 3096; *ostel* ('hostel', that is, 'lodging'): 1056; *om* ('home'): 2270; *oten* ('called'): 1131.

List B   *hagte* ('wealth'): 431; *hagt* ('grief'): 486, 2044, 2082; *halle* ('all'): 2340; *ham* ('am'): 926; *helde* (that is, *elde*: 'age'): 457, 1527; *her* ('before'): 801; *herf* (that is, *erf*: 'cattle'): 2991; *herðe* (that is, *erde*: 'land'): 806; *hic* ('I'): 34, 2783; *his* ('is'): 2935; *hore* (that is, *or*: 'before'): 958; *hunframe* (*unframe*): 554; *hunkinde* (*unkinde*): 534; *hunne*: ('grant'): 2249; *hunwreste* ('wicked'): 537; *hure* ('our'): 322, 2206.

The most immediate 'explanation' for such substantial instability in the use of *h* is that syllable-initial [h] was not present, or only variably present, in the speech of the relevant regions. The letter was, however, present in the orthographic tradition (regardless of the mixed origins of the tradition in Old English, Anglo-Norman and Latin orthography): thus, in the absence of strong orthographic standardization, the scribes would omit it on some occasions and insert it 'hypercorrectly' on others.

As instability of *h* is extremely common, it is remarkable that careful scholars could have been so much aware of this type of evidence, but could nevertheless have rejected it. Wyld (1936), for example, cites a large number of spellings from around 1200 onwards in which the letter *h* is 'wrongly' omitted or inserted, but concludes that there is no reliable evidence for 'the present day vulgarism' before the eighteenth century (p. 296). Writers of standard hand-books are also inclined to dismiss the early evidence. Ekwall (1975), citing Walker, notes that [h]-loss might have occurred as early as 1791; Brunner (1963: 5) dismisses early ME spelling evidence with the remark that Anglo-Norman scribes were prone to use initial *h* 'incorrectly'. Dobson is also inclined, for similar reasons, to give the impression that ME evidence for [h]-loss is sporadic and unreliable (see, for example, Dobson, 1968 II: 991). Many more authorities who accept the same view could be cited. In fact, the evidence for [h]-loss in the texts I have mentioned above is anything but sporadic. However, as the citation from Brunner suggests, *h*-instability is one of the putative 'Anglo-Norman' features distinguished by Skeat (1897), and this is another of the reasons why it has been dismissed.

Frequently, this orthographic evidence for variation in Middle English is rejected not on the grounds that the scribe was literally an Anglo-Norman (which is what Skeat argued), but that uses such as variable *h* are originally scribal importations from French or Latin usage. However, the origin of scribal habits is not in itself valid proof that variable use of the conventions in written English do not *also* relate to variable usages in spoken English. This is because variable scribal usage is likely to be functional in some way, just as spoken variation is functional (as suggested in chapter 2), and the most immediately obvious function of an alphabetic writing system is to relate writing to speech-forms, however complicated this relationship may be. Thus, *especially in a time of unsettled orthography*, it is extremely likely that current sound-changes will be admitted into writing, whatever the historical origins of the writing conventions may be.

Moreover, the *prima facie* evidence for [h]-dropping continues well into EModE – long after there can be any suspicion of direct Anglo-Norman scribal interference. In addition to the non-literary sources cited above, there is rather strong evidence in Shakespeare and Marlowe – especially in puns of the type *air, heir, hair* – that [h]-dropping was salient in the speech community: clearly, the puns could not have worked if the 'groundlings' had not recognized them (see, for example, *Comedy of Errors*, III.ii.122–3; *Dido and Aeneas*, I.i.10). But as it was accepted into this relatively formal literary genre, [h]-loss seems to have been much less overtly stigmatized than it is today. All this evidence strongly suggests that (h) has been a *variable* in English for many centuries: [h]-loss may have gone to completion in some varieties at particular times and places, but in general speech communities have used the variation over these centuries for stylistic and social marking. In other words, whatever the linguistic origin of the phenomenon may be – in phonotactic constraints (Lutz, 1985), in rapid speech processes, in language contact, or in a combination of these – variation in (h) has probably had social and stylistic *functions* in the language for centuries.

We should bear in mind, however, that underlying the 'colonial' chronological argument and the Anglo-Norman argument, there is a more fundamental reason why scholars have been so willing to reject the evidence for [h]-loss. Many historians of English seem to have shared the attitude of Oliphant (above) and have therefore been inclined to think that apparently non-standard linguistic forms are somehow not to be taken seriously as evidence for 'genuine' linguistic change. Even such an excellent scholar as Wyld, who was extremely interested in the social motivations of change, did not give sufficient weight to the evidence for [h]-loss. What these scholars did was to place their own (negative) *evaluations* of [h]-loss on to the speech communities of earlier centuries in which evaluations of this pheno-menon were not necessarily the same. It was difficult for them to appreciate that [h]-loss could ever have been anything else but a stigmatized form: in so far as they knew of evidence for it in earlier centuries, they tended to dismiss it, seemingly in the belief that 'vulgar' and 'careless' usage is not implicated in linguistic change. This attitude to [h]-dropping is, of course, symptomatic of a more general attitude to non-standard English, and it can be seen as an effect of the 'standard ideology'.

Plainly, there is no compelling *linguistic* reason why, in a particular language at a particular time, loss of a segment should be considered less beautiful or less 'correct' than its insertion. For example, loss of pre-consonantal [r] (as in *car, card*) is widespread in many English vernaculars, but it is not stigmatized in southern Britain. Although it is a consonantal loss, it is not said to be ugly or careless in England generally. Unlike /h/, however, [r] seems to have been lost quite early in a forerunner of the institutional British accent (RP) at a time when consciousness of the standard ideology was beginning to develop, and it is this difference in the social evaluation of (r) and (h) which seems to be the explanation for dominant attitudes to it. In dismissing [h]-loss in the manner described, however, scholars may also have dismissed important evidence for the study of how linguistic changes are implemented and diffused. It is also relevant to observe, in a wider dimension, that English is the only *Germanic* language that is widely subject to [h]-loss.

It has also been clearly established that in the course of time evaluation of particular variants can change or even be reversed. It is therefore most unlikely that present-day stigmatized forms have always been stigmatized, or that present-day elite forms have always been elite. Even the RP 'broad' [a] (as in *path, dance*) seems to have acquired its high evaluation only recently: Mugglestone (1989) cites evidence from the nineteenth century to the effect that it was stigmatized as a vulgarism by some commentators: it looks as though it may have been 'borrowed' from a low-status dialect (such as 'Cockney'). As for [h]-dropping – I have suggested elsewhere (J. Milroy, 1983) that in the Middle Ages it may have been a marker of more cultured speech.

What is clear is that, when compared with literary OE, some varieties of Early ME (including those that show variation in (h)) were *contact varieties*. They were spoken in those parts of the country that had been massively subject to Scandinavian settlement in the late OE period, and they were subsequently used in areas where the elite language became Norman French. It is not impossible that [h]-loss became fashionable because of its loss in French, but this cannot be demonstrated. However, one outcome of contact is simplification and loss of distinctions, and [h]-loss results in loss of a distinction – as in the pair *hall* and *all*. Thus, the loss of [h] could be associated with the contact situation in general, regardless of the specific properties of the contact languages. But there is another circumstance that strongly suggests that [h]-dropping was not a low-status feature in ME, and that is its association at that time with East Anglian texts.

Figure 5.1 shows that East Anglia is one of those areas in which the rural dialects have remained generally [h]-ful up to the present day. The evidence for early *loss* of [h], however, is quite strongly associated with this part of the country. The texts of *Genesis and Exodus, Havelok the Dane* and certain other Early ME works that I have cited, are almost certainly East Anglian. As for late ME, among the best sources for variable spelling (including variation in *h*) are the *Norfolk Gilds* (late fourteenth century) and the *Paston Letters* (fifteenth century, Norfolk). The *Gilds* contain records from Norwich, (King's) Lynn and other towns, and these include some quite magnificent spellings such as *alpenie* ('halfpenny'), *hoke lewes* ('oak leaves'), and many more.

We might therefore advance the hypothesis that the medieval evidence (unlike the modern dialect evidence for [h]-fulness in Norfolk) is from a relatively high social stratum – this is certainly true of the *Paston Letters* at the very least – and that [h]-loss was current at that level but not amongst the rural population. This is the kind of hypothesis that would be suggested by a specifically sociolinguistic interpretation of the evidence, but it is offered here as a suggestion, not as a definite conclusion. In the following sections, I shall revert to questions that are less socially-oriented than this, but still variationist. I want to consider how far we can use descriptions of the Belfast and Hiberno-English vowel system to reflect on the past – specifically on aspects of the Early ModE vowel system.

5.6 Projecting Backwards: Vowel Systems

So far we have focused on the time-depth of vernacular variants in English, using (h) as an example and treating it as a binary variable (we have assumed that in such words as *hall, hit* it is either pronounced or dropped). In this section I turn to the configuration of vowel systems, and this of course is phonologically more complicated than (h). As we noticed in chapter 3, vernacular vowel systems such as the Belfast one may display patterns that are not comfortably accounted for by standard or traditional methods. In particular, traditional descriptive and analytic methods find it difficult to contemplate such phenomena as: (1) close approximation of phones without merger; (2) overlapping allophones; (3) flip-flops, and (4) reversal of merger. Indeed, in some cases evidence that seems to point to one of these things may be rejected on the grounds that the phenomenon is impossible. In what follows, I would like to bear in mind two general points. The first is the difficulty of stipulating when a sound-change is completed (this is amply demonstrated by the history of (h), above), and hence the difficulty of saying precisely what is meant by 'sound-change'. The second is the traditional binary distinction between 'sound-change proper' and 'borrowing': this distinction, or something similar to it, still seems to be be assumed in many orthodox accounts. That is to say that some changes are believed to arise internally within the system and are motivated by system-internal factors, whereas others are said to arise from the influence of neighbouring languages or dialects. Leaving these (and other) theoretical generalizations aside for the moment, we turn first to the history of what is usually known as short /a/ in English, and to possible historical patterns of overlap and merger with /ɛ/ and /ɔ/. In later sections I present a fuller discussion of *merger*.

It is generally known, of course, that standard English enshrines sporadic residues of approximations between these vowels, for example in doublets of the type *strop/strap, catch/ketch*, but there has been a good deal of dispute about EModE evidence for overlap and merger in this part of the vowel-system. Orthodox accounts, as we have seen, tend to ignore or explain away evidence for variability when it does not have reflexes in present-day RP. The systematic study of a non-standard system, however, supports the argument that there could have been orderly variation in EModE involving merger and reversal patterns of /a/ and /ɛ/ (or /ɔ/) in certain consonantal environments, and suggests that the usual account of the history of /a/ (fronting to [æ] and subsequent split into two RP phonemes) is oversimplified. Amongst other things, this type of study can contribute to problems in English etymology, for example in dealing with pairs of the type: *pack/peck*. The following account will suggest that many such pairs are etymological doublets, and we shall consider this further in an appendix to the chapter.

The history of ModE /a/ is a traditional bone of contention, and views have been expressed on it by a gallery of famous names from Henry Sweet onward (for a review, see Lass, 1976). Some scholars have argued that despite the front quality of OE /æ/, ME *a* was a back vowel (or perhaps merely a fully low vowel: it is not always clear what is meant by 'back vowel'), and on this basis have postulated a change around 1600 from a back (or low) value to front-raised /æ/, which is of course the modern conservative RP value. Others (such as Lass, 1976) have preferred to argue that a generally front vowel had already existed in ME. Much of this argumentation is, of course, concerned with very broad states of language, and, as I have pointed out, can apply only at a rather high level of generality, because it is likely that in EModE, as in PresE, there were varying conditioned allophones of /a/ (perhaps some front and some back, or some low and some low-mid). The regular patterns of variability observable in (a) at the present day suggest this strongly. In what follows, we focus on one particular modern vowel system, that of Belfast vernacular.

5.7 Orderly Heterogeneity in Vowels: the Low Vowels in Belfast

One of the purposes of the Belfast study of variation in (a) was to project our observations on to past language states in which patterns of heterogeneity must also have existed. In the event, the inner-city study demonstrated that (a) in this vernacular is phonetically and phonologically much more complicated than standard accounts of EModE /a/ (such as Dobson, 1968). It is more complicated also than (a) as studied in New York (Labov, 1966), and more complicated than descriptions of /æ/ in present-day RP (Gimson, 1970, etc.). We noticed the wide range of realizations in chapter 4 (table 4.2, p. 97) and commented on its regularity. The variation exhibited is constrained within definable limits: following velars predict a front vowel, following voiceless stops predict a low front vowel; fricatives and voiced obstruents allow variation between front and back, but strongly favour backing. What table 4.2 does not show, however, is that there is also variation in *length* in the /a/ system, which is equally rule-governed. As many of the apparent overlaps between the low vowels occur in environments where the vowel is *short*, a brief review of the vowel-length system is necessary.

Like Scots, the Belfast vowel system does not use length phonemically: most vowels have long and short allophones, and the variation in length can be very marked. Thus, /a/ in monosyllables such as *back, bat, can't* (before voiceless stops and before sonorants + voiceless obstruent) is very short, whereas before fricatives and voiced obstruents (as in *grass, mad, bag*) it is markedly longer. We remarked in chapter 3, however, that within the vowel system as a whole (including /a/), length tends to co-vary with quality, that is, long-vowel realizations are usually noticeably qualitatively different from short-vowel allophones of the same phoneme. Furthermore, whereas the short-vowel allophones commonly exhibit patterns of overlap, merger and near-merger with one another, the long-vowel realizations of different phonemes tend to be much more distinct from one another: short-vowel realizations of /a/ overlap with /ɛ/ and /ɔ/ in the same environments (for example, in *pet, pat, pot*), whereas the long vowel realizations are fully distinct. Thus, whereas pairs such as *sat/set, can't/Kent* are commonly realized with the same, or very similar, low-front short vowel, the pairs *sand/send, bad/bed* have markedly different vowels, /a/ being long low-back and /ɛ/ long mid-front in such pairs. This commonly results in vowel alternations in morphologically related pairs with /ɛ/ and /ɔ/, as in table 5.1.

Within the /a/ system, and in terms of its overlap with the other low vowels, the areas most relevant to interpreting EModE data are: (1) the short-vowel environments; and (2) the *velar-raising* rules. In section 5.8, we examine these patterns in Belfast vernacular in a degree of time-depth by appealing again to the evidence of Patterson (1860).

Table 5.1

	mid, long	low, short
	send	sent
	twelve	twelfth
	Ed	Eddy
	Tom	Tommy
	Prod*	Protestant

(* 'Prod' is a slang term for Protestant)

5.8 Short /a/ in Belfast Vernacular

One of the most salient characteristics of present-day Belfast vernacular is the rule for raising /a/ to [æ, ɛ] before the three velar consonants /k, g, ŋ/ (these consonants are themselves normally fronted to some degree). As we noticed in chapter 4.2, this is quite well preserved in BV as a stable marker of membership of inner-city communities. However, there is also a rule for raising *after* /k, g/, which predicts that such items as *cabbage, castle, cab* will appear with front vowels. Unlike pre-velar raising, post-velar raising is highly recessive. A common inner-city pattern is for the fronting rule to be superseded by a lowering rule (before voiceless stops and in polysyllables), or a backing rule (in other environments) in the speech of younger speakers. Thus *cab* for example will appear as [kɛ·b] for some speakers on some occasions and [kɑ·b] for others or on other occasions. In the community as a whole, therefore, we can speak of alternation between front-raised values and lowered (mainly backed) values, according to which of the rules is applied. The 'change' here is phonetically sudden, not gradual, and the alternation is age-graded. However, *real-time* evidence shows that in nineteenth-century Belfast raising of /a/ was well established both before *and* after velars: the rules are clearly stated by Patterson (1860) and cited in chapter 4.6.

Patterson attests that /a/ was raised after *both* velars (/k/ and /g/), and Gregg's (1964) lists for Larne (20 miles north of Belfast) indicate that the same pattern has applied there. In present-day Belfast, however, we have attested no cases of raising after /g/ or before /r/. Thus, although Patterson has *gellon* for 'gallon' and *care* for 'car', and although similar pronunciations are heard in Ulster rural dialects, our Belfast data show that the rule has receded in an orderly way through a series of environments. It now remains as a variable rule after /k/ before all consonants except /r/. The rule for raising *before* velars, however, is strong and active and does not seem to have begun to recede lexically: in word-list style (which is usually considered to be formal) it persists much more strongly than post-velar raising; neologisms undergo the rule, and it affects spelling (see the discussion of 'occasional spellings' below). In 1976, for example, I noticed a car-park sign in West Belfast which displayed the legend: NO EXCESS ('no access'), and some of our inner-city informants refused to believe that there is an orthographic item *fag* ('cigarette') in the language: for them, it was *feg*.

The fact that velar-raising is, or has been, so well established, bears directly on the question of time-depth. What we are observing is a late stage in the recession of formerly well-established rules. And there is one well-known fact of present-day RP and SBE that points to the importance of the velars in the ancestral forms of those dialects also. Just as the velar environments prevent backing in BV, so they have also prevented *rounding* after [w] in RP: hence, *wax, quack*, but *want, swat*. This suggests that, as in present BV, so also at some point in the development of SBE, velar environments were fronted and raised ahead of other environments and were not accessible to the back-rounding rule. However, if raising of /a/ is so well established in BV velar environments, the tendency to front-raising may formerly have been present in both BV and EModE in other environments also, receding from these environments before receding from the velars. There are indeed indications in Patterson (1860) that raising of /a/ was, or had been, more widespread.

Patterson comments that the sound of *e* is substituted for *a* 'in some places' in almost every relevant word. It is not clear what this means, but it is possible today to observe mid-front values of /a/ before all or most consonants in many rural west of Ireland dialects. We shall see that there are other indications that the Belfast /a/ system was formerly more inclined to the front than it is now, and as we have noted above, the EModE front-raising rule may have affected some dialects later than others. What we observe in Belfast may therefore be the reflex of a raising rule that was originally 'metropolitan' or 'mainstream', together with some admixture of Scots raising rules which account for Scots [glɛs, kɛrt] 'glass, cart', and which are now partly superseded in Scots by lowering and backing rules. Patterson's evidence plainly indicates that there has been a gradual swing away from front values in the past century or so. What is relevant to EModE, however, is that Patterson's word-lists suggest that a raising rule still applied in *pre-nasal* environments (which often have a *back* vowel today).

Patterson spells many *a* words with *e*, and some of these (such as *rether* 'rather') are plainly sporadic residues of rural Scots (which has [ɛ, e] in, for example, *father, rather, gather* and in other pre-dental/alveolar positions); before nasals, however, *e* for *a* is more evident in Patterson. It appears in polysyllables before single nasals in *exemine, Jenuary,* and before nasal + voiceless obstruent in *demsel, exemple, Entrim* ('Antrim'); it also appears in monosyllables before nasal + voiceless obstruent in *slent, brench*: all of these now have a fully low vowel in Belfast. We shall see repeatedly in what follows that polysyllables are particularly resistant to change and that a following sonorant + voiceless obstruent is also relatively resistant. For this reason, Patterson's data (being chiefly polysyllables) most probably attest to a late stage in the loss of raising before nasals, a change that had formerly affected a wider range of environments. We shall not be surprised, therefore, to find evidence of pre-nasal raising in related dialects, at earlier times and in other environments. For the moment, however, it is reasonable to conclude that raising of /a/ formerly affected other environments besides velars – the pre-nasal environment in particular. In the next section, we proceed to consider variation in /ɛ/, as our discussion up to this point has obviously raised the possibility that tokens of /a/ and /ɛ/ can *merge* in certain environments.

5.9 Short /ɛ/ in Belfast: Overlap and Merger

Although 'classical' phoneme theory does not allow allophonic overlapping and approximation without merger, the Belfast research suggests that overlap and merger of phones in particular environments are common, and that they are amongst the patterns noticed when linguistic change is observed in progress. An example of this is the pattern of allophonic interchange between /a/ and /ɛ/.

Just as /a/ can be *raised* to [ɛ] in velar environments, so /ɛ/ can be *lowered* to [a, æ] before voiceless stops and before sonorant + voiceless obstruent. These latter environments are precisely those in which /a/ is also most likely to have a low front short value. Thus, such pairs as *sat/set, bat/bet* commonly occur with a vowel around [æ, a], and there is little, if any, difference between the vowels in *ant, can't, want, dance,* on the one hand, and those in *Kent, went, rent, pence* on the other. The pattern of /ɛ/ lowering in these 'short' environments is extremely well established: as table 4.9, p. 111, shows, it is categorical in some inner-city male groups. However, the pattern of merger/approximation that this suggests is complicated by the existence of the *raising rule* by which /a/ is raised before velars. The lowering and raising rules can be stated as follows:

Rule 1 /ɛ/ > <a>/ {voiceless stop}
Rule 2 /a/ > <ɛ>/ {velar}

If these rules are interpreted categorically, they predict a *flip-flop* in the case of voiceless velar stops: whereas the vowel in *neck* will lower to [a] (Rule 1), the vowel in *back* will raise to [ɛ] (Rule 2). This does, in fact, happen very commonly in casual speech, as in the following examples from the Belfast data:

1 The b[ɛ]ck of my n[a]ck;
2 Will you pay by [ɛk]cess ('Access') card or by ch[a]que?;
3 T[a]xtile f[ɛ]ctory.

These rules, however, are not categorical, but variable. Thus, speakers can also realise /a/ as [a] and /ɛ/ as [ɛ], although inner-city speakers *very rarely* do this in casual speech. More importantly, speakers can also use a further strategy in this case: *merger*. On word-lists inner-city speakers all merged *pack* and *peck* ; when pressed to differentiate, they often seemed unable, in the interview situation, to do so. However, as items that were merged on word-lists were commonly differentiated in conversational styles (and speakers some-times actually commented on that fact), it seems possible that some speakers may favour the flip-flop rule in casual style and the merger in word-lists. Thus, the voiceless velar environment exhibits merger in some instances and flip-flops in others; no doubt, it would be possible to observe other varying patterns of approximation (as for the *meat/mate* 'merger', below). Before we discuss further implications of these patterns, however, we need to look briefly ·at raising before *voiced* velars, and at the rules for short /ɔ /.

Unlike the /ɛ/ lowering rule, the velar-raising rule is not confined to short-vowel environments (that is, before the voiceless velar stop), but also applies when a voiced velar follows (that is, in long-vowel environments): thus *bag, bang* are realized with [ɛː]. When the vowel is long, it is usually front-raised much farther than when it is short and may be as high as [eː]. The routine application of the rule, however results in flip-flops with /ɛ/, so that *jet-lag*, for example, is realized with [a] in *jet* and [ɛː] in *lag*. The short /ɔ/ rules, however, are formally identical to those for /ɛ/: /ɔ/ is realized as a short vowel near [a] when it occurs before a voiceless stop or sonorant + voiceless obstruent, for example in *pot, font*; both /ɛ/ and /ɔ/, therefore, show patterns of overlap with /a/ in these environments and, under certain conditions, in polysyllables, as we shall see below.

5.10 Syllabic Alternations

For the sake of clarity in the argument so far, I have largely ignored the disyllabic/polysyllabic rules that affect /a/, /ɛ/ and /ɔ/, and have confined most of the discussion to monosyllables. However, the effects of polysyllabic environments are of the greatest interest, both for the study of sound-change in progress and for historical explora-tion. In the early stages of the inner-city study it was already evident that these rules were of historical and theoretical importance, as they lead to a regular series of *alternations* in derivationally related items.

(They are discussed in J. Milroy, 1976a.) It seems that when a change is in progress, polysyllabic environments will be amongst the last to be affected: thus, the vowel observed in the polysyllable today may be the vowel that was formerly found in other environments. It is possible to suggest an implicational series, using the symbols suggested in chapter 4.5: as the rule diffuses through the lexicon, monosyllabic T environments are the first to be affected by it, followed by monosyllabic D environments, with the polysyllables being the last to be affected. In preserving the conservative form in polysyllables, the language enshrines time-depth differences in the phonology – a kind of 'apparent time'.

In the inner-city data, the (synchronic) rule for shortening of /ɛ/ and /ɔ/ applies not only in the monosyllabic environments described, but also in the stressed syllable of disyllables, when that syllable is penultimate or pre-penultimate. The rule applies in all pre-consonantal environments including those that would have a long vowel in monosyllables (fricative and voiced obstruent environments and liquids), except apparently before [s] clusters (as in *hospital*). Thus, shortening applies to the stressed syllables of *fellow, intention, intentional,* but not to *fell, intend* (as in the last case the stressed syllable is not penultimate). These short disyllabic realizations of /a, ɛ, ɔ/ converge on a vowel near [a] (as in such monosyllables as *went, pot*). One result is homophony or near-homophony in such pairs as *phonetic/fanatic, erratic/erotic.*

The rule is plainly phonological, as it affects phonetically similar pairs that are not morphologically or semantically related, as in table 5.2. However, as it applies to all phonologically similar pairs, it inevitably has consequences for derivationally related items, such as in table 5.3. The rule does *not* apply, however, in disyllabic/polysyllabic inflected forms. Thus, while *mess/message, intend/intention* have the alternation, *mess/messing, intend/intended,* have [ɛ:] in both items in each pair. Furthermore, if /a/ is followed by a velar in these disyllabic environments, we again have a flip-flop: words like *factory, access* have [ɛ], whereas *intention, message* have [a]. The remarkable predictability and regularity of these inner-city rules suggests that they have deep historical embedding: their existence in well-established form may help to interpret evidence for the configuration of the low vowels of EModE.

The evidence that we have briefly reviewed above for various patterns of flip-flop and phonologically conditioned interchanges

Table 5.2

[ɛ]	[a]
mess	message
fell	fellow

Table 5.3

[ɛ, ɔ]	[a]
Ed	Eddy
Tom	Tommy
John	Johnny
offend	offensive
intend	intention
	intentional
	intensive
	superintendent

between adjacent vowels is much richer than anything we can hope to recover from history. Nevertheless, we shall see in the next section that EModE evidence strongly suggests a vowel system that exhibits patterns of a similar type to those we have reviewed. These are patterns which resemble *vernacular* states of language in which change and variation are inherent, and which do *not* resemble standard language states, which are uniform.

5.11 The Belfast Pattern and the Vowels of Early Modern English

Amongst traditional scholars, H. C. Wyld was particularly inclined to place a high value (for reconstructing EModE pronunciation) on 'occasional spellings' and rhymes/puns in written English, and to consider the evidence of contemporary commentaries (the work of the 'orthoepists') to be of less immediate value, as these can often be difficult to evaluate. Dobson's study (1968) of orthoepic evidence, on the other hand, relegates occasional spellings to a secondary position, and relies more closely on the descriptions of the 'best' orthoepists. Although such testimony is important, it is a little unfortunate that Dobson's influence led for a time to an undervaluing of occasional spellings, rhymes and puns. The kind of variation revealed by occasional spellings as primary evidence does not always fit comfortably into the standard historical linguistic mould, and so it has often seemed convenient to ignore it or explain it away, sometimes on the grounds that variability of the kind apparently attested is 'impossible'. The best-known difficulty of this kind is the apparent EModE merger of ME 'open' /ɛ:/ (the *meat* class) with ME /a:/ (the *mate* class), followed by apparent reversal of merger and subsequent merger of the MEAT class with ME close /e:/ (the *meet* class). In the concluding sections of this chapter we briefly consider in sociolinguistic terms: (1) phonemic overlap of /a/ and /ɛ/ in EModE; (2) the question of reversibility of merger, with reference to the *meat/mate* 'merger'; (3) lexical diffusion patterns and the Neogrammarian problem of gradual versus sudden phonetic change.

The value of EModE occasional spellings is given considerable support by the Belfast evidence, put together as it is on the basis of detailed observation of the spoken variety and real-time evidence (Patterson, 1860). In view of this, many of the spellings cited by Wyld from sixteenth-century sources (1936: 198–9) seem oddly familiar. It is not necessary to be unduly selective to find indications of pre-velar and pre-nasal raising of /a/, and polysyllabic lowering of /ɛ/, as in present-day Ulster English. Spellings that fall into these categories are the majority of those cited by Wyld. Velar items include *wex* ('wax'), *seck* ('sack'), *thenking* ('thanking'), *wexe* (verb), *renk* ('rank'), *beck* ('back'), *ectes* ('acts'). Pre-palatal raising may also be indicated by *wesshe* ('wash'): this would not be surprising, as it is also characteristic of stereotypical Lowland Scots and is found in the Belfast data. Wyld also cites a number of such spellings in nasal environments that recapitulate Patterson's *Jenuary, exemine*: they are *Jenewary, axemyne* ('examine'), *exemynyde, Crenmer, Frencis*. Apart from the proper names, the items cited are the same as those in Patterson. All of them are in polysyllables before the single nasal and before nasal clusters. It is possible that the range of the nasal-raising rule was wider than in nineteenth-century Belfast, as some other spellings indicate it in monosyllables before nasal + *voiced* obstruent: these are *hendes* ('hands'), *bend* ('band'). We cannot at the moment reconstruct with certainty what the ordering of relevant environments in EModE might have been, or whether it was always nasals that were decisive: as Lowland Scots preserves evidence of a raising rule before *dentals/alveolars* (for example in *glad, gather, Saturday*), it is not impossible that *hendes, bend* attest to pre-dental raisings. However, there is no doubt that the EModE items cited coincide closely with Patterson's environments (many similar examples are cited by other commentators, such as Kökeritz and Dobson, and they are quite common in texts with non-standard spellings from the *Paston Letters* to the *Diary of Henry Machyn*). As the EModE evidence for /a/ raising is systematically related to the Belfast evidence, it is worth considering whether the flip-flop pattern affecting /a/ and /ɛ/ in Belfast can also be paralleled in EModE.

Wyld (1936: 198) provides evidence for this. He also cites a series of what he calls 'inverted spellings' that strongly suggest a 'flip-flop' lowering of /ɛ/ to /a/: these are also in the environments most affected in Belfast, namely polysyllables. They include *a* for *e* in, for example, *Wanysday* ('Wednesday'), *massynger, massage* ('message'), *zastyrday* ('yesterday'), *mantion* ('mention'). The similarities to modern Ulster vernacular (see p. 151, above) are very striking to anyone who knows Ulster vernacular: lowering of /ɛ/ seems to have applied in polysyllables in EModE (as in BV), and there seems to have been a flip-flop, as the lowering of /ɛ/ applies in environments where raising of /a/ also applies – again as in Belfast. Thus, we have apparent flip-flops before nasals as between *Jenewary, Frencis*, in which /a/ is raised to [ɛ], and *Wanysday, mantion*, in which /ɛ/ is lowered to [a]: if raising before dentals also applied, then *massage* and others suggest a further possibility of a flip-flop rule, and a wider range of environments in which the mid and low vowels are exchanged. Thus, there is strong evidence that EModE, like modern Ulster, had rules for raising of /a/ before velars, palatals and nasals, together with a rule for lowering of /ɛ/ in certain polysyllabic environments, and possibly elsewhere. It also appears that just as Belfast speakers can merge pairs like *pack* and *peck*, so it is possible that patterns of merger, or near-merger, of such pairs might have been observable in EModE.

The most celebrated case of dispute about an alleged EModE merger, however, is not *pack/peck*, but what we have elsewhere called the *meat/mate* problem (J. Milroy and Harris, 1980). This is the problem mentioned above – the question whether the ME open /eː/ class merged in EModE with ME /aː/, only to separate again and undergo subsequent merger with ME close /eː/. Evidence from rhymes and occasional spellings gives some support to this, and the view taken by Wyld (1936) and followed by Kökeritz (1953) and Dobson (1968) is that there was a merger followed by a reversal and re-merger. Other prominent historical scholars (Jespersen, Luick and others) however, have rejected the evidence for the *meat/mate* merger by invoking the theoretical principle of *irreversibility of merger*. This principle, which became strongly characteristic of structuralist thinking, continues into post-generative 'mentalist' historical linguistics. Clearly, if the knowledge that classes A and B were once distinct is no longer present in speakers' minds, they cannot pick out the class B items and so cannot separate them from the merged class and then re-merge them with a completely different class. Thus, if the historical evidence seems to suggest that *meat* merged with *mate*, this cannot be a valid interpretation according to this principle, because if it had happened then both *meat* and *mate* would subsequently have been eligible for merger with *meet*: speakers would not have known the difference.

The Belfast and general Hiberno-English system seems to display a situation similar to EModE, and they cast considerable doubt on the principle of irreversibility of merger. Hib-E speakers appear to have access to two systems here, one in which *meat* merges with *mate* and one in which *meat* merges with *meet*; that is, they know both mergers. For most speakers the *meat* class belongs to both systems in that it is an alternating class; thus, on different occasions the same speaker may pronounce words of the type *seat, peace, leave* with [eː] or with [i]. Hib-E scholars have apparently always been quite happy to accept that the *meat/mate* merger is a true merger (see citations in J. Milroy and Harris, 1980: 200), and Bliss (1979: 208–10) cites evidence to show that these two classes had merged in Hib-E by around 1700. Seemingly, they are also happy to accept that the *meat/ meet* merger is also a true merger, and that some people alternate between these two merged classes. If we take a social view of language, and accept that it is the possession of the community as well as internal to speakers' minds, we must be prepared to accept that reversal of merger can take place in this way, so long as speakers know that *meat* is an alternating class. The EModE scenario as envisaged by Wyld, Kökeritz and others is therefore a possible scenario, and there is a sense in which merger is reversible. Normal language states are not uniform, and in vernacular (non-standardized) states we expect alternations and other kinds of variation to exist. Thus, the potential for this kind of reversal is always likely to be present in vernaculars. Whether a second merger (in this case *meat* to *meet*) occurs in the community, and the direction it moves in, will be determined not linguistically but socially.

Generally relevant here also is the (*pull*) set, which I discussed in chapters 3 and 4. In BV the RP long and short /u/ classes (as in *pool, pull*) are the same and are both realized as a short vowel; however, the restricted lexical set of *pull, bull, foot* etc., is an alternating set, rhyming alternately with *cut, dull* and with *soon, pool, good*. As we also noticed in chapter 3, we cannot predict the full membership of the set on phonological grounds. One group of alternants clearly originates with the extension of the general unrounding of ME *u* (as in *cut, dull*) to initial labial items, such as *pull*, but it is not clear how the words originating from shortening in the ME ō set can be predicted phonologically (for example, if *took* belongs to the set, why not *cook*?). I have listed the number of occurrences of each individual word occurring in the data in table 5.4. Although it looks from this as though each word has its own history, certain generalizations can be based on these figures. First, disyllables are in general more resistant to transfer into the incoming /u/ class than are monosyllables, and this is in line with our findings for other vowels. The fact that in this case the transfer is trans-phonemic whereas the other cases are usually tensing rules within the same phoneme does not make any difference. It seems that we reach a better generalization about direction of vowel change in BV if we override contrastive phoneme theory here. Second, items with initial labials are more resistant to transfer than the other items; we can suggest, therefore, that the initial labial is a constraint on change – it encourages maintenance. Finally, labial items with initial [b] are more resistant to transfer than other initial labial items. We have noted elsewhere (J. Milroy, 1980) that the vernacular unrounded vowel is persistent in word-lists, that it also persists into middle-class speech, and that polysyllables are the most resistant environments. A rough implicational ordering of resistance to change would be *bulletin–bullet–bull–pull–football–foot*, with the leftmost item the most resistant and the rightmost the most susceptible to transfer. The disentangling of ancient mergers that we observe here has taken a very long time, and the best explanation for the persistence of this alternating class is again a social explanation: the 'vernacular' alternant carries an identity function and strong connotations of closeness and intimacy.

Table 5.4   The (*pull*) alternating set in Belfast.

Occurrences of [ʌ]: reading styles

Items from ME short *u*				Items from ME ō and other sources			
	[u]	−N−	[ʌ]	%		[u]	−N−	[ʌ]	%

Items from ME short *u*	[u]	−N−	[ʌ]	%	Items from ME ō and other sources	[u]	−N−	[ʌ]	%
butcher	23		27	54	shook	40		1	2
bush	21		11	34	took	64		0	0
bull	27		14	34	foot	35		0	0
pudding	36		4	10	could	56		0	0
put	49		4	8	look	7		0	0
pull	34		1	3	would	41		0	0
Totals					should	10		0	0
b-items	71		52	42	*Total*	253		1	0.4
p-items	119		9	7					
disyllables	59		31	39					
monosyllables	131		34	21					

Occurences of [ʌ]: conversational styles

Items from ME short *u*	[u]	−N−	[ʌ]	%	Items from ME ō and other sources	[u]	−N−	[ʌ]	%
bullet	2		8	80	football	5		4	44
pull	18		51	74	stood	10		7	41
full	17		15	47	foot	22		12	35
put	189		120	39	took	99		49	33
push	11		5	31	could	186		82	31
butcher	0		1	−	look	140		51	27
bush	1		2	−	would	453		88	16
bull	2		1	−	should	54		5	8
pudding	1		0	−	shook	0		1	−
Totals					*Totals*				
disyllables	3		9	75	disyllables	5		4	44
monosyllables	235		191	45	monosyllables	964		295	23

As we have shown elsewhere, however, it is not always the case in such examples that full merger within the language system has come about. The unreliability of reported mergers has been argued for most strongly by Labov and his colleagues (Labov, Yaeger and Steiner, 1972; Labov, 1975 etc.), and for inner-city Belfast it can be argued that *meat* is not really merged with *mate*, despite the fact that people believe that it is a merger. We demonstrated this statistically (J. Milroy and Harris, 1980): the data in table 5.5, were subjected to the chi-squared test, and the difference between the distributions of *meat* items and *mate* items was found to be very highly significant. This means that although realizations of these overlap and are sometimes identical, it does not really make sense to say that this is a merger in the language system in BV (of course, it may be in other dialects). If it were a full merger, the variation observed (as in variation in RP *meat/meet*, for instance) would be insignificant and random. Thus, at least one of the systems that children have been learning over the centuries in the ancestral forms of BV must have incorporated a three-way distinction of *meet/meat/mate*.

Table 5.5 Distribution of *mate* and *meat* items: vowel-height.

	mate	*meat*
[ɪe]	33	0
[e][ee]	60	20
[ɛ][ɛe]	6	38
[ɛ]	0	2

5.12 Conclusions

In this chapter, the general underlying issue with which we have been concerned is the question of what a sound-change actually is. In observing states of language, at what point can we specify that what used to be A is now B? From a sociolinguistic perspective, we may accept that a change is complete when some community agrees that it is and reflects this change in their usage; it is a change in community norms and so it is not adequately described if it is presented in the traditional way as a phonetic movement. However, if we recall the history of [h]-loss, it will be clear that the change from one phonetic realization to another may take many centuries and may never be complete. We must therefore extend our definition of change to include *change in the distribution of variants*. Thus, if at one time [h] was categorical before vowels, the change to socially-marked variation in (h) is itself a linguistic change. Similarly a change in the social evaluation of a variant is also a change. It seems that questions of this kind (especially: what do we mean by a linguistic change?) should now be given more prominence than the more traditional Neogrammarian questions, as discussed by Labov (1981) and more recently by Kiparsky (1988). The most relevant Neogrammarian question here is the question whether sound-change is (1) phonetically gradual and lexically sudden, or (2) phonetically sudden and lexically gradual. I end this chapter by turning briefly to this question.

My own studies of dialect divergence have repeatedly encountered examples that fit with (2), that is, lexical diffusion. The (*pull*) and (*meat*) sets are examples: the transfer from [ʌ] to [u] in *pull, stood* etc. is achieved by a leap across phonetic space, and the process is lexically gradual in that different lexical items are transferred at differential rates. Observable change in the BV system is overwhelmingly like this – phonetically sudden and lexically gradual. It is, however, much less clear that we can demonstrate unequivocally that sound-change can also be implemented in a phonetically gradual fashion, although linguists still usually argue that this can happen. To take an example from Belfast, we might attempt to argue for phonetically gradual change on the basis of our data on /a/, which in present-day Belfast is undergoing retraction to [ɑ]. However, within the /a/ system we repeatedly find that some parts of the backing process are phonetically sudden and implemented through alternating sets: initial velar items such as *cab, can* are realized alternately by a fully front low-mid vowel and a fully back low to low-mid (sometimes rounded) vowel. This is plainly phonetically sudden, and not confined to the initial velar set: it seems that subsets of phonologically defined items within the system undergo a process of transfer one after the other. So it is possible that the swing to the back in the /a/ system is triggered in a phonetically sudden manner, and that patterns in the data that appear to be gradual are secondary patterns dependent on the primary sudden impetus to change. Thus, in cases where the evidence available at a given time suggests that the process is phonetically gradual, we may simply not have looked at the phonology in sufficient depth and detail.

The Neogrammarian position on phonetically gradual change was, of course, purely theoretical in the sense that they did not have the technology to observe change in progress empirically. They may therefore quite simply have been wrong. It is possible that sound-change in the narrow traditional sense (in which A 'becomes' B) must be phonetically sudden (involving movement from one allophone to another, lexical diffusion and/or, sometimes, phonemic restructuring), and that the apparently phonetically gradual patterns that we are now able to observe are not sound-changes in progress, but simply variation. This variation, when subjected to fine-grained analysis, may at a given time appear to be moving in a particular direction, but the direction may change, and the realizations may all drift back again to where they started off. If there is to be a change, it seems that this will be determined socially. Bearing in mind the points I have made above about what a sound-change actually is, it may therefore be useful to consider a possible socially based definition of language change, dependent on a prior distinction between *innovation* and *change*. In chapter 6, I will have more to say about this, amongst other things.

Appendix: Etymological Applications of Variation Studies

Whereas relatively standardized varieties suppress alternative pro-nunciations of the same word (with a few exceptions), vernaculars that are less affected by the 'mainstream' variety are rich in lexical alternants. In Belfast, for example, post-velar /a/ can be realized even by the same speaker on different occasions as [ɛ] or as [ɑ]. T.M. (Clonard) pronounces *can* with [ɛ], and then follows it with three tokens of *can* with [ɑ]. EModE seems to have been in this respect similar to Belfast vernacular and dissimilar to post-eighteenth-century relatively standardized varieties: as Kökeritz points out, it was more tolerant of variation than PresStE is. It is as residues of the EModE alternating state that PresStE preserves 'fossilized' pairs such as *strop/strap*, with semantic differentiation that has rendered the alternation functional in conveying meaning.

As for variation between /a/ and /ɛ/, etymologists consistently recognize doublets resulting from post-velar raising of the kind attested in present-day Belfast (see, for example, Onions, 1966, s.v. *catch/ketch*). The *pre*-velar raising rule, however, is not so consistently recognized. *Margaret/Meg* and *hackle/heckle* are given by Onions as alternants, the second item in each pair being 'Northern' or 'Scottish'. However, the pairs *drag/dregs* and *pack/peck* (quarter of a bushel) are not thought to be etymologically connected. Rather than appealing to rules that may have played some role within the English language, scholars have been inclined to look outside of the language for their inspirations – often to Old Norse, and sometimes (in desperation?) to Middle Dutch.

For *dreg(s)*, Onions says: 'prob. of Scand. origin (cf ON pl. *dreggjar*...)', and he adds that 'the problem of immed. origin is complicated by the occurrence in early mod. E. of the forms *dragges* and *dredges*.' Patterson (1860), however, had no doubt that it was an alternant of *drags*: he interpreted *dregs* as an Ulsterism deriving from the operation of pre-velar raising, and recommended the hypercorrection *drags*, a hypercorrection which is still current in Ulster. It is possible, of course, that the *ultimate* origin of the alternate form was Old Norse, as that language did have pre-velar (probably palatalized velar) raising of /a/, but this applied only when /i/ or /j/ followed in the next syllable. So it is wise to be sceptical about wholesale explanations based on Old Norse.

As for *pack/peck*, Onions says that both occur in the thirteenth century, *pack* being from Middle Dutch and *peck* from Anglo-Norman. Both ultimately are of unknown origin, that is, it is not known how *pek* got into Anglo-Norman (could it have been from English?). It could, of course, be an alternant of *pack*, a *peck* being the measure appropriate to a donkey's *pack*. If so, the alternation may be due either to post-velar raising of /a/ or to pre-voiceless stop lowering of /ɛ/ at some early stage of English. The etymology of *wrack* (cf. *wreck*) is similarly obscure, according to Onions (possibly 'Middle Dutch' – again!). Middle-class Ulster speakers often interpret *wrack/wreck* as alternants: *nerve-wracked* is often 'corrected' to *nerve-wrecked*, presumably on the assumption that *wracked* manifests stigmatized lowering of /ɛ/ before the voiceless stop. Surely we must consider the possibility that many such pairs are merely alternants, arising from the operation in early English of the rules that we have discussed. Origins in Old Norse and Middle Dutch in such cases seem to be far more speculative than explanations based on alternating pairs, especially when (as in this case) we can support the explanations by appealing to *both* historical and contemporary sources.

6
Speaker-innovation and Linguistic Change

6.0 Introduction: Actuation and the Speaker

The discussion so far has been mainly about the embedding of language in society and about the patterns, including historical patterns, that can be revealed by systematic and accountable methods. Much of the discussion has been about patterns of maintenance: it has not been exclusively focused on linguistic change. In this chapter I *am* concerned with change – specifically with the most intractable of the five problems distinguished by Weinreich, Labov and Herzog (1968). This is 'the very heart of the matter' – the actuation problem itself – essentially the problem of explaining the causes of language change. It is appropriate to start by recalling their statement of the problem (p. 102):

> Why do changes in a structural feature take place in a particular language at a given time, but not in other languages with the same feature, or in the same language at other times?

This is such a challenging formulation that (as we have seen above) many linguists do not address it directly. We noted in chapter 2 that, strictly speaking, the problem is insoluble, but that this is not an excuse for neglecting it entirely. The point of view adopted here is that linguistic change originates with speakers and is implemented in social interactions between speakers, so it is reasonable to suggest that by systematic observation of language in use we can come closer to understanding actuation. But, recalling Principle 1 (that language use – except in literary modes – is *always* observed within social contexts), we must accept that our analysis and interpretation must take account of society, situation and speaker.

To clarify this, I would like to take up again the methodological distinction between *speaker* and *system*, which I have mentioned several times so far. It is important to specify when we are talking about speakers and when we are talking about systems, and I shall attempt to show that observing this distinction can lead to important insights that we would be unlikely to achieve if our approach were purely language-internal.

6.1 Speaker and System

One clear difference between historical and social linguistics is the methodological centrality of the speaker in sociolinguistic investigations. The database is not derived from written records, but from live speakers in social contexts. It does not follow, of course, that more direct access to speakers (on the part of field linguists) necessarily implies direct access to linguistic 'facts'. As we noted in chapter 2, we do not observe linguistic patterns directly: we observe people talking. Similarly, the 'products' of our analyses (Kibrik, 1977) are idealizations in the form of 'grammars'; in this sense, Labov's graphs of linguistic change in New York City are 'grammars', just as generative rule-statements are. Thus, the output of all linguistic investigations can be regarded as 'grammars of language' constructed by linguists, and not necessarily what any *individual* speaker of a language uses or 'knows'.

In the process of data-analysis, the non-congruence of speaker-based and system-based accounts becomes very obvious. We have seen some examples of this from outer-city Belfast in chapter 4: vowel realizations that we describe systemically as 'long' turn out to be 'short' in individual instances, and West (1988) has shown that Harris's (1985) characterization of Ulster vowel length does not turn out to be correct for certain individual instances collected in Bally-gawley, Co. Tyrone. But that does not invalidate Harris's description of the system, and I would be extremely surprised if these systemic descriptions ever turned out to be correct for all speakers. For these reasons, it can be quite misleading not to draw the speaker/system distinction in studies of language change. The following example may make the necessity for the distinction clear.

I showed in chapter 4 (Sections 4.6 and 4.7) that /a/ (as in *pat, bad*) and /ɛ/ (as in *set, bed*) have been undergoing change for some time: /a/ is becoming backed and lengthened, while /ɛ/ is being front-raised and lengthened. However, both seem to have started off from much the same (low to low-mid front) position in phonological space, and these older variants (apparently merged in many cases) are still common, especially before voiceless stops. Thus, at the level of language *system* we are able to make a suitably abstract and correct statement about these changes. Rule 1 and Rule 2 describe the changes affecting /a/ and /ɛ/ respectively:

Rule 1 (/a/)   −Back > +Back
                      +Low > +Low
Rule 2 (/ɛ/   −Back > −Back
                      +Low > −Low

This seems to capture what is currently happening to this part of the vowel *system*, and it conveys the impression that the two vowels are moving apart in phonetic space, leaving the low-front region untenanted. Viewed at the abstract level, we may interpret this as an attempt on the part of the *language* to disentangle a merger of such items as *pat/pet, can't/Kent*. But if we look at the output of speakers, a very different pattern emerges. We can get a clue to this by noticing that the implementation of the changes is sex-differentiated (see table 4.9, p. 111). Although the differences between males and females here do not predict absolutely that females will always behave in one way and males in another, the figures are nevertheless based on a close analysis of the speech of individuals. It is clear that in general those speakers (usually male) who have considerable /a/-backing do not also have /ɛ/-raising, and that those who have /ɛ/-raising (almost always female) do not normally have /a/-backing. Therefore, what appears to be a grammar of change does not predict the manner in which individual speakers are implementing the change, and it appears that not all members of the speech community are participating in the same changes. Thus, it seems that a speaker-based account does not necessarily support Labov's view of 'speech community', or the recent characterization by Labov and Harris (1986) in terms of the two Philadelphia ethnic communities not 'participating' in the same changes. It may be that members of the *same* inner-city Belfast communities do not always participate in the same changes.

As we wish to use sociolinguistic findings to throw light on more traditional system-oriented approaches to language change, it is necessary to clarify further the implications of drawing a distinction between speaker-activity on the one hand, and grammars of language or of linguistic change on the other. In so far as linguistic changes are in some sense brought about by the activities of speakers, it seems appropriate to distinguish sharply between *speaker-activity* and the linguistic *system*, to which speakers have access and which they can influence. But here I want to show that whereas the approach to language change advocated in this book is both speaker-oriented and system-oriented, the approach of most quantitative social dialectology has agreed with the tradition in being primarily system-oriented.

Traditional historical linguistics, as we have seen, has generally presented linguistic change as something that can be described (or, ultimately, explained) as a language-internal phenomenon, that is, without primary reference to speakers in social groupings as the agents of change: it has also tended to impose constraints on the kind of historical data that can be adduced as evidence, focusing on what Lass (1980: 87n.) calls 'native languages of the usual type'. When speakers have been referred to, it has usually been in post-generative accounts that have recognized 'idealized native-speaker competence', and the idea of speakers' internalization of rules and capacity to bring about rule-change (an example is Andersen, 1973). Sociolinguistics, on the other hand, has recognized the centrality of speakers in a more thoroughgoing way – very often in studies that need to take account of language-mixing and code-switching in contact situations, that is, by studying situations that do not necessarily focus on nativeness of languages at all and that therefore do not have any place for the Chomskyan idealized 'native' speaker. But sociolinguists have differed amongst themselves in the emphasis they have given to the centrality of speaker-behaviour in their methodologies.

The position adopted by different sociolinguistic investigators ultimately depends on the aims of their research. One approach is to produce an account based primarily on speakers (without obligatorily attempting to map their output on to a grammar), and to focus on the discourse strategies they use in interaction. This is associated with the work of Gumperz, and the introduction to Gumperz (1982) is in fact one of the clearest accounts of the differences between speaker-based and system-based approaches.[1] The quantitative paradigm, however, is primarily system-oriented and in Gumperz's view devoted to the production of 'grammars'. Although it uses social (or speaker) variables, and so takes account of the speaker, the main aim of Labov's work is to discover and describe linguistic patterns of variation: this is very clear from the fact that the graphs and diagrams of Labov's early work (themselves mini-grammars of variation) were then developed into variable rule descriptions, using an intra-linguistic generative framework, and subsequently adopted in Kiparsky's (1988) account of phonological change. Labov has replaced uniform grammars with variable grammars, and this in itself is a tremendous achievement. In the present perspective, however, it is fair to say that the quantitative methodology has refined our understanding of variable language systems much more than our understanding of speaker-innovations.

Clearly, it is by using the system-oriented approach of Labov that we have made most progress in looking at the traditional problems of historical linguistics (which, as I have pointed out, seldom took account of the speaker's role in change). As my concerns in this book are with these traditional problems, I am, like Labov, necessarily concerned with historical grammars. It seems, however, that a solution to the traditional question of how changes are *actuated* requires that the speaker's activities in innovating should be in principle distinguished sharply from the language state affected by the innovations. For that reason, we must give a principled position to the speaker in accounts of change, and the distinction between speaker and system is fundamental in this book as a perspective from which we interpret our findings. We can, of course, take the argument somewhat further than this and claim that the speaker's position in, and relation to, broader social structures and processes should be more systematically studied than it has normally been in sociolinguistics. We shall look at this in chapter 7.

For the moment, it is sufficient to observe that, as we are using both system-oriented and speaker-oriented approaches in our work, we need to draw a clear distinction between them, so that in any discussion we will know which of these orientations we are actually adopting. One obvious consequence of making this distinction is that we can separate speaker-*innovation* from linguistic *change*, and we now turn to this.

6.2   Speaker-innovation and Language Change

On the basis of the speaker/system distinction, we can propose an associated distinction that bears directly on the actuation problem – the distinction between speaker *innovation* on the one hand, and linguistic *change* on the other. Innovation and change are not conceptually the same thing: an innovation is an act of the speaker, whereas a change is observed within the language system. It is *speakers*, and not *languages*, that innovate.

We can therefore approach the *actuation problem* in the following way. We can describe *speaker-innovation* as *an act of the speaker which is capable of influencing linguistic structure*. The innovation may, or may not, enter the language system: thus, part of the solution to the actuation problem will be to explain the conditions in which an innovation is unsuccessful in addition to those in which it is successful. This is one reason why it is important to associate our account of change with a prior account of language maintenance: incipient changes can be *resisted* in the speech community, and we must attempt to understand the conditions under which this happens. If, however, the innovation is successful, the reflex of this speaker-act is *change in the language system*, which of course is always observed after the speaker-act of innovation has taken place. Once a new linguistic structure is created – that is, once change has entered the system – it appears to penetrate in an orderly fashion and to constrain individual and collective behaviour in the manner that has been shown in quantitative analysis by Labov (1966) and many others. We must notice here, however, that what the graphs, diagrams and variable rule statements of the quantitative paradigm actually model is not the behaviour of speakers, nor is it the act of actuation: what they model is the *linguistic system*. This quantitative modelling of the system is, of course, much more sophisticated than the homogeneous and uniform systems that are postulated in other branches of linguistic inquiry, as it incorporates the *orderly heterogeneity* of the community 'grammar', but it is nonetheless a linguistic system – one that characterizes the *constraints on the linguistic behaviour of groups and individuals*. It can be interpreted as modelling the effects of the linguistic system on speakers rather than the effects of speakers on the system. This is conceptually quite a different matter from the modelling of *how speakers introduce an innovation into the system in the first place*. These relationships are expressed graphically in figure 6.1.

It seems that while investigators may observe something quite close to speaker-innovation, they have no principled way of determining whether what they have observed is the beginning of a linguistic change in the system. As figure 6.1 shows, what the quantitative linguist describes is a change that has already assumed a regular pattern of social variation in the community. For these reasons, intra-linguistic approaches generally dismiss actuation as unobservable. It is, for example, discussed by Lass (1980: 95–6) in the following way. Suppose I have observed that a speaker utters [e] in a 'word of etymological category X' on one day, and utters [i] in the same environment on the next day, all that I have observed (according to Lass) is a diachronic correspondence: I have no way of determining whether it is a change. But there are some distinctions that sociolinguists customarily make that Lass does not make here; the 'change' from one day to the next might, for example, be stylistic – an instance of orderly heterogeneity. But what is noticeable in the present context is the absence of the speaker/system distinction: it appears from Lass's example that a change in the output of a *single* speaker might

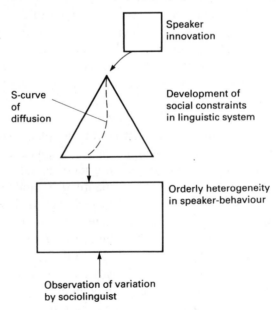

Figure 6.1 Model of transition from speaker-innovation to linguistic change.

be regarded as the locus of a change in the system, whereas of course a change is not a change until it has been adopted by *more than one* speaker. Therefore, we cannot deal with actuation by positing examples like this, based on a single speaker. But it does appear that we *can* observe a speaker-innovation (perhaps completely accidentally): the problem is that we do not know whether it will be a *successful* innovation – we cannot demonstrate systematically that it leads to a linguistic change until after it has spread. Yet, as we have already noted, the quantitative methodology does not in itself give us the means to deal with *actuation* and the very early stages of a change.

The distinction I am trying to make here can be further clarified by referring to some recent work by Trudgill (1986b), which strongly suggests that we need methods quite different from the standard quantitative ones to study *actuation* of change (depending on speaker-behaviour) as distinct from *the effect of the system on speakers*. Returning to Norwich eighteen years after his original survey, Trudgill noticed that one particular linguistic feature (a labio-dental variant of /r/) was by then firmly embedded as a patterned sociolinguistic variable. In his 1968 fieldwork, however, he had noticed this feature sporadically, but had thought that it might be pathological – perhaps a speech problem experienced by a few younger speakers. Now, although actuation of this change must already have taken place when Trudgill observed it in 1968, it had not yet become embedded in sociolinguistic structure in the way that is accessible by quantitative methods, but was near the beginning of the S-curve of diffusion (see figure 6.1). Therefore, using the classic quantitative methods, it was not possible at that point to show the patterning of this change in the sociolinguistic system.

In fact, the quantitative methodology predisposes us to overlook cases like the Norwich one, and this example draws attention in a clear way to a familiar difficulty. When we were selecting phonological variables for quantification in Belfast, there were many variables that had to be rejected from the quantification precisely because tokens of them were sporadic or relatively rare. Using the standard methods, we would not have been able to show large-scale patterns in these variables. As I pointed out in chapter 3, some of these were recessive forms (such as the *meat/mate* distinction). Others, however, seemed to point to the early stages of change. For example, we noticed in a pilot survey that the glottal stop for /t/ (as in *water, what*) – which is emphatically *not* part of traditional Belfast vernacular – occurred now and again, chiefly among female adolescents. I am fairly sure that this is the leading edge of a change (the beginning of the S-curve), because I know that urban central Scots English (which has glottal stops) can influence Belfast – and because I believe that there is a general tendency ('drift') towards glottalling in Cisatlantic English – but I cannot convincingly demonstrate this by standard quantitative methods. This is because (as we noted above) the classic methods are designed to examine the effect of the system on speaker-behaviour rather than vice versa, and so it is hard to see how anyone using these methods could make a systematic attempt to handle *actuation* or the very early stages of a change.

Bearing in mind the speaker/system distinction, therefore, we have tried to approach the problem in a more abstract way by attempting a *social* characterization of those persons, or sections of society, who are responsible for the actuation of change, in terms of the social links that can exist between speakers. We might call this a characterization of the *idealized speaker-innovator*. In the following sections, I am concerned with how this might be modelled.

6.3   The Speaker-innovator according to Labov

It is useful to begin with the best-known attempt to determine the social characteristics of the speaker-innovator, which is that of Labov. Labov's characterization is based directly on the findings of neighbourhood studies of socially cohesive groups, and his main conclusions can be summarized as follows:

1   Speakers who lead sound change are those with the highest status in their local communities as measured by a social class index.

2   Among persons of equal status 'the most advanced speakers are the persons with the largest number of local contacts within the neighborhood, yet who have at the same time the highest proportion of their acquaintances outside the neighborhood.' Labov then goes on to comment 'Thus we have a portrait of individuals with the highest local prestige who are responsive to a somewhat broader form of prestige at the next larger level of social communication' (1980: 261).

According to this account, linguistic innovation is accomplished by persons who have many ties within the community but who simultaneously have a large number of outside contacts. This raises some issues concerning the nature of social ties between persons, and we shall return to this point below. But this characterization seems also to rely on certain presuppositions about the broader social structure: there is heavy reliance on stratificational social class and the associated notion of *prestige*. Clearly, all this raises a number of general issues that are central to sociolinguistic explanation, and we shall discuss these more general issues in chapter 7.

Here, the most immediately relevant point is that Labov uses the notion of prestige in two different ways: the innovators are said to have prestige in two dimensions – both inside and outside the communities. First, there is a superordinate locus of change, with prestige depending on the broader socio-economic class distribution in the wider community (this is implicit in measuring the status of the innovator by a social-class index); within this, however, Labov presents a more refined or micro-level locus of change within a neighbourhood group of roughly equal status, in which the innovator has 'local prestige'. On the one hand, we have a kind of prestige that is somehow agreed on by the wider community, but on the other a more fine-grained kind of local prestige, which is presumably not the same, but which must depend on the way in which this innovator is subjectively evaluated by his or her peers in day-to-day encounters within the local social networks.

These two kinds of prestige belong to two different orders of conceptualization. In so far as socio-economic class is used in the Labov paradigm to access the social structure in which change is embedded, the first kind of prestige is macro-level: it is accessible through a theory of abstract social structure, it often appears in practice to be institutionalized, and it is associated with unequal distribution of power in society at large. The second kind of prestige is micro-level and subjective: it is predicated on personal attitudes developed in the situations in which speakers interact as individuals, and it is something of a truism that people who are accorded prestige in this second sense frequently do not have prestige in the first sense. In fact, these two kinds of prestige are often in conflict: the social values that confer prestige on prominent members of street gangs, for example – such as skill in street-fighting and playing truant from school (Labov, 1972a) – are clearly in conflict with the values of mainstream society.

But there is another aspect of Labov's characterization that leads to a difficulty, and this difficulty arises from the nature of social links as modelled by a network-based account. In this perspective, we have pointed out elsewhere (J. Milroy and L. Milroy, 1985b), following Granovetter (1973), that it is doubtful whether an individual can be a central member of a close-tie community and at the same time have large numbers of close-tie outside contacts, or carry both kinds of prestige (J. Milroy, 1989), and furthermore that even if this type of person does exist, it is not clear that he or she, as described in Labov's account, is actually the innovator (Labov's innovator in fact looks very much like Boissevain's (1974) *broker*, who by definition is not central to the network). But this is a difficult point, to which I shall return below; we have preferred to argue, not so much in terms of characterizing a type of personality, but more abstractly in terms of characterizing the kind of social ties that can exist between individuals. In this argument, it is *weak ties* and not strong ties that are crucial.

Before I go on to develop this further, it is relevant to comment briefly on Labov's use of the concept of socio-economic class, as this is a crucial factor in his model of the innovator. This use of socio-economic class (as I shall further explain in chapter 7) derives from a particular consensus-based theory of class (Parsons, 1952), which is not self-evidently the only or correct theory of social class structure. The relevant point here, however, is not so much the rightness of the model as the fact that the theoretical category of social class is basic to Labov's methodology. As a result of this, descriptions of 'speech community' and interpretations (or explanations) of change tend also to be expressed primarily in terms of social class, and this is probably why the notion of prestige looms so large in interpretation. We produce a community grammar that is modelled in terms of social class, and we then use social class (and the related notion of prestige) to interpret the patterns that we have revealed. This has many effects. One of these is that other social categories are frequently interpreted as subsidiary to social class, and so patterns of gender-differentiation, for example, are interpreted as being enacted within this class framework: as female speech patterns usually tend upwards in the social hierarchy, females are said to be exhibiting 'prestige' in their speech. But what is especially important here is that Labov's characterization of the speaker-innovator is measured against the social-class hierarchy and expressed in terms of it. To judge by other comments (Labov, 1980: 154), it looks as though the innovator is conceived of within this model as being a lower-middle to upper working-class individual. Taking all these points together, it is not at all clear from Labov's account how we could locate the innovator in a community that is *not* stratified in this way. Indeed, the Labov model may even be interpreted as containing the entailment that change is possible only in socially stratified societies.

The model of the innovator that I shall propose differs in many ways from Labov's characterization. It is not based primarily on the idea of prestige, or on the operation of prestige in the social class dimension, but on the rather different model of *speech community* that I have been explaining in this book. This model is based on the strength of social ties that can exist between individuals, and innovation is conceived of as passing through relatively weak ties. The model is therefore less personalized than Labov's model appears to be: it is not so much about a kind of person as about the kind of links that exist between persons, and between groups of persons. It is in this sense more abstract than Labov's model. It therefore seems to be applicable to a much broader range of language situations and is capable of casting light on patterns of change at both the micro- and macro-levels and at all points between these. In section 6.4, my purpose is to introduce this model by first explaining the functions of weak ties in facilitating language change.

6.4   Network Structure and Linguistic Change

In chapters 3 and 4, I attempted to give some idea of how an extensive array of linguistic variants can be associated with a variety of intersecting and overlapping social functions in close-tie communities. I also explained the reasoning behind the extension of our analysis in the second phase of the Belfast project to outer-city locations and to a city-wide survey. Essentially, the prediction is that to the extent that the strong localized norm-enforcement of the inner city is reduced, there will be a movement away from localized vernacular norms of language. As we have seen, this means not only a movement away from what are usually known as 'stigmatized' forms in the direction of supra-local forms which are sometimes, but by no means always, more similar to the 'standard': it also means a decline in the incidence of the *variable* norms discussed in chapter 4. That is to say that to the extent that alternant forms (especially the phono-lexical ones) marking close-tie situations become less functional in the outer city, they recede, and we are left with (amongst other things) a reduction in the alternative choices that mark symbolic functions. So it is relevant to recall that linguistic change is conceived of here as being observable in different patterns: not only in the traditional pattern of sound change from A to B, but more broadly in movements towards greater or lesser consensus on community norms of usage, for example movements towards greater or lesser convergence on uniform norms.

Recall that the Belfast research design here depends on the idea of norm maintenance, which we have operationalized in terms of *social network*, and within this model we have distinguished between relatively weak and strong network links. In any real community individuals and groups will vary in the relative intensity of ties, and this is what makes it possible to compare them in these terms. But behind this there lies an idealization which predicts that in a community bound by maximally dense and multiplex network ties linguistic change would not take place at all. No such community can actually exist, but the idealization is important, because it also implies that to the extent that relatively weak ties exist in communities (as in fact they do), the conditions will be present for linguistic change to take place. This perception was partly borne out even in the inner-city research. We noted that a very few individuals had markedly low network strength scores, and furthermore that these individuals tended to use language much less close to the core Belfast vernacular, with a much lower use of the 'close-tie' variants (such as [ʌ] in words of the (*pull*) class). The idea that *relative strength of network tie* is a powerful predictor of language use is thus implicit in the interpretative model we have used throughout: it predicts, amongst other things, that to the extent that ties are strong, linguistic change will be prevented or impeded, whereas to the extent that they are weak, they will be more open to external influences, and so linguistic change will be facilitated.

Weak ties are much more difficult to investigate empirically than strong ones, and the instinct of the network-based ethnographer is usually to study relatively self-contained small communities that are internally bound by strong links and relatively insulated from outside influences. The ethnographic work reported in Cohen (1982), for example, focuses on peripheral areas of the British Isles that have a strong sense of local 'community'. Although we may surmise that urban situations (such as Belfast) are likely to exhibit lower density and multiplexity in personal ties than remote rural ones (and are by the same token also likely to be more open to outside influences), many studies, both urban and rural, have shown that a close-knit network structure functions as a conservative force, resisting pressures for change originating from outside the network; conversely, those speakers whose ties to the localized network are weakest approximate least closely to localized vernacular norms, and are most exposed to external pressures for change (J. Milroy and L. Milroy, 1985b). This second observation suggests that since strong network structure seems to be implicated in a rather negative way in linguistic change, a closer examination of *weak* network ties might be profitable.

The difficulty in studying weak ties empirically means that the quantitative variable of network (which can be readily applied to close-knit communities) cannot be easily operationalized in situations where the population is socially and/or geographically mobile. The networks of mobile persons tend to be loose-knit; such persons form (relatively weak) ties with very large numbers of others, and these are often open-ended, seldom forming into close-tie clusters. It is therefore difficult, in studying loose-knit situations, to produce direct empirical (quantitative) evidence of the kind usually used to support sociolinguistic theories, and indeed (as we noted above) the speaker-innovator cannot easily be directly observed and located. However, we have argued (J. Milroy and L. Milroy, 1985b) that the speaker-innovator is a necessary theoretical construct if we are to clarify what is involved in solving the actuation problem. Therefore, as we are again dealing with an idealization here, we use a mode of argumentation that differs from the usual inductive mode favoured by quantitative linguists, and to support the argument we adduce evidence from various sources.

6.5 Weak Ties

This evidence is of several different kinds. As is the case so often in network analysis, we find that anthropological and sociological studies of small-scale communities (as in Cohen, 1982) are illuminating. On the basis of evidence from a number of such studies, Mewett (1982) has observed that *class* differences in small communities begin to emerge over time as the proportion of *multiplex* relationships declines, (multiplexity being an important characteristic of a close-knit type of network structure). This observation, in addition to associating social class stratification with the decline of close-knit networks, suggests a framework for linking network studies with larger-scale class-based studies in formulating a more coherent multi-level sociolinguistic theory than we have at present, and I shall return to this point in chapter 7. But we have also derived insights from important work by Granovetter (1973, 1982), who has argued that 'weak' and uniplex interpersonal ties, although they may be subjectively perceived as unimportant, are in fact important channels through which innovation and influence flow from one close-knit group to another, linking such groups to the wider society. This rather larger-scale aspect of the social function of weak ties has a number of important implications for a socially accountable theory of linguistic change and diffusion, some of which I shall briefly outline.

Granovetter's working definition of 'weak' and 'strong' ties is as follows: 'The strength of a tie is a (probably linear) combination of the amount of time, the emotional intensity, the intimacy (mutual confiding) and the reciprocal services which characterise a tie' (1973: 1361). This is probably sufficient to satisfy most people's feeling of what might be meant by a 'weak' or 'strong' interpersonal tie, and it fits in fairly well with our indicators for measuring network strength in the Belfast inner-city communities. It also fits in with the principles followed in comparing inner-city with outer-city Belfast (on which see chapter 4): broadly speaking, the former is characterized by stronger and the latter by weaker ties. Thus, although *strength of tie* is a continuous variable, for the purpose of exposition Granovetter treats it as if it were discrete, and we need always to bear in mind that we are speaking in relative terms: a tie is 'weak' if it is less strong than the other ties against which it is measured. Granovetter's basic point is that weak ties between groups regularly provide bridges through which information and influence are diffused. Furthermore, these bridges between groups cannot consist of strong ties: the ties *must* be weak (that is, relatively weak when measured against internal ties). Thus, weak ties may or may not function as bridges, but no strong tie can. This is shown in figure 6.2.

Strong ties, however, are observed as concentrated within groups. Thus, they give rise to a *local* cohesion of the kind that we explored in

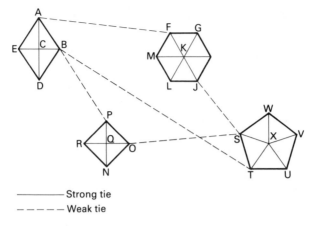

Strong tie
— — — — Weak tie

Figure 6.2   Weak ties as bridges.

inner-city Belfast; yet, at the same time, they lead paradoxically to overall fragmentation. Clearly, this perception is potentially very illuminating in accounting for different language states at different times and places at many levels of generality, ranging from the interpersonal situations, through dialect-divergent, bilingual and code-switching communities to the very broadest of language situations, and it throws light on the question of convergence and divergence that we discussed in chapters 2 and 3. The model of strong and weak ties presented graphically in figure 6.3 can be thought of as an idealized representation of (for example) an urban community which consists of clumps connected by predominantly strong ties, which in turn are connected to other clumps by predominantly weak ties, but it can of course represent other kinds of language situation that we might conceive of.

The important point (from our perspective) that follows from all this is that weak inter-group ties are likely to be critical in transmitting innovations from one group to another, despite the common-sense assumption that *strong* ties fulfil this role. For example, Downes (1984: 155) suggests that the network concept is important in developing a theory of linguistic diffusion, but assumes that it is strong ties that will be critical. This assumption seems to be shared by many linguists who have considered the matter; indeed, as we have noticed above, Labov (1980: 261) presents a model of the innovator as an individual with strong ties both inside *and* outside a local group.

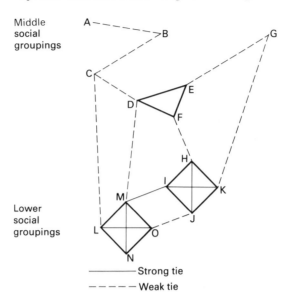

Figure 6.3 Idealized representation of an urban community in which weaker ties are more numerous in middle social groupings and between the groups.

Clearly, this conflicts with the arguments presented here, which predict that to the extent that ties are strong, linguistic change will be impeded, not facilitated.

Granovetter's principle seems at first sight to go against 'common sense', and for this reason I need to expound it a little further. First of all, it is likely that weak ties are much more numerous than strong ties, simply because the time and energy invested in the maintenance of strong ties must place an upper limit on how many it is possible to have, whereas weak ties require little effort. Second, many more individuals can be reached through weak ties than through strong ties; consider for example the bridges set up by participants at academic conferences, which link cohesive groups associated with each institution and through which new ideas and information pass. Conversely, information relayed through strong ties tends not to be innovatory, since persons linked by strong ties tend to share contacts (that is, to belong to overlapping networks). So they may, for example, hear the same rumour several times. This general principle entails that mobile individuals who have contracted many weak ties, but who as a consequence of their mobility occupy a position marginal to some cohesive group, are in a particularly strong position to carry information across social boundaries and to diffuse innovations of all kinds.

In view of the norm-enforcing capacities of groups built up mainly of strong ties, it is easy to see why innovators are likely to be persons weakly linked to the group. Susceptibility to outside influence is likely to increase in inverse proportion to strength of tie with the group. Where groups are loose-knit – that is, linked mainly by weak ties – they are likely to be generally more susceptible to innovation. We might note that this contention is consistent with the principle enunciated by Labov and Kroch that innovating groups are located centrally in the social hierarchy, characterized as upper-working or lower-middle class (Labov 1980: 254; Kroch 1978). For it is likely that in British (and probably also North American) society the most close-knit networks are located at the highest and lowest strata, with a majority of socially and geographically mobile speakers (whose networks are relatively loose-knit) falling between these two points.

One apparent difficulty with the proposal that innovators are only marginally linked to the group is in explaining how these peripheral people can successfully diffuse innovations to central members of that group, who are of course resistant to innovation. One part of the answer here is that central members often *do not* accept the innovation: hence, for example, the persistence of regional varieties and minority languages in strong-tie situations (compare here Andersen's (1986) idea of *endocentric* dialect communities). But to the extent that they do accept innovations, two related points are relevant. First, since resistance to innovation is likely to be strong in a norm-conforming group, a large number of persons will have to be exposed to it and adopt it in the early stages for it to spread successfully. Now, in a mobile society, weak ties are likely to be very much more numerous than strong ties (especially in urban communities), and some of them are likely to function as bridges through which innovations flow. Thus, an innovation like the London merger between /ð,θ/ (as in *brother, thin*) and /v,f/ reported in Norwich teenage speech (Trudgill 1986b: 54ff.) is likely to be transmitted through a great many weak links between Londoners and Norwich speakers, and Trudgill suggests tourists and football supporters as individuals who might contract such links. Quite simply, before it stands any chance of acceptance by central members of a group, the links through which it is originally transmitted *need* to be numerous (compare Granovetter 1973: 1367). Thus, the existence of numerous weak ties is a necessary condition for innovations to spread: it is the quantity as well as the quality of links between people that is crucial here.

The second point we need to make in explaining the success of marginal members of a group as innovators relates more directly to Labov's view of the innovating personality type. As Granovetter suggests, persons central to a close-knit, norm-enforcing group are likely to find innovation a risky activity (indeed it is probably more in their interests to maintain and enforce norms than to innovate); but adopting an innovation that is already widespread on the fringes of the group is very much less risky. There is of course a time dimension involved, and in this dimension a point may be reached at which central members begin to accept that it is in their own interests to adopt the innovation. Informal observation of cultural and political innovation suggests that this is generally true. As an example we may cite the final adoption of a marginal cult (Christianity) in ancient Rome: it took centuries for this innovation to penetrate to the centre. Central members of a group diminish the risk of potentially deviant activity by adopting (after a lapse of time) an innovation from persons who are already non-peripheral members of the group, rather than by direct importation from marginals, who tend to be perceived as deviant. Thus, we can in this way understand how accep-tance – under certain conditions – can be a rational strategy on the part of central members of the group.

Within the network model, therefore, the existence of numerous weak ties is a necessary condition for innovation to be adopted. But there must be additional conditions, and at least one of these is psycho-social: this is that speakers from the receptor community want to identify for some reason with speakers from the donor community. Thus, the Norwich speakers cited by Trudgill in some sense view London vernacular speakers as persons with whom, in Andersen's (1986) terms, they wish to express solidarity. Ultimately, for an innovation to be adopted, it seems that the adopters must believe that some benefit to themselves and/or their groups will come about through the adoption of the innovation. The cost of adopting the innovation in terms of effort will thus be perceived by the adopters as less than the benefit received from adopting it. It also seems that an explanation based on the idea of group identity and solidarity is more satisfactory than one that relies on prestige in a social class dimen-sion, and we shall return to this question in chapter 7.

Bearing all these points in mind, it is appropriate now to return to Labov's account of the innovator and compare it with our own. The most general difference is that Labov's account is about a type of person, whereas ours is abstract and structural, focusing on the nature of interpersonal links: it is based on relationships rather than on persons. We might describe Labov's innovator as a person who is sociable and outgoing, and who has many friends both inside and outside the local group. Intuitively, it seems very likely that information of all kinds (including linguistic innovation) can be diffused by such persons, for the reason that they have many contacts. But according to our account, such individuals could not be near the centre of a close-knit group and at the same time have many strong outside ties. More probably, they would have relatively few multiplex links with others, and many of their links would be open-ended and hence low on density; they would have a predominance of weak links, including many that constitute bridges between groups. In class terms such persons would probably be mobile, and their profile would therefore fit in with Labov's view that socially mobile sectors (upper-working to lower-middle class) are the ones in which linguistic innovation and change are carried. It seems, however, that this profile is not that of the innovator at all, but that of an *early adopter*, and I shall consider this point fully in the next section.

What I have presented here is an abstract model, supported by the insights of Granovetter, which in effect implies that a community characterized by maximally strong network ties (and hence maximal norm-enforcement) will not permit change to take place within it. Real communities, however, contain varying degrees of internal cohesion and varying degrees of openness to outside influence through weak ties. The speaker-innovator within this model is not a close-tie person, but one who is marginal to more than one (relatively) close-knit group and who therefore forms a bridge between groups across which innovations pass. In the next section, I shall adduce some further support for the model; I shall then go on to look at some case studies that demonstrate how the model can be used to interpret patterns of variation, including some that are very difficult to make sense of in any other way.

6.6   Innovators and Early Adopters

Empirical support for our modelling of the speaker-innovator is provided by Rogers and Shoemaker's (1971) studies of about 1500 cases of innovation in many areas of life, including, for example, innovations in agricultural, educational and technological methods. In the present discussion, the most important principle emerging from this work is the distinction between the *innovator* and the *early adopter*. As the innovator has weak links to more than one group and forms a bridge between groups, he or she is, in relation to the close-tie groups, a marginal individual. Rogers and Shoemaker's studies confirm the marginality of innovators and further suggest that innovators are often perceived as underconforming to the point of deviance. If this is correct, the innovator does not resemble Labov's (1980) characterization (an individual who has 'prestige' both inside and outside the local group), but actually seems to have more in common with the famous 'lames' of the Harlem study (Labov, 1972a). Conversely, Labov's 'innovator' resembles what Rogers and Shoemaker call the 'early adopter'.

Early adopters are relatively central to the group and relatively conforming to the group norms. Once the innovation reaches them, it diffuses to the group as a whole, and at this stage it moves into the middle part of the S-curve structure that is associated with the diffusion of innovations generally. Thus, although linguistic processes are much more complex than many of the other processes that have been studied from this point of view, they share this pattern of diffusion with other kinds of innovation. Later, once the new forms are established in the group, they may diffuse from the centre outwards. At the macro-level, therefore, it is tempting to see these patterns in broad sweeps of cultural and linguistic history (the history of Christianity comes again to mind), but we must leave this speculation aside and return to the matter in hand, because there seems to be no easy way for empirical studies of change in progress to identify in the data the crucial distinction between innovators and early adopters.

However, we should again recall that we are not attempting to describe the characteristics of personality types, but of relations between groups and individuals, and these may vary considerably according to different social and cultural conditions. That is to say that we are not thinking of identifying some individual who lurks around the margins of a group and labelling him or her 'the innovator'. Nor is it a case of 'once an innovator, always an innovator', and it is obviously true that people who are innovative in some ways may not be innovative in others. We are thinking in structural terms, and so we are concerned with the kinds of *relationship between persons* that determine the conditions in which linguistic innovations can be accepted or rejected. Thus, the whole question is relative, just as the definition of the weakness of a tie is relative. What is clear, however, is that if innovations are transmitted across relatively tenuous and marginal links in fleeting encounters that are perceived as unimportant, we are unlikely to observe the actuation of a change. However sophisticated our methods may be, we are much more likely to observe the take-up and diffusion of the innovation by the more socially salient early adopters.

Bearing these difficulties in mind, we now turn to some detailed examples in order to demonstrate how the model developed here affects the interpretation of linguistic variation in speech communities. First, I shall consider two cases of phonological variation from the Belfast inner-city study, and then move on to suggest a tentative analysis of some parts of the Philadelphia data, as reported by Labov and Harris (1986) and Ash and Myhill (1986). Finally, I shall consider a number of more general patterns of change that may be illuminated by the model.

6.7   Weak Ties: Crossing the Peace-line in Belfast

It is usual to suppose that the diffusion of linguistic change is encouraged by relatively open channels of communication and discouraged by boundaries or weaknesses in lines of communication. In Belfast, however, there are many patterns that are difficult to explain in this apparently common-sense way, and we shall consider two of them here. They are: (1) the social configuration of the spread of /a/-backing from the Protestant east of the city into the Clonard, a West Belfast Catholic community; and (2) the city-wide younger generation consensus on the evaluation of the (*pull*) variable, as against conflicting patterns in the older generation. The details of these variables are more fully discussed in chapters 3, 4 and 5, and in various publications referred to there. Table 4.10 (p. 116) and figure

6.4 show respectively the stylistic patterning in East and West Belfast and the crossover pattern in casual conversational style for (a).

We have already noticed that the backing of /a/ is led by East Belfast males. Figure 6.4 shows this, and it also shows that the movement of back /a/ into West Belfast is not led by Protestant males in the Hammer, as might be expected, but by the younger female group in the Catholic Clonard area. This is the group that exhibits the crossover pattern and reverses the generally expected 'stable norm' patterns (of the kind demonstrated in chapter 4). In this group the city-wide female movement *away* from /a/-backing is reversed: the incidence of /a/-backing in the group is higher than in the other older and younger female groups, higher than amongst older females in the same area, and – surprisingly – also higher than amongst their young male counterparts in the Clonard. When measured against other groups, these young women are deviant.

When stylistic patterning (table 4.10) is additionally taken into account, this young female group appears as the only Clonard group with noticeable stylistic differentiation on the same pattern as in East Belfast: they favour backing appreciably more in casual style than in careful style. This pattern is innovatory in West Belfast in that it is not established in the other Clonard groups: the social value attached to the variants by the Clonard young women is the same as the social evaluation evident in East Belfast: they seem to have adopted this evaluation as a community norm. The linguistic change that they are carrying is thus manifested as a change of norms in addition to a

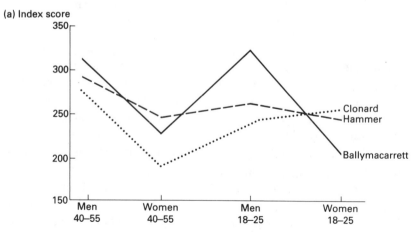

Figure 6.4   Backing of /a/ in Ballymacarrett, the Clonard and the Hammer.

change in phonetic realization. Thus, while superficial inspection of the data in figure 6.4 might suggest that the young Clonard female pattern is modelled on that of the older Clonard males (who have fairly high backing scores), such an explanation would fail to account for the *reduction* of /a/-backing in other groups, and (more importantly) it would not explain the adoption of (a) as a *stylistic* marker by the young Clonard females.

The social barriers that inhibit contacts between working-class communities have been well described for many locations throughout the world (examples are cited by L. Milroy, 1987), and they were evident in our inner-city fieldwork even *inside* sectarian boundaries. Inter-ethnic conflict in Belfast, however, has had the effect of strengthening the barriers that are present in all such communities (Boal, 1978). In fact, the major sectarian boundary in West Belfast is now marked physically by a brick and barbed wire structure, which is described by the military authorities, apparently without intentional irony, as the 'Peace Line'. The puzzle is that an East Belfast pattern can be carried across these boundaries, evidently by a group of young women whose movements and face-to-face contacts have been constrained from a very early age. As we noted in chapter 4, there is a long term shift in the vowel system towards back /a/, and this diffusion pattern from east to west is a continuation it. That this shift is continuing across the iron barriers (both physical and psychological) that separate the Protestant east and Catholic west, is a fact for which we are obliged to seek a principled explanation.

The most accessible, and possibly the only, explanation is one that takes account of weak ties and the distinction between the marginal innovators and the early adopters. It seems that the Clonard young women are central members of the group, and so they resemble early adopters rather than innovators. This is quite clear from their Network Strength score (as reported by L. Milroy, 1987: 204): they all score extremely high on this – much higher than the young Clonard males. Their average score is 4.75 out of a possible maximum of 5.00.

Further personal information about this group points rather clearly to innovation through multiple weak ties. These young women, unlike their male counterparts, were in full employment: they all had regular jobs outside the Clonard community at a rather poor city-centre store. Here they were very likely to be in weak-tie contact with large numbers of people from all over the city, both Catholic and Protestant. Thus, they would be well placed to adopt innovations transmitted by persons peripheral to their core networks, and as a result exposure to innovatory forms would be frequent. Given the large number of service encounters in the store, it becomes possible for the weak-tie encounters with back [a] users to exceed greatly the number of strong-tie encounters with non-back [a] users. Hence the capacity of innovation-bearing weak ties to compete with, and in this case overcome, the innovation-resisting strong ties.

If we have a theoretical perspective such as the one developed here, which explicitly predicts that an innovation will be transmitted through (frequent and numerous) weak ties, we have a solution to the problem of explaining how back [a] can diffuse in this way, and we can present a plausible account of how the innovation can appear to jump across a barrier of brick and barbed wire. If, however, we make the usual assumption that innovations are diffused through strong ties, the pattern is very difficult to explain. Yet, it is only if we make this strong-tie assumption in the first place that [a] diffusion appears to be a puzzle at all.

Whereas back [a] diffusion is mainly a change in a phonetic segment, the change of pattern in the (*pull*) variable is a change of evaluation (or of agreement on norms). This variable is quantified on the basis of a small phono-lexical set consisting of items such as *pull*, *push*, *took*, *shook*, *foot*, which exhibit vowel alternation between [ʌ] and [u]; we discussed it in chapter 2. Although the [ʌ] variant is recessive, it has very strong affective values and is a very salient marker of casual speech between close acquaintances. But here I wish to point out only one thing – the change in consensus on norms over the generations. Whereas the (*bag*) variable referred to in chapter 4 shows consensus across the different groups – old and young, male and female – the (*pull*) variable (shown in figure 6.5) shows consensus only in the younger generation, where it has become a marker of gender-differentiation. The question is: how can this normative consensus come about in this divided city?

The pattern here is one in which the older groups do not agree on the gender marking in use of the 'in-group' variant [ʌ]. In Ballymacarrett, males favour [ʌ], but in the two West Belfast communities, gender preference is reversed: the [ʌ] variant is favoured by the females. The younger groups, however, show the same pattern in all three communities: in all cases [ʌ] preference is stronger among males and weaker among females.

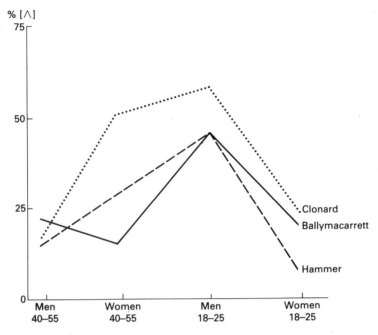

Figure 6.5 Distribution of the (*pull*) variable (percentage of [ʌ] variants are shown) by age, sex and area in inner-city Belfast.

Again the puzzle is to explain how young people living in closed communities, whose outside links are quite tenuous, could reach cross-community consensus on the social value to be attached to the two variants of (*pull*). In their parents' youth there was greater freedom of movement, and people frequently formed friendships across regional and sectarian divisions; however, since the beginning of the civil disorder in 1969, people have been much less able to form strong ties outside their communities. Yet, despite this, the absorption of the (*pull*) variable into the regular sociolinguistic structure of Belfast vernacular has continued unhindered. Again, it is only if we accept that weak ties are the normal channel for the diffusion of innovations that the apparent paradox is resolved.

In these examples, I have selected instances based on extensive quantified information which is very fine-grained and which is fully accountable to the data, but the general pattern here had already become evident from observation of other cases, and the (*pull*) variable can be regarded as testing out a hypothesis that had already been formed. There are many other examples involving different dimensions of variation (including, for example, phonological mergers) that can be observed fairly easily and that appear to show this general pattern of consensus in the inner-city younger generation. Indeed, once you are 'clued in' to the possibilities (especially with regard to gender-differentiation), it is remarkable how readily you can observe the trends in everyday encounters. Perhaps the most dramatic of these trends is the progressive loss of localized lexical items and reduction of phono-lexical variable sets of the (*pull*) type (J. Milroy, 1981). Another example is the three-way merger (or apparent merger) of words of the type *fur/fir/fair*, which are very close to being fully merged amongst younger speakers. The few elderly speakers that we studied (around 70 years old in 1975), however, exhibit a three-way differentiation, and middle-aged speakers often have a two-way differentiation. As indications of this greater consensus amongst younger people had already been observed before we started our quantitative analysis, we spoke in terms of 'the rise of an urban vernacular': the first research application in 1975 proposed the hypothesis that we were witnessing in Belfast a fairly early stage in the development of a focused urban vernacular, in which there is a generally observable trend towards greater consensus on norms.

However, we have also emphasized in this section the psycho-social barrier of the *sectarian* difference in Belfast, which we might expect to inhibit the trend towards consensus, and from the beginning of our research we naturally wished to discover whether the ethnic difference was consistently and reliably reflected in language. In our pilot research, therefore, we looked at two East Belfast communities, one Catholic and one Protestant (Catholics being a small minority in this part of the city). In our analysis of the tapes, however, we could find no appreciable differences between the two groups: the Catholics spoke with an East Belfast accent (including back varieties of /a/) just as the Protestants did, and their speech was more similar to East Belfast Protestants than it was to West Belfast Catholics. Subsequently, after comparing different communities very fully in our inner-city study, I was able to state, rather cautiously, that 'there is as yet no persuasive evidence to show that the two ethnic groups in Belfast (and Ulster) can be clearly identified by differences in accent' (J. Milroy, 1981: 44). Indeed, it seems that those features of differentiation that in the past could have been seized upon as ethnic markers, have been abandoned in favour of greater inner-city agreement on norms of age, sex and contextual style. In general, the

Catholic immigrants arrived in the city later than the Protestants and brought from mid and west Ulster a number of features (such as palatalization of initial [k]) that *could* have been used to reinforce differences, but this does not seem to have happened. Both groups seem to be moving in the same direction in the younger generation even though there may be divergent movements in small details; similarly, both groups appear to evaluate variants in much the same way (and this evaluation is often quite divergent from 'standard' evaluations). Thus, whereas our findings indicate a trend towards city-wide working-class consensus which overrides the ethnic difference, the Philadelphia findings (Labov and Harris, 1986) show a trend towards greater divergence between the two ethnic groups. In the next section, therefore, I would like to examine the findings reported by Labov and his colleagues in terms of the theoretical model of innovation proposed in this chapter.

6.8 Weak Ties: Inter-ethnic Patterns in Philadelphia

The most general finding of the Philadelphia studies (Labov and Harris, 1986) is that the speech of the two ethnic groups is diverging, and not converging. The researchers express this in terms of participation in linguistic changes: the black community is not participating in the changes that are in progress in the white community. It can also be expressed in terms of the model I have been developing in this book. This would emphasize consensus and conflict: the two communities do not agree on norms of usage, and so in broad terms we can say that the sociolinguistic situation is one of conflict rather than consensus.

In the Philadelphia reports, however, the idea of prestige is still very influential in interpreting the variation revealed, and the idea of social stratification is prominent in the argumentation. Labov and Harris (1986: 20–1) mention the 'prestige' of the localized 'innovator' (pointing out, quite rightly, that the activities of this type of person have much more influence than the 'mainstream' norms such as radio and television); yet, at the same time they speak of the 'dominant' dialect as against the 'dominated'. This dominance model is used in interpreting their findings (Ash and Myhill, 1986) on four groups of speakers: a core white group, a core black group and two marginal groups – a group of blacks who have considerable contact with whites (let us call these WBs) and a group of whites who have considerable contact with blacks (henceforth BWs). The findings are that the WBs converge towards white morpho-syntactic norms more markedly than the BWs converge towards black norms (see figure 6.6), and this is where the idea of dominance comes into the argument. The pattern discovered here is described in terms of dominance: the white dialect is seen as dominant and less subject to change in a non-prestige direction. Although this may be quite plausible in this case, where power-structures are likely to be relevant, it cannot be generally applicable as an explanation, because it does not account for the converse pattern that has been so frequently noticed: historians of language often point out that dominant (or 'elite' or 'high prestige') dialects can be influenced 'from below', and Labov has also pointed this out (Labov, 1972b). This kind of explanation for linguistic patterning is therefore insufficiently general: it does not take into account the fact that 'dominant' dialects do not always dominate. Therefore, although Labov and Harris explicitly reject social network as an interpretative category, it seems that some of these findings are open to interpretations based on strong/weak ties, the identity function of linguistic variation, and models of linguistic accommodation and politeness. Furthermore, it also seems that this type of interpretation can have greater explanatory power than one based on 'prestige', as it is applicable to a wider range of different language situations.

What is particularly noticeable about the two contact groups mentioned above (white-oriented blacks and black-oriented whites) is that on morpho-syntactic variation their scores average about the same: on copula-deletion and *ain't* for *didn't*, the whites actually out-perform the blacks on 'black' variants. What is also noticeable from figure 6.6 is that, whereas the core black group uses these features quite variably (presumably also using the 'white' variants), the core white group does not use the 'black' variants at all. Thus, the core black vernacular (whether or not it is 'dominated') incorporates a resource not available to mainstream white speakers – the capacity to alternate between 'black' and 'white' morpho-syntactic variants according to occasion of use. To this extent, there is a structural resemblance to the inner-city Belfast speakers described in chapters 3 and 4, who also have at their disposal alternating forms which carry different symbolic functions according to occasion of use. I have also

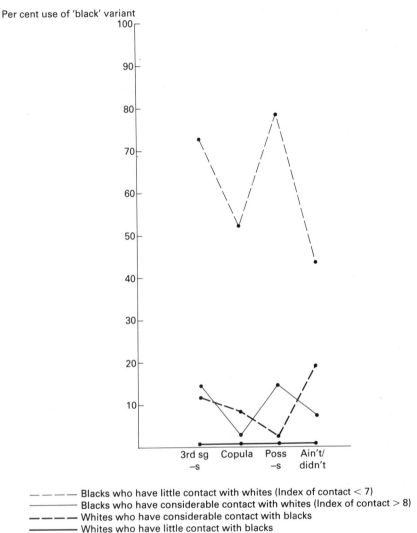

Figure 6.6 Average per cent use of 'black' morpho-syntactic variants by four groups of speakers. (Adapted from Ash and Myhill, 1986)

suggested in chapter 3 that this kind of situation is actually a normal situation: *it is the more uniform state of language that is abnormal.*

From this perspective, however, the convergence of WBs towards 'white' norms is not so remarkable, *as these 'white' norms are already available to them within core black vernacular variation.* The reason why WBs use the 'white' norms *more often* than other blacks is plainly accessible through a theory of weak ties, as it is clear from the authors' descriptions of these speakers that they are a contact group and that their contacts with whites are of a classic weak-tie type: they are described as con-men, hustlers and political activists. Their contacts through these activities must generally be weak contacts, as it is hardly possible to pursue these activities within dense and multiplex networks where everyone knows everyone else. The degree to which these speakers use the white norms is increased by the range and number of situations in which they have these weak-tie contacts outside their core community, and for them the adoption of more 'white' usage is functional in their weak-tie contacts. Con-men do not directly threaten the 'face' of their victims, but try to gain their confidence, and they will normally accommodate to the victims' norms and expectations. Hence the broader models of accommodation (Giles and Smith, 1979) and politeness (Brown and Levinson, 1987) are relevant to interpretation here. The suggestion (Ash and Myhill, 1986: 41) that 'prestige' is the explanation for this shift towards 'white' norms seems, on the other hand, to be quite a weak explanation, which merely begs the question of what 'prestige' can actually mean in this case.

The convergence of BWs to 'black' norms is in a sense more remarkable, as the core white dialect does *not* possess the new variants (copula-deletion, etc.) that the BWs adopt (to a certain extent) in carrying out their act of accommodation: *these outside variants have to be acquired*, and so some affirmatory effort (or some 'cost') is involved. Although the researchers do not give precise information as to the strength of these speakers' participation in black culture, a theory of innovations (Rogers and Shoemaker, 1971) and weak ties (Granovetter, 1973) would predict that their ties with both communities are likely to be relatively weak. It is this group, and not the WB group, who most resemble the peripheral innovators characterised by Rogers and Shoemaker, and who, as have I pointed out above, may be 'underconforming to the point of deviance'. This looks very much like innovatory behaviour in terms of the model I have suggested, and these data are particularly relevant to the argument as we are dealing here with contact groups in which weak ties must be involved. I think that Labov and his colleagues have succeeded here in locating an innovating group.

Of course, we may well consider it to be very unlikely that these particular innovations by marginal whites will penetrate deeply into white society. However, our model is designed to deal with this kind of situation also. It is based on the idea of language maintenance, and, as I pointed out above, it must account for situations in which innovations are unsuccessful as well as for those in which they are successful. The model predicts that, for these innovations to penetrate, they will have to be taken up by early adopters, who in this case would have to be more central to white society. Thus, whether these 'black' norms will ever penetrate will depend on the amount of access these peripheral white speakers are likely to have to central members, and the willingness of central members to adopt the innovations. Unlikely as this eventuality may be, it is worth remembering that forms originating in black usage have been accepted into 'mainstream' English in the past, and it is sometimes suggested that these have been originated by, and diffused through, jazz musicians. These are normally underconforming people, as the Rogers and Shoemaker model would predict.

Thus, although it is unlikely that these particular innovations will ever show up as regular variants in white society, this does not make the behaviour of these speakers any less innovatory. If we are to understand the phenomenon of language change, we need to observe the distinction between innovation and change, and we must recognize that innovations do not always lead to change: as Tarde (1903: 140) points out, we need to learn why, if 100 innovations are conceived simultaneously, 10 will spread while 90 will be forgotten.

The data I have used in sections 6.7 and 6.8 are drawn from extensive fine-grained analysis of present-day speech communities; there are, however, many language situations in the world in which a model of strong and weak ties might help to illuminate broader patterns of change. In section 6.9 therefore, I go on to discuss a number of more general situations in which the model may be helpful. At this broader level, the majority of situations that I shall discuss are those generally regarded as *language-contact* situations.

6.9   Weak Ties as an Explanation for Change: Some Examples

There are many patterns of linguistic maintenance and change that have been widely observed, but that are not easy to explain in a consistent way if we depend on the usual assumptions about diffusion being brought about through strong links. These patterns can be observed at widely differing levels of generality, and I shall review a small number of them here. At the macro-level, it can be noted that while some languages (such as English and Danish) have been structurally innovative (mainly in the direction of inflexional simplification), other related languages (such as Icelandic) remain highly conservative. In such cases we may be able to show that the conservative communities are characterized by close-knit networks and the innovatory ones by the development over history of numerous loose-knit ties, and we have attempted to demonstrate this in the case of English and Icelandic (J. Milroy and L. Milroy, 1985b). Although the relative stability of Icelandic through the centuries may be largely attributable to its geographical isolation, its uniformity throughout the country requires further explanation. In a sparsely populated country in which communities have been traditionally isolated from one another by climate and terrain, one might expect that dialectal diversity, rather than uniformity, would result. We attempted to throw light on this by adducing evidence from the Icelandic Family Sagas of the twelfth and thirteenth centuries, which show very clearly the high value placed on the maintenance of strong-tie relationships over long distances, and we therefore suggested that the maintenance of strong ties may be crucial in explaining the failure of Icelandic to split up historically into divergent dialects. English, on the other hand, has changed radically and exhibits gross dialect divergence: this may be largely attributable to the development of weak-tie patterns.

It can also happen that within a particular language, some dialects of the language are innovative, whereas others are conservative. The conservative dialects are often (but not always) regionally peripheral, and therefore likely to be relatively strong-tie communities that are less exposed than centrally located dialects to influence from mainstream norms. Relevant here is the case of the Scots vowel systems (Catford, 1957), in which the regionally peripheral dialects have a greater number of vowel phonemes than the central ones, the latter having innovated by merging vowel phonemes that were previously distinct. In a wide-ranging discussion of innovatory and conservative patterns in a large number of dialects of different languages, Andersen (1986) proposes a distinction between *open* and *closed* dialect communities, and further proposes that within these categories some communities are *endocentric*, whereas others are *exocentric*. It seems that endocentrism and exocentrism may have to do with psycho-social *attitudes* within the communities towards the maintenance of local identities and resistance to external influence, with the endocentric communities strong in these respects and the exocentric communites weak. However, it is not easy to see how we could undertake an empirical investigation of personal attitudes in such a wide range of relevant language situations, although it does appear that once we have supported a theory of weak and strong network ties by fine-grained sociolinguistic analysis of the kind we have described in sections 6.7 and 6.8, we may be justified in projecting the model on to these more general instances. This will predict that the closed communities will be characterized by strong internal cohesiveness with relatively few weak external links, and the open ones by more loose-knit networks, with more external links. It is then a matter of adducing supporting evidence to assess the degree of network strength in the relevant communities.

There are other situations which are also clearly amenable to weak-tie explanations. For example, it has been widely noted that neighbouring languages which are unrelated or distantly related may share similar linguistic changes. Trudgill (1983b: 56–9) draws attention to the wide distribution of uvular /r/ in north-west European languages, and certain Balkan languages are known to share specific grammatical features even though they are very distantly related. Trudgill suggests that we come closer to an explanation for the cross-language distribution of uvular /r/ if we focus on urban centres which have it: Paris, The Hague, Cologne, Berlin, Bergen and others (indeed, in French, alveolar /r/ is overtly perceived as a rustic feature). One of the most important ways in which this innovation has been implemented is by 'jumping' from one urban centre to another. Within specific languages also, it is known that innovations tend to spread from one centre of population to another without immediately affecting the intervening countryside (which is of course more sparsely populated). Urban development seems therefore to be implicated in the maintenance and diffusion of vernacular features within a language. The adoption of London features by Norwich teenagers (see above, p. 181) is a case in point, and the historical spread of /h/-dropping and (probably) glottal-stopping in British English seems also to be urban. There is support for this in the fact that, despite the long history of /h/ dropping, there are still rural (but not urban) dialects in southern England which do not /h/-drop (see, chapter 5 and Trudgill, 1974). As for slang and colloquial expressions, it is (for example) a matter of common observation in Belfast that many of these are diffused from Glasgow, which is 150 miles away across the sea, but which is associated with Belfast through numerous weak ties.

In an extended discussion of the process of innovation, Trudgill (1986a: 54) raises problems rather similar to the ones raised here; he suggests that it is difficult to account for the London-based Norwich innovations if *close* ties are postulated between members of the innovating and donor communities. It seems to be adolescents who are implementing the merger of [ð,θ] with [v,f], and this is an age group that does not normally contract strong ties over long distances. We have also carried out informal tests on British adolescents in Sheffield, who appear to be diffusing the use of *well* as an intensifier before certain adjectives, as in *well nice, well happy*. The indications are that this is well established in London vernacular: if this is so, its spread to distant parts amongst adolescents must be due to weak, rather than strong, ties. Trudgill further cites a report by the dialectologist, Gary Underwood, that persons who moved from his home area of Memphis and then returned were influential in spreading urban speech-forms to their rural friends. These persons were effectively weakly linked to the rural network. Similarly, Trudgill reports the notion of the 'language missionary', developed by the Norwegian social dialectologist, Anders Steinsholt. Discussing the spread of urban forms from Larvik into the rural dialect of Hedrum, Steinsholt comments:

> The urban dialect spreads into Hedrum partly as a result of the influence of particular individuals living in different parts of the area. Such individuals – we can call them 'language missionaries' – may be village people who have been particularly heavily influenced by the urban dialect. The most important language missionaries are first the young girls who come home after living for some time in the town, and, second, the whalers. (Trudgill, 1986a: 57)

All these situations involve relatively weak links, but they are also often connected with spread from urban centres. Thus, on the basis of such observations, it might be proposed that urbanization is in itself the main 'cause' of such phenomena. This does not, however, seem to be satisfactory, as at least some of the phenomena discussed appear to apply in some circumstances to non-urban situations, or to situations that are rather marginally urban (involving very small towns and villages). For example, one possible case of the spread of innovations from one language to another is the occurrence of *pre-aspiration* of consonants in two geographically peripheral and very distantly related languages – Scots Gaelic and Icelandic. While this development could be independent in these languages, it is neverthe-less true that they were in prolonged contact in medieval times. Many Norse speakers settled in the Western and Northern Isles and northern mainland of Scotland, intermarried with Gaelic speakers and subsequently emigrated, often with Celtic servants, to Iceland. We cannot appeal to urbanization in this case, but we *can* appeal to language contact in a more general way. Therefore, as urban situations are a sub-type of contact situation, the correct generaliza-tion is that contact situations (including urban ones) result in an increase in the number and frequency of weak ties existing within populations.

As we have raised the question of language contact, it seems appropriate to comment here that a theory of weak ties at the level of *speaker* may help to illuminate language-contact situations generally. What we call *close* contact situations, which lead to linguistic change, seem to be characterized not by *close* networks, but by open ones – not by numerous strong ties, but by the development of numerous *weak* ties. Clearly, if we do not distinguish between speaker and system, this might appear to be contradictory or paradoxical, because the influence on the language situation concerned is *strong*, rather than weak. For example, the influence on Scandinavian and Norman French on medieval English was strong, and the consequences of the shift from Hungarian to German speaking in Oberwart, reported by Gal (1979) are considerable. However, if we bear in mind the fact that although change is observed in systems, it must be brought about by speakers, the apparent contradiction is resolved. When linguists speak of a close contact situation, they are usually thinking of contact between *systems*, but what actually occurs is contact between *speakers* of different languages: the changes that result and that are then observed in the system have been brought about by the speakers, who form weak and uniplex ties when two populations first come into contact. So, strictly speaking, it is not really *language* contact at all, but *speaker* contact. In such situations the model would predict that the innovators in close contact situations are those who form weak ties both inside and outside their own community, and not the central members of either community.

We also speak of different *types* of language contact, which lead to different results, for example: stable bilingualism, gradual language shift (Gal, 1979, Gumperz, 1982), survival of one of the languages after it has been influenced by the other, rapid language-mixing, pidginization. It would seem that these different situations may all be approachable in terms of the relative strength of the ties that are formed between the relevant populations in given cases. For example, we might predict that the survival of stable bilingualism in a community will be associated with the maintenance of dense and multiplex networks within each community in roughly equal balance, and that language shift (for example, the shift to German in Oberwart) will be facilitated by the development of numerous and frequent weak-tie contacts. The model of weak ties gives us a basis for interpreting the results of many such studies, and it seems to be illuminating in a wider range of situations than those that have been approached mainly in terms of hierarchical social stratification and 'prestige'. In the final section of this chapter, I want to recall some of the general points about intra-linguistic theories of change that I have already made (particularly in chapter 2), and consider the general relevance of the weak-tie model to orthodox theoretical positions.

6.10   Conclusion: On Linguistic Change as a Social Phenomenon

In this chapter I have attempted to explore the consequences of a network-based approach for our understanding of how linguistic change can happen, and I have suggested that the model is more powerful than sociolinguistic models based primarily on social status or class, in that it is capable of dealing with a wider range of language situations. But I do not pretend that by using this model alone we have solved the actuation problem. What I have tried to do, therefore, is to approach actuation by first making a distinction between speaker and system, and within this a distinction between speaker-innovation and linguistic change. At the very least, this has the merit that it clarifies what is actually involved in solving the actuation problem. We are forced to consider carefully what we actually mean by 'linguistic change'. We are also forced to try to explain why some innovations are successful, while others are not, and the notion of resistance to change which is inherent in the network model is crucial here.

As many approaches to linguistic change still appear to assume that changes pass through strong links between communities, I have also summarized the arguments of Granovetter (1973) on the importance of weak ties in the diffusion of change, and I have used the findings of Rogers and Shoemaker (1971) on innovations. On the basis of these, I have suggested a model of the speaker-innovator that differs from Labov's model, and have further suggested that the individuals or groups that we identify as carrying linguistic changes are likely to be early adopters of the change, rather than innovators. I have then attempted to apply the model to fine-grained language situations of the kind studied in Belfast and Philadelphia, and have tried to explain its effect on how we interpret such data. It is fairly clear from all this, however, that since the model appears to emphasize the notion of *external* influences on communities, there are some implications for orthodox notions of language change.

It is noticeable that, after a period of quiescence, the Neogrammarians have returned in recent years to a prominent position in the theory of sound-change (see especially Labov, 1981; Kiparsky, 1988). In chapter 5 we briefly considered the distinction between Neogrammarian phonetically gradual sound-change and phonetically sudden change, and we have noted from a sociolinguistic point of view that although changes do not appear to be phonetically gradual, they are certainly socially gradual. Here, it seems that the Neogrammarian distinction between *blind* exceptionless change and linguistic 'borrowing' is also relevant, as it would be easy to conclude that what I have proposed accounts mainly for patterns of diffusion and contact (that is, 'borrowing') rather than for internal 'spontaneous' change within speech communities. I do not think that this is quite correct: it seems that the social model actually cuts across the traditional distinctions and may even call into question the validity of the Neogrammarian distinction. The distinction between innovation and change is not merely terminological: it has consequences for what we mean by a sound-change and for the manner in which questions about sound-change are put. In the weak-tie model *all* sound-change is socially conditioned, simply because those so-called changes that arise spontaneously are not actually changes: they are innovations, and they do not become changes until they have assumed a social pattern in the community. If, as often happens, these innovations are not adopted by a community, however small that community may be, then they do not become changes at all. Thus, we are not asking how spontaneous innovations arise, but how we are to specify the conditions under which some of these innovations, and not others, are admitted into linguistic systems as linguistic changes.

This interpretation of what is actually meant by a change differs considerably from what is usually assumed. It is usual to suppose that sound-change is an internal linguistic phenomenon, perhaps explainable with reference to the mental capacities of the idealized speaker, but not a social phenomenon. It does not become social until it is observed to show a social pattern in the community, and this comes about when the community latches on to the variants that have already arisen and imposes social meanings on them. Andersen's insightful account of deductive and abductive change is one of those that differ in emphasis in this way, in that linguistic constraints are seen as primary: his 'implementation rules' are structurally motivated within the language system and therefore productive ((1973) 1978: 332). The present account, on the other hand, would suggest that while all variants must be constrained by aspects of linguistic structure and may be produced by deductive and abductive generalizations (as argued by Andersen), language-internal arguments or mentally-based idealizations do not account for change (or indeed stable variation), although they help to account for innovations. What has to be explained is the manner in which speaker-based variants actually feed into the system as established changes (Andersen handles this aspect by postulating 'adaptive rules'). A linguistic change is a social phenomenon, and it comes about for reasons of marking social identity, stylistic difference and so on. If it does not carry these social meanings, then it is not a linguistic change: it is a random variant stuck somewhere near the beginning of the S-curve in figure 6.1 (p. 170). Since our perspective differs in these ways, it is appropriate to examine this point a little more fully.

Suppose we observe at a given time that a spontaneous innovation (for example, a common one such as palatalization of /k/ before front vowels) occurs in the speech of a small number of persons who do not have any social contact with one another, and suppose also that we can demonstrate that this really is an innovation in the community (like the glottal stop in Belfast). The question is how we are to determine whether and in what manner the innovation will feed into the system as a patterned change. It is clear that the structural conditions exist in many languages for palatalization of initial /k/ to take place: in some languages (or dialects) we can observe that it has taken place, whereas in others it has not, but has remained at the stage of a sporadic innovation that is always a potential change. At billions of moments throughout history, the change has been possible in these varieties, but has not been realized. This is the point: the likelihood of any specific event occurring at any given place or time is close to zero; therefore, no specific sound-change is ever likely to happen at any particular time even when favourable structural conditions exist in the language (for example, when it might be regarded as 'natural'), and when there have been innovations which might favour the initiation of a change. It appears that for the change to take place it is necessary for the *social* conditions to be favourable.

Such conditions must have applied to the case discussed by Andersen (1973) – the attested change from sharped labials to dentals in the Teták dialects of Czech, which Andersen explains as arising from the acoustic similarity between sharped labials and dentals. The difficulty that our account raises here is the question why this change, which was always possible for these acoustic reasons, took place at the time and place that it did, and not at other times or places. The acoustic similarity adduced by Andersen defines the Teták innovation as one of a class of innovations that must have been possible candidates for change at any time or place, so long as the linguistic conditions (in this case, acoustic similarity) existed within the language system. The historian's problem, of course, is that in historically attested, but highly specific, instances like this, we cannot have sufficiently precise social information to explain the social conditions that favoured the change and then (in the nineteenth century) helped to bring about its recession. But it is unlikely that social identity factors were not involved, as Andersen's subsequent work would itself suggest (for example, Andersen, 1986). In sociolinguistic inquiries into present-day states of language, we can pursue these social questions more fully.

The distinction between innovation and change may have further relevance to some general assumptions that linguists commonly make about the origin of language changes, for example the proposal that the locus of change is in child language-learning phenomena. One difference between this and a sociolinguistic or discourse-oriented model is in the nature of the information available. Whereas social dialectologists can demonstrate the patterning of change in progress in adolescent and adult populations by large-scale investigations and quantitative techniques, mentalist accounts depend on more idealized data and on theoretical positions that take little note of heterogeneous databases. It would clearly be very difficult to demonstrate, beyond reasonable doubt, which of the many innovations observed in child language (for example) will actually be accepted by speech communities and become linguistic changes, as most of the innovations observed in such circumstances (as in others) will never become changes. We are thinking here of present-day communities and assuming that innovations can be directly observed in them, but as so much of our knowledge has depended on history, it should also be remembered that phonological innovations cannot be observed in historical data; what historical data normally display are changes at a late stage of development – usually late enough to be accepted into writing systems and message-oriented styles. Thus, much historical linguistic argumentation has depended on the observation of completed changes and not directly on the origins of innovations. As for the Neogrammarian axioms, if we accept that a change is not a change until it assumes a socially regular distribution of some kind, we have no criteria for determining absolutely that there is an axiomatic distinction between sound-change and borrowing (or contact change) because, as we have defined them, all changes must arise from contact between speakers. But we can certainly save the Neogrammarian hypothesis that change is regular, provided we allow social regularity to be counted as regular: in this perspective it is innovations that may have an irregular distribution, and change must be regular by definition. This implies, amongst other things, that phenomena of the type that appear to be irregular in an intra-linguistic account may turn out to be regular in relation to a more fully developed sociolinguistic model of social structures, processes and relationships.

Finally, we need to make a few comments on the social model of change proposed here and some suggestions as to how it might be extended. The weak-tie model is not in itself sufficient to provide a full social explanation of linguistic change. What it proposes is a set of conditions that are necessary – but not sufficient – for linguistic change to take place. There are certain things that are important socially about which social network has nothing to say. It is not about psycho-social attitudes to language or about language-learning processes, and so it has nothing directly to say about these things.

Similarly, it is not about social stratification, and so it has nothing directly to say about that either. In order to make progress towards a fuller account of the social embedding of language change, we have turned our attention to exploring the connection between network and wider patterns of social structure (L. Milroy and J. Milroy, forthcoming). As we have noted above, ethnographers, such as Mewett (1982), have suggested that social stratification is observed to develop in cohesive communities to the extent that the strong ties are weakened. This is where we also make the link: in the Belfast outer-city research, we hypothesized that movement away from the core vernacular would be associated with this decline in close-knit networks. It may therefore be possible to show a link between the interpersonal concept of network and the broader dimensions of social structure that are often spoken of in terms of social class.

However, it also appears that whereas a network approach can be approached through the idea of shared values and consensus in social groupings, social class (together with other stratificational concepts such as rank or status), if it is to be fully understood, involves conflict and inequalities of power. It is reasonable to point out that the social models on which sociolinguists have relied have not always been noticeably sophisticated, and there has been much vagueness in the use of important socially-based concepts such as social class, language standardization and prestige. In order to reach a fuller understanding of social aspects of language change, therefore, we need a more sophisticated understanding of social structures and relationships. In chapter 7 I shall pursue this point: I shall be concerned there with the relationship between social network and the phenomena of power, status, class and prestige in society.

7

Towards an Integrated Social Model for the Interpretation of Language Change

7.0   Introduction: Two Scenarios for Language Change

In chapter 6 I proposed a condition, based on the social network model, which is a necessary condition for linguistic change to take place: this is that there must be weak ties in a population through which influence can pass from one close-knit group to another. It is assumed that (relatively) weak ties exist in all situations and that the maximal strong-tie scenario, in which density and multiplexity are 100 per cent for all members, is an idealization and does not exist in reality. There are two broad types of scenario that do actually exist in reality: in scenario 1, the group has some external contact (through weak ties) but is resistant to external influence: it is norm-maintaining and 'conservative'. The changes that do take place in this scenario, therefore, may include changes that tend to *differentiate* the in-group from external contact groups rather than changes that make it more similar to them, and the effect of such changes may be to maintain and assert the separate identity of the in-group. Andersen (1986) discusses situations that seem to be like this, in which the dialects undergo 'exorbitant' internal changes seemingly as acts of separate identity. Here, the influence of external groups is negative to the extent that the in-group moves away from them, and we can speculate that the number of weak ties in this scenario may well be fewer than in scenario 2. In scenario 2, the group admits external influence more readily, and contact-changes result. In Andersen's terms, these two scenarios are those of the *endocentric* and *exocentric* speech communities.

In any given case, of course, the two scenarios may be mixed, in that the group may admit some external influences and resist others, and a group that is norm-enforcing at one period of time may become norm-changing at another (and vice versa). What we need to do, therefore, is to explain the different social conditions under which the alternative strategies of scenarios 1 and 2 are adopted by different groups, in different places or at different times. We have attempted to make progress here by using the social network model, but it appears that this in itself is not sufficient to account satisfactorily for all situations: it needs to be supplemented by something else. This final chapter is intended merely to suggest how we might go about supplementing the model, and it is based on current work (L. Milroy and J. Milroy, forthcoming).

The need to extend the model is partly a result of methodological difficulties in measuring weak ties, on which I commented in chapter 6.4. Social network is most readily operationalized to account for solidary, strong-tie patterns, which normally contribute to language maintenance rather than change and which involve consensus on norms rather than conflict. But even if we could measure weak ties satisfactorily, there would still be inadequacies, because there are certain things that are socially important which lie outside a consensus-based model of this kind. These have to do with the broader structures of society, involving patterns of social stratification, or of social rank, class, status, power or economic wealth. But although it would be difficult, if not impossible, to include social network systematically in an integrated model alongside certain other matters of importance (such as psycho-social attitudinal studies or language-acquisition studies), it does seem to be feasible to work towards an integrated sociolinguistic model of social network and social class.

7.1 Consensus and Conflict

Social network has sometimes been represented in sociolinguistics as an alternative model to social class and considered to be incompatible with it. Because of this it may seem to be surprising that I should propose an integrated model here. However, if we are to move towards a fully-fledged social model, it is clearly necessary to relate in some way the study of micro-level social relationships (as, for example, accessed through social network) with the study of the wider social structures within which these micro-level relationships are enacted. For it must be made clear that the forms that various network groupings take are not arbitrary: they are in some sense dependent on the wider organization of society. The particular type of solidary network structures that is found in the shanty towns studied by Lomnitz (1977), for example, does not spring up for no reason: it is related to socio-economic inequalities at a macro-social level, which make it necessary for people to form solidary groupings for mutual support, protection and even survival. The purpose of this chapter is to suggest what an integrated model might be like, and to examine the consequences of adopting such a model for interpreting attested language changes.

We can make a start here by relating our own findings on the relationship between social network and language variation (as discussed in chapters 4 and 6) to a broader theory of social class which can account for larger-scale social structures and processes. But this does not amount to accepting the conceptualization of social class that is current in much contemporary sociolinguistics. I think we can agree with Kathryn Woolard, who has recently commented on the integration of sociolinguistic and social theory; her view is that much of the social theory implicitly adopted by sociolinguists is in need of explicit formulation and critique: ' . . . sociolinguists have often borrowed social concepts in an ad hoc and unreflecting fashion, not usually considering critically the implicit theoretical frameworks that are imported wholesale along with such convenient constructs as three−, four−, or nine-sector scalings of socioeconomic status' (1985: 738). Other investigators (such as Rickford, 1986) have expressed broadly similar views, and of course the avoidance of social class measures in the Belfast inner-city research was based on a similar critique of my own (J. Milroy and L. Milroy, 1978, and elsewhere).

In developing a suitable social model, we start with sociolinguistic findings and then look for a coherent theory which accounts for them. Proceeding in this way allows us to make principled decisions about the kind of framework that seems to be required, without binding us to a particular social class model that has been superimposed beforehand as a means of organizing the data. But we do not claim to have found the ideal social class model; we are simply attempting to integrate existing findings and suggest the *kind* of social model that seems to be practical and capable of giving insights. However, many sociolinguistic findings suggest that the kind of social class model required differs quite sharply from that underlying Labov's work, which is most clearly manifested in his New York City study, but still influential in interpreting at least some of the findings of his more recent work in Philadelphia. Labov's definition of *speech community* (his key sociolinguistic notion) depends, as we have seen, on the idea of shared values throughout the community at all levels of social structure. But as the community shape implicit in Labov's analysis is a stratified shape with agreement across the different strata, it assumes a consensus model of the type associated with Parsons (1952), in which the community is envisaged as fundamentally cohesive, and where speakers are said to agree on the evaluation of the very linguistic norms that actually symbolize the divisions between them. My own sociolinguistic research started with the view that divergence and conflict are synchronically more salient than consensus, and I think the findings of much sociolinguistic research now give support to this view. The reality and persistence of non-standard vernacular communities uncovered by many researchers, constitute evidence not primarily of consensus, but of conflict and sharp divisions in society. This view seems to be shared by some others: for example, Rickford's work on Guyanese Creole has led him to call for more attention to conflict models of class (Rickford, 1986). And despite the characteristic focus of Labov's work on shared values, support for a conflict model of society is provided by some of the Philadelphia findings showing progressive segregation and linguistic differentiation between black and white networks (Labov and Harris, 1986). Furthermore, a conflict-based social theory seems to be essential if we are to account for the phenomenon of linguistic change, because if values are fully shared throughout a community there will be no reason to change them. In fact, pointing to the social conflict associated with linguistic change, Labov himself has suggested that 'a thoroughgoing structural-functional approach to language could be applied only if linguistic systems did not undergo internal change and development' (Labov 1986: 283).

From these points it seems reasonable to conclude that a social class model based on conflict, division and inequality will account best for patterns of language variation at the macro-level. This has consequences not only for interpretations based on shared values (following Labov), but also for the idea of the linguistic market (Bourdieu, 1977). This has been widely used (see especially Sankoff, et al., 1989), the argument being that language represents a form of social and cultural capital, which is convertible (in varying degrees) into economic capital. Dittmar, Schlobinski and Wachs (1988) provide a useful exposition of the concept in relation to their analysis of Berlin vernacular. Woolard (1985), however, has discussed standard/vernacular opposition in terms of alternative linguistic markets, rather than adopting Bourdieu's view of a single dominant linguistic market where the rule of the 'legitimate' language is merely suspended by the 'vernacular' user. This is our view also: we have argued that the use of the vernacular cannot be seen simply as a relaxation of tension, a temporary absence of domination of the standard, as Bourdieu posits. Indeed, much of the argumentation of this book has suggested that standard languages are not 'normal' states of affairs, and that variability is normal and primary. A major reason for rejecting Bourdieu's assumptions about the standard is that much sociolinguistic work (including our own) has shown that, just as there is strong institutional pressure in formal situations to use varieties approximating to the standard, so also effective sanctions are in force to promote 'vernacular' use in non-standard domains. The vernacular in this view is a positive force in itself, and if you study highly divergent vernaculars, you cannot help being impressed by the sheer irrelevance of the 'standard' or the 'legitimate' language in many situations (for some relevant comments, see chapters 3 and 4).

The orthodox account of the linguistic market appears to offer a unidimensional analysis of the speech community, in which the control of the 'legitimate' language is basic. Woolard (1985), however, suggests that much recent sociolinguistic work which has concentrated on competing social values using a bi-dimensional analysis – such as one based on contrastive *status* and *solidarity* (we specifically developed such an analysis in inner-city Belfast) – offers a particularly promising bridge between sociolinguistic and social theory. Within this status (power)/solidarity framework, close-knit social networks are seen as mechanisms enabling speakers to maintain a vernacular code, which itself constitutes an actively constructed, symbolic opposition to the 'dominant', legitimized code. But it should also be borne in mind that the dominance of a given legitimized code is not necessarily maintained through time. It is quite common for forms and varieties that were at one time non-standard to take over as the basis of legitimized codes and, on the other hand, for legitimized forms to recede and/or become vernacular forms. Unidimensional models (including standard-based modelling of the linguistic market) do not offer much help in explaining these historical changes.

It is these patterns of symbolic opposition (present or past) that make it necessary for us to to move beyond network and look for an appropriate model of wider social structure, because, as Gal (1988) argues, the success, persistence and precise form of the symbolic opposition will depend not upon internal linguistic or interactional factors, but upon the relation of the resisting group to the national economy and to like groups in other states. The outcome in terms of language survival or shift in Belfast may be different from that in Brighton; in Catalonia different from Gascony. It will necessarily be constrained by local historical contingencies.

So far I have tried to outline some general prerequisites for a socially coherent sociolinguistic theory, constructed to take account of sociolinguistic findings – particularly those that have emphasized the strength and persistence of local vernaculars in opposition to legitimized languages. In order to put this together, we need to recall briefly the chief principles underlying a network analysis of language variation, looking first at close-knit communities and then at more loose-knit network situations. I shall attempt to show that the structure and social function of both types of situation need to be considered if we want to integrate a network model with a sociolinguistically and socially adequate model of social class.

7.2 Close Ties in Rural and Urban Communities

Dialectological research has generally drawn a sharp distinction between rural and urban dialectology, and in some cases (such as Andersen, 1986) between 'central' and 'peripheral' dialect situations. Before we go on to suggest a way of integrating class and network, it seems necessary to comment on the relation of social network to these distinctions. Fundamentally the concept of network is neutral with regard to such situations, but it is sometimes felt that close-knit networks are receding under the impact of modern urban life, and that the analysis of close-knit network situations will therefore become less and less relevant to the explanation of observed linguistic and social variation. This is probably not correct.

It has been argued (for example, by Wirth, 1938) that urban conditions give rise to impersonality and social distance. But this 'urbanist' thesis does not contradict the model I have suggested: it fits in with the arguments in chapter 6 on the role of weak ties (urban communities being a sub-type of contact situation where numerous weak ties are bound to arise). However, weak ties do not tell the whole story about urban life. It may well be true that the Italian American 'urban villagers' described by Gans (1962), or the close-knit mining communities described in Yorkshire by Dennis, Henriques and Slaughter (1957), are less salient in American and British cities than they once were. But there are still close-tie situations in cities, as these traditional communities are gradually replaced by similar types of community created by newer immigrants. More importantly perhaps, as Giddens (1989) points out, neighbourhoods involving close kinship and personal ties seem to be actually *created* by the conditions of city life. It is easy to understand that when people settle in a strange (and possibly frightening) environment, they will seek security by developing ties with people of their own ethnic and cultural background – people they understand. And as Fischer's work (1984) suggests, it is in large cities rather than in small towns that cultural diversity will be enabled to develop in this manner.

It seems, therefore, that those who form part of urban ethnic communities will gravitate to form ties with, and often to live with, others from a similar linguistic or ethnic background. These ethnic groups use the close-knit network as a means of protecting their economic and social interests while their community develops the resources to integrate more fully into urban life. For example, differences in the network structure of members of the Chinese community in Newcastle upon Tyne correlate with different patterns of language choice and with different levels of integration into non-Chinese domains of urban life (L. Milroy and Li Wei, forthcoming). Bortoni-Ricardo (1985) makes a similar point with regard to rural migrants into Brasilia. Thus, the type of close-knit community that is most easily conceptualized in (close-tie) network terms is as likely to be a product of modern city life as it is to be a residue of an earlier type of social organization. It is an instance of a recurrent phenomenon – a phenomenon favoured by the conditions of urban life and therefore likely to renew itself cyclically as new populations move in – and of course these close-tie communities are functional for their members in that they offer security and mutual support.

These close-knit groups are important in providing a focal point for 'stigmatized' urban vernaculars and other non-legitimized linguistic norms, and so need to be accounted for in any sociolinguistic theory. That is why some form of network analysis that examines the relationship between the individual and the primary group is so important. But the indicators of strength and intensity of network tie, which is the variable relevant to the kind of analysis we are discussing here, will vary in kind with community organization. For example, membership of religious groups might be irrelevant in a contemporary northern English coal-mining community, but highly relevant in a Midlands black community.

The link between network and class, however, is not provided by strong ties, but by weak ties. As I have suggested in chapter 6 (following J. Milroy and L. Milroy, 1985b), those speakers whose network structures are least close-knit are also less likely to approximate closely to conservative vernacular norms of language and are more exposed to external influences, which in many cases will be – relatively speaking – standardizing influences. The link between network and class pointed out by Mewett (1982) suggests a route for constructing a two-level sociolinguistic theory, linking small-scale structures such as networks, in which individuals act purposively in their daily lives, with larger-scale and more abstract social structures (classes) which determine relationships of power at the institutional level. The relationship between weakness of ties and the development of class structure also gives us a consistent explanation for the

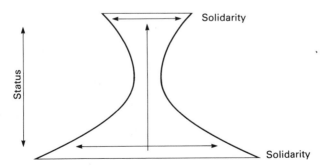

Figure 7.1 The anvil-shaped status/solidarity model.

openness to innovation of the socially mobile middle groups in the social hierarchy, as against the conservatism of the uppermost and lowermost groups. During the Belfast projects I suggested a status/ solidarity model measured against social class, which gives us the anvil-shaped diagram of figure 7.1. In this perspective, network-based and class-based analyses are not contradictory (as is sometimes suggested); rather, they complement each other. Figure 7.2 is a more elaborate attempt to indicate the pattern of relationships that are likely to exist in the community in terms of both strong and weak ties.

7.3   Towards an Integrated Model: The Concept of Life-modes

I commented above that the findings of sociolinguistic research, particularly small-scale network studies of ethnic minority and working-class groups, constitute evidence of conflict and sharp division in society, rather than of cohesion. We also commented above that we need a social theory that links our network analysis to an analysis of social structure at the political, institutional and economic level. Such a link may be provided by 'life-mode' analysis (Højrup, 1983), which we develop further below.

What is required here is a model representing various ethnic and class groups as *both* internally structured *and* connected to each other with varying proportions of strong and weak ties, which we have attempted to show in figure 7.2. For example, ethnic subgroups in Britain such as the black speakers studied by Edwards (1985) have a predominantly strong-tie internal structure, but seem to be linked by relatively few weak ties to white working-class groups. These white groups in turn might have a similar internal network structure but have *more* weak tie links with other white working-class groups. Vertical links to middle-class groups might be fewer (this seemed to be the case in Belfast) and moreover to be frequently institutional to such persons as doctors, lawyers, teachers, welfare personnel and the like. Middle-class groups for their part – professional, neighbour-hood and friendship groups – are characterized by a higher propor-tion of weak ties *internally* than working-class groups; hence the problems of studying them systematically in network terms in Zehlen-dorf – a middle-class suburb in Berlin (Dittmar, Schlobinski and

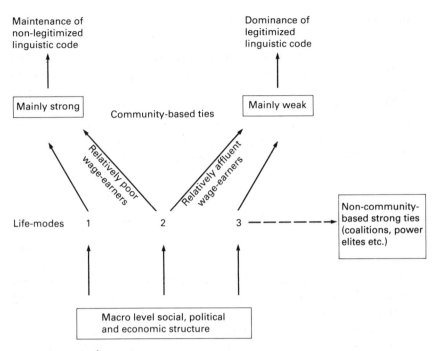

Figure 7.2 Macro and micro levels of sociolinguistic structure.

Wachs, 1988) – and in outer-city Belfast. Thus, however we interpret the concept of class, and however we model these localized networks, we can use Granovetter's concept of the weak tie to link close-knit community level groupings to more abstract institutional structures.

In the model we are developing, the behaviour of speakers is attributed to the constraining effects of the network, or the diminution of those effects which enables supra-local norms (including the legitimized language) to permeate networks, rather than to any direct effect of 'prestige' as defined by the perceived attributes of speakers who are seen to 'belong' to different status groups. Social class is viewed here as a structural concept, not as a set of labels which might be attached to particular individuals. Thus, local and individual social behaviour is not seen as directly related to class but as mediated through these smaller-scale structures. However, while network analysis can delineate various economic, political and subcultural groupings in society, it cannot say anything about the varying potentials of such networks to exercise the economic and political power that is the source of conflict and inequality in society. In linguistic terms, of course, this means that powerful networks have the capacity to impose their linguistic and cultural norms on others, while powerless ones do not, but can merely use the resources of the network to maintain and at best renew their own linguistic and cultural norms.

This last comment takes us back to the discussion of norms and prescription in chapter 1. As we noticed there, Jones's *English Pronouncing Dictionary* (1955) is an account of RP which, although it claims to be descriptive and not prescriptive, is nonetheless used by readers as a prescriptive guide. If it is used in this way, however, this does not arise from Jones's intentions, but from the social factors I have just alluded to. If the accent described were not RP, but Belfast inner-city vernacular, the description would not be used prescriptively. Like other accents, RP is a network accent, and like other accents it is also a badge of identity. But there is one overriding difference: RP is also the possession of a network that has the greatest socio-economic power, and that is why some socially mobile persons (mainly in life-mode 3, below) may wish to acquire it.

We cannot really understand all this without reference to the broader structures of society, and for this reason we need a social theory that links a network analysis of subgroups within society to an analysis of social structure at the political, institutional and economic level. These two levels correspond to what Gal (1988: 247) describes as 'the interactional and socio-political level of analysis'. The most helpful analysis of this kind we have encountered is that of Højrup (1983), who proposes a division of the population into subgroups which are described in terms of three life-modes.[1] These life-modes are seen as *necessary* and *inevitable* constituents of the social structure as a whole. Højrup's conception of this larger social structure is Marxist, and the initial analysis is in terms of modes of production and consumption. Thus, crucially, these subgroups are not seen as socially or culturally arbitrary, but as the effect of 'fundamental societal structures which split the population into fundamentally different life-modes' (Højrup, 1983: 47). The analysis is particularly useful from our point of view, since the different types of network structure that we have distinguished emerge naturally from differences in the life-modes of different individuals. Although the argumentation in support of his analysis is lengthy and complex, Højrup uses a limited number of straightforward concepts to distinguish the three life-modes, and we shall look at these briefly. Life-mode 1 is the life-mode of the self-employed, life-modes 2 and 3 of two different types of wage-earners. Of critical importance is the ideological orientation of the three groups to *work, leisure* and *family*. We shall focus a brief description of each of them on points of contact with our network analysis.

Life-mode 1   Here Højrup is thinking of any simple commodity producing unit, be it agriculture, fishing, a corner shop or a restaurant. In this life-mode, social relationships in the form of family ties or co-operative relations among colleagues bind the producers into a cohesive production unit. The primary concern is to keep the production rolling, and all the family and other affiliated producers are involved in this. The purpose of the enterprise is to be able to remain self-employed, a means that is its own end. The concept of free time has little meaning in this life-mode, since the producer is not put to work but puts himself to work to gain independence. This is done to the extent that it is necessary and beneficial for himself and his family to maintain or expand their enterprise. The concepts of 'leisure' and 'work' thus have a totally different meaning from that which they assume for wage-earners, and it is clear that a close-knit type of network structure and a solidarity ethic will be associated with this life-mode, which itself follows from the type of economic activity in which the producers engage. Højrup does not see this kind of life-mode as a relic of an earlier period (see my comments, above, on close-knit networks in modern cities) but as highly efficient and competitive given its flexibility of operation and the commitment of the producers. He uses the Danish fishing industry as an example, but his description equally well applies to Chinese family restaurant businesses, Pakistani corner shops, or small painting and decorating businesses in Britain.

Life-mode 2   Wage-earners are different from life-mode 1 commodity producers, in that they are incorporated in a long and complex process of production which they do not own or control. Life-mode 2 is that of the ordinary wage-earner, the purpose of whose work is to provide him with an income that will enable him to live a meaningful life during his free time. The family differs from life-mode 1 families in being separate from his work activities; it is the framework within which non-productive leisure activity takes place. The life-mode 2 worker lacks the commitment to his work characteristic of life-mode 1. He is prepared to sell his labour, thereby becoming mobile and severing existing close-knit network ties if there is an adequate inducement to do so. If wages are low, however, he has to demand enough to survive. Hence, the solidarity that arises amongst workers who earn little – a solidarity reflected at the institutional level in the establishment of trades unions. At a neighbourhood level this solidarity is embodied in the close-knit networks of the traditional working-class society of the kind we studied in Belfast. Following through Højrup's analysis, we would surmise that the solidarity ethic would collapse and network ties become loose-knit if economic and political conditions allowed workers to feel secure in their future prospects, if they earned enough to become mobile, to buy better houses and cars, to take holidays abroad and so on. There do in fact appear to be differences of this kind in behaviour between different groups of wage-earner, as we noted in our analysis of the outer-city versus inner-city areas in Belfast. Lockwood's (1966) classic investigation of images of class structure in Britain fits in broadly with such an analysis, particularly in its distinction between the outlooks described respectively as *proletarian traditionalism* and *privatized worker* (see Giddens 1989: 224). Privatized workers, exemplified by the Luton car workers studied by Goldthorpe et al. (1968–9), live apart from traditional working-class areas in the suburbs, and see work as a way of achieving a satisfactory life style for themselves and their families. They apparently reject the traditional working-class solidarity ethic, but given a certain level of grievance it tends to reinstate itself as does the us/them, insider/outsider imagery characteristic of close-knit communities and traditional proletarian ideology. The persistence and renewal of this imagery (and associated network structures) seem to spring from changes in economic and power structures in society.

Life-mode 3   The life-mode 2 wage-earner performs the routine tasks of the workforce at a given daily or hourly rate. The life-mode 3 wage-earner is, however, a higher professional or managerial employee with a high level of skill which is itself a saleable commodity, and he or she is paid to arrange, monitor and control the production process. Typically, the concept of work and leisure and the role of the family are in sharp contrast to those of life-mode 2. The life-mode 3 goal is to rise up through the hierarchy, to obtain control through managerial and professional roles, to exercise more and more power and ultimately escape from the control of others so as to control resources and exercise power on one's own account. This process demands an immersion of the individual in work, a competitive attitude to colleagues and a blurring of the boundaries between work and leisure. The family and its way of life fulfils a supportive role in relation to the career. Work therefore *is* life to a high degree, and the concept of freedom is not one of free time but is associated with the work situation and the career perspective. This will be uncomfortably familiar to those who, like me, are university teachers.

Just as different types of network structure emerge from the economic conditions associated with life-modes 1 and 2, so a certain type of personal network structure seems to follow from life-mode 3. These wage-earners will be socially and geographically mobile as they pursue their careers, forming many loose ties, particularly of a professional kind, through which innovations and influence may be transmitted. However, they will also form close-knit clusters and coalitions within their personal networks, through which they control considerable resources. This seems to fit in with our general characterization of the differing role of loose-knit and close-knit network ties; the primarily loose-knit network of the life-mode 3 individual ensures that the dominant linguistic market holds sway without hindrance from (in Woolard's (1985) terms) alternative vernacular markets. Thus, to the extent that it is true that the standard language influences speakers, it will be life-mode 3 speakers who are open to that influence, and not the economically powerless people that we studied in inner-city Belfast, for whom the standard language is almost irrelevant. In a totally different dimension, and recalling my comments on the consequences of standardization in chapter 5, I find it very tempting to suggest here that orthodox historical linguistic description has been dominated by the perspective of life-mode 3 individuals, who have believed their own attitudes to language to be based on 'common sense', and have not been aware that their perspective is in conflict with that of other sectors of society. That is why we have the emphasis on dominant linguistic markets or dominant dialects, the focus on 'shared values' throughout the community, and repeated unanalysed appeals to the concept of 'prestige'.

It is important to emphasize that the concept of life-mode, like that of social network, is a structural one. People cannot be neatly slotted into pre-determined life-modes like letters into pigeon-holes. Their ideological and cultural characteristics will be determined by their contrast to the other life-modes in the social formation. The interrelationships between the three life-modes and the cultural practices associated with each one will therefore take different forms in, for example, Denmark, Ireland, England and Germany. In each of these countries the three fundamental modes of production which the life-modes reflect 'will appear in different variants and in different combinations of opposition and independence' (Højrup, 1983).

One consequence of this chain of dependence running from political and socio-economic structure through life-modes to network structure and ultimately to sociolinguistic structure, is that close-knit networks will be associated with life-mode 2 individuals in some states more than in others. This seems to be the case if we compare Belfast with Copenhagen, where wage-earners are apparently more mobile and prosperous and less inclined to organize themselves into close-knit groups of the kind described in Belfast (Gregersen and Pedersen, forthcoming). This in turn will give rise to locally contingent sociolinguistic patterns, with urban vernaculars varying in their degree of 'focusing', opposition to mainstream norms, and general vitality. But to analyse the life-modes we need to look simultaneously at cultural practices and specify more completely the modes of production that give rise to them. It seems, however, that Højrup's analysis has the capacity to help us develop a socially sensitive sociolinguistic theory which links the macro and micro levels of analysis in a coherent way. It is offered here as a way forward towards an integrated social model of language variation and change, and it is discussed more fully in L. Milroy and J. Milroy (forthcoming).

7.4 Conclusion: Towards a Historical Sociolinguistics

In this chapter I have tried to build on our social dialectological research and further developments in the social network model in order to suggest how a broader social framework for the interpretation of language change might be constructed. There are other conceivable social models, some of which might be complementary to this and some of which might be alternatives to it. What this model does is to indicate the kind of relationship that might exist between micro-sociological concepts and macro-sociological concepts as they relate to interpreting language variation and change. There can be little doubt that some form of integrated social model is necessary.

Even from within sociolinguistics there have been constant complaints about the naïveté of the social underpinning of the subject (a recent one is Cameron, 1990). In interpreting data, such terms as class, prestige and standard language are frequently used but seldom adequately defined, with the result that there is much vagueness, ambiguity and circularity in the use of these terms in explanation.

The view of historical sociolinguistics that I have developed in this book is, like other approaches (for example, Romaine, 1982a), variationist. As language is variable at all times, an adequate historical account must be an account of changing patterns of variation. However, the approach advocated here is also much more *social* in nature than any other sociolinguistic approach (as far as I know). The changing patterns of language are not seen exclusively as changes in the linguistic shape of a language variety, but also as changes in social agreement on the linguistic norms of communities. In this account, much more attention is given to the social side than is given in the Labov paradigm, which is mainly system-oriented, as I have tried to show, despite its strong emphasis on fieldwork methods. Other approaches also are less social than ours. Romaine (1982a), for example, proposes a version of 'socio-historical linguistics' which is mainly system-oriented and concerned with philosophy of science issues of an abstract idealizing kind, rather than the experimental 'realist' brand of philosophy of science that has influenced our work (Plutchik, 1974). Similarly, although John Harris worked with us in Belfast, his treatment of similar data (Harris, 1985) is also less social and less speaker-oriented than ours.

The main theme that I have tried to develop in this book is that a strongly social approach is justified because linguistic change is a social phenomenon. It is negotiated by speakers in face-to-face encounters, and an innovation in a speaker's output is not a linguistic change until it has been agreed on and adopted by some community of speakers, however small the community may be. By further developing our social model of language change we can hope in time to reach a better understanding of the conditions in which innovations are sometimes adopted as changes and sometimes rejected, and models of social identity (Le Page and Tabouret-Keller, 1985), accommodation (Giles and Smith, 1979) and politeness (Brown and Levinson, 1987) will not be irrelevant to these developments.

In the meantime we may wish to consider how far we can be satisfied with mainly mentalist or language-internal explanations for language change, and within sociolinguistics we may also wish to consider more carefully than has been usual what is really meant when we appeal to concepts like class and prestige as explanations for attested changes. Finally, within the tradition of historical linguistic theorizing, our social approach seems in certain respects to supersede some of the axioms of the Neogrammarians. From a social point of view, linguistic change, when it is carefully observed by accountable methods, is always gradual.

A major task, therefore, is to link linguistic change with social change in such a way as to explain the conditions under which linguistic change takes on particular patterns, including patterns of rapid and slow change. This is a very different task from that of orthodox historical linguistics, and I hope that I have shown in this book that it is a very exciting challenge.

Notes

Chapter 1   *Introduction: Language Change and Variation*

1   I have in mind here languages such as ancient Greek, Latin or Sanskrit, the classical forms of which survived the demise of native speakers. It is true that they developed into vernacular languages and were used for ritual purposes, but in these later forms they displayed changes only when they had speakers or writers.

Chapter 2   *Social and Historical Linguistics*

1   There is evidence that both Danish and English had a higher incidence of palatization of velars in the past than they have now. For English, McKnight (1928: 456) lists examples (e.g. *cyar, gyet* for 'car, get') from 1653 until 1791, noting that one writer at least regarded palatalization as 'essential in polite pronunciation'. The recession of palatalization here is just as much a sound-change as its implementation, and a solution to the actuation riddle would involve explaining cases of recession as well as cases of implementation of the phenomenon. We have been able to observe a late stage in the recession of palatalization in Belfast. See J. Milroy (1981) and chapter 3.

2   This is particularly true of the Chomskyan 'idealized native speaker/listener'.

3   To give a socially-based explanation of the merger of *bird/fern/hurt* in seventeenth-century English, we would need detailed information of a kind that is not normally directly recoverable from historical sources. See my comments on the limitations of historical inquiry in section 2.7, below. However, we can observe similar patterns of merger in present-

day English, particularly in urban dialects: see chapter 5 for some discussion.

4   Smith (1989: 181) suggests that it is unlikely that a homogeneous input (to the language-learner) would make language learning impossible. Perhaps not quite, but a person who had acquired a first language from a homogeneous model would surely be perceived as a very odd person. But it is widely believed by linguists that variation and change are non-functional. Consider Postal (1968: 283): '. . . there is no more reason for languages to change than there is for automobiles to add fins one year and remove them the next . . . the 'causes' of sound change without language contact lie in the general tendency of human cultural products to undergo 'nonfunctional' stylistic change.' Manufacturers normally have good reasons to alter designs that they want to sell to the public. However, beside the strong feelings that speakers express about language variation, this intra-linguistic view seems to me to be rather pallid.

5   Jespersen, of course, did not use the term 'transparent'.

6   Vennemann (1989) has recently claimed that language change is 'meliorative'. This seems to be a non-social view: languages become better in themselves, independently of society. Vennemann links this to the idea of evolution: languages are seen as evolving to a better state, in common with biological evolution generally. As for 'drift', which has recently come to the fore again, one problem with this, as possibly with some of Vennemann's ideas also, is that it can only be discerned retrospectively.

7   I discussed some of these in J. Milroy (1978). They were subsequently further discussed in the wider context of conversational breakdown by L. Milroy (1984).

8   One of the most naïve assumptions of early transformational-generative theory is the idea that different dialects of English can be derived from the base form by the addition of relatively 'low-level' or 'late' rules. This was still being seriously proposed as recently as 1981 (Smith and Wilson, 1981).

9   I have used the distinction between message-oriented and listener-oriented speech as a very general distinction here. There is no suggestion that it would be possible to define every part of a conversation as belonging to one category or the other. One might also adduce Bernsteinian distinctions here – for example, between context-free and context-sensitive discourse.

10 In J. Milroy (1982a) I have discussed the absence of Verner's Law voicing from the Gothic strong verb, where according to the theory it should occur. There are two alternative traditional explanations for this (see Wright, 1954: 369–70). In my paper, I suggest a third explanation,

which fits the facts equally well. Because the phenomena lie deep in history, we do not have reliable criteria for choosing amongst these three explanations, and any preference we express is likely to be influenced by some theoretical consideration. Verner's own explanation (analogical levelling), for example, was derived from Neogrammarian theory.

Chapter 3 *Analysing Language in the Community: General Principles*

1   We can say that the conclusion based on this instance of hypercorrection is 'warranted' by the data, very much as conversational analysts use the term 'warranted'.
2   The back /ɑ:/ in RP is so socially salient that people tend to believe far too readily that backing in other dialects is RP-influenced. For a rebuttal of this view in the case of Tyneside English, see Beal (1985).
3   Social network did not form part of the original research design; it was not mentioned in our application for funding in 1975. Misinterpretations of the role of social network in the research design have been common enough to require comment. Sometimes the hypothesis – about language maintenance through normative consensus – with which we started out (before we thought of using the social network model) is presented as if it were a finding arising *after* quantitative analysis. Cameron (1990: 87), for example, says that the quantitative (network) analysis 'led Milroy to conclude that people in her (*sic*) survey behave linguistically as they did because of the normative influence of their peer group', and describes the language/ close-tie hypothesis as a 'finding'. This is not quite right: our data analysis supported our hypothesis. Unfortunately, the Belfast work (which was not mainly a survey) is also misattributed here to Lesley Milroy, and 'social networks' are wrongly equated with 'peer groups'. Unlike Labov (1972a) in Harlem and Cheshire (1982) in Reading, we did not carry out peer-group studies in Belfast. The social network model covers person-to-person relationships generally, and not solely within bounded groups. See further Chapter 4.1.
4   Some additional guidance was in fact available from the prescriptions made by the elocutionist David Patterson (1860) (see chapters 4 and 5 for further references to Patterson) and from descriptive work on Ulster dialect generally by Adams (1964), Gregg (1964, 1972) and others.
5   It is possible also to quantify variables of a supra-phonemic type: for example, Rigg (1987) has quantified glottal-stopping and glottal reinforcement for three consonants ([p, t, k]) in Tyneside, and it would have been possible to quantify supra-phonemically in Belfast. Centring

glides, for example, occur under similar conditions for several different vowels, and several vowels show similarities to one another before [r]. In my judgement at the time, it was possible to deal adequately with these features descriptively and without quantification.

6 It is important to note that there is nothing new in using co-variation arugments in linguistics. Traditional comparative linguistics has been based on observed co-variation and correlation (without quantification, of course), and well-known 'sound-laws', such as Grimm's Law, are based on these perceptions. I have elsewhere discussed the correlational arguments that account for 'Verner's Law' (J. Milroy, 1982a). The notion of causality tends to get involved here as Germanic accent shift correlates very closely with Verner's Law voicing, so there may be a 'causal relationship', but we would be on shaky ground if we claimed that accent shift was *the cause* of the voicing. Proposed solutions to actuation have to recognize that it is multi-causal, and that is why we look at numerous social and linguistic conditions when we study sound-change in progress. And, of course, the use of quantification is irrelevant to any substantive claims that are made on the basis of co-variation patterns.

Chapter 4   *Interpreting Variation in the Speech Community*

1 It is easy to give examples of strongly expressed feelings about language variants and to show that such views often have a 'gate-keeping' function. Edwards (forthcoming) quotes a letter sent to a teacher who had been rejected for an appointment after an interview in which his use of 'aspirates' ([h]) was objected to. She also mentions the stigma against 'Cockney' in particular: Walker (1791) describes it as 'offensive and disgusting'; Matthews (1938: x) points out that even 'philologists' deny Cockney the status of a dialect and 'describe it as vulgar speech based on error and misunderstanding'. In my own experience a university Dean once objected to the appointment of the best candidate for a particular post on the grounds that the candidate had a 'London accent'. In chapter 2 (note 4), we noticed that despite the strong feelings that people express about language, linguistic scholars often believe that variation and change are non-functional (see especially Postal, 1968: 283).

2 Horvath (1985) has re-graphed Labov's New York City data in terms of sex-difference, and has shown that differentiating in terms of sex works at least as well as differentiating in terms of class. In fact, Nathan B, who seems anomalous in terms of class, is 'normal' if the data are presented in terms of sex-difference. Rigg (1987), analysing the

incidence of glottal-stopping in Tyneside, has presented figures that show that the use of the glottal stop is related to sex, rather than class, as reported by L. Milroy (1989):

	Working class			Middle class		
	(p)	(t)	(k)	(p)	(t)	(k)
Males %:	99.5	97.0	94.5	96.5	91.0	80.5
Females %:	60.0	31.0	28.0	27.0	32.5	11.0

3 The term 'marker' is used here in a general sense, and not in the more technical sense used by Labov, which requires that the variable is marked in terms of both class and style. So it should be borne in mind that the variables are not selected in the belief that some are *indicators*, some *markers*, and others *stereotypes* (Labov, 1972b), or that some are 'low-consciousness' and others 'high-consciousness' variables (Johnston, 1983). These taxonomies are not involves at this stage, but we can perhaps regard our procedures as helping to test to what extent they are valid.

4 Gregg (1972: 110) speaks of the 'ubiquitous Ulster "light" [l]'; Jones (1956: 92) states that 'in English as spoken in Ireland [l] is always clear', and a similar view is expressed by Gimson (1970: 204) and O'Connor (1973: 149).

Chapter 6   Speaker-innovation and Linguistic Change

The arguments in this chapter about weak ties, speaker-innovation and diffusion of innovations are largely based on a paper jointly authored by James and Lesley Milroy, 'Linguistic change, social network and speaker-innovation', which appeared in the *Journal of Linguistics* in 1985. I am extremely grateful to Lesley for the continuing collaboration out of which this paper emerged.

1 Gumperz points out that Labov shares with other linguists an interest in understanding the character of *grammars*; a speaker-oriented approach, on the other hand, 'focuses directly on the strategies that govern the actor's use of lexical, grammatical, sociolinguistic and other knowledge in the production and interpretation of messages in context' (Gumperz, 1982: 35). Thus, a display such as the graph of the famous cross-over pattern for /r/ in New York City is not aimed primarily at accounting

for speaker-behaviour: it is a grammar of change which locates a change in progress within the system.

Chapter 7   Towards an Integrated Social Model for the Interpretation of Language Change

1   My thanks to Inge-Lise Pedersen, Copenhagen, for noting the possible usefulness of Thomas Højrup's life-modes model and for calling our attention to it in 1987. I am also grateful to Lesley Milroy for the continuing collaboration on the social aspects of our research and in particular for her collaboration on the forthcoming paper on which this chapter is substantially based.

References

Abdel Jawad 1987. Cross-dialectal variation in Arabic: competing prestigious forms. *Language in Society*, 16, 359–68.

Adams, B. (ed.) 1964. *Ulster Dialects: a symposium*. Holywood, Co. Down: Ulster Folk Museum.

Adamska-Salaciak, A. 1989. On explaining language change teleologically. *Studia Anglica Posnaniensia*, 22, 53–74.

Ahlqvist, A. (ed.) 1982. *Papers from the 5th International Conference on Historical Linguistics* (Current Issues in Linguistic Theory, 21). Amsterdam: Benjamins.

Alahdal, H. 1989. *Standard and Prestige: a sociolinguistic study of Makkan Arabic*. PhD thesis: University of Reading.

Alatis, J. (ed.) 1978. *International Dimensions of Bilingual Education*. Washington DC: Georgetown University Press.

Andersen, H. 1973. Abductive and deductive change. *Language*, 49, 765–93. Reprinted in Baldi and Werth (1978: 313–47).

Andersen, H. 1986. Center and periphery: adoption, diffusion and spread. Paper delivered to the Conference on Historical Dialectology, Poznan, Poland.

Anderson, J. and Jones, C. (eds) 1974. *Historical Linguistics*. Amsterdam: North-Holland Publishing Company.

Ash, S. and Myhill, J. 1986. Linguistic correlates of inter-ethnic contact. In Sankoff, D. (ed.), *Diversity and Diachrony*, Amsterdam: Benjamins, 33–44.

Bailey, C. J. 1973. *Variation and Linguistic Theory*. Washington, DC: Center for Applied Linguistics.

Baldi, P. and Werth, R. N. (eds) 1978. *Readings in Historical Phonology*. University Park: Pennsylvania State University Press.

Beal, J. 1985. Lengthening of *a* in Tyneside English. Current issues in Linguistic Theory, 41. Amsterdam: Benjamins.

Berdan, R. 1977. Polylectal comprehension and the polylectal grammar. In Fasold, R. and Shuy, R. W. (eds), *Studies in Language Variation*, Washington DC: Georgetown University Press, 12–29.

Bertz, S. 1975. *Der Dubliner Stadtdialekt*. Doctoral dissertation: Albert-Ludwigs-Universität, Freiburg in Breisgau.

Bliss, A. 1979. *Spoken English in Ireland*. Dublin: Dolmen Press.

Bloomfield L. 1933. *Language*. London: Allen and Unwin.

Blom, J.-P. and Gumperz, J. J. 1972. Social meaning in linguistic structure: code-switching in Norway. In Gumperz, J. J. and Hymes, D. (eds), *Directions in Sociolinguistics*, New York: Holt, Rinehart and Winston, 407–34.

Boal, F. W. 1978. Territoriality on the Shankill-Falls divide, Belfast: the perspective from 1976. In Lanegran, D. A. and Palm, R. (eds), *An Invitation to Geography*, 2nd edn, New York: McGraw Hill, 58–77.

Boissevain, J. 1974. *Friends of friends; networks, manipulators and coalitions*. Oxford: Basil Blackwell.

Bolton, W. F. 1966. *The English language: essays by English and American men of letters, 1490–1839*. Cambridge: Cambridge University Press.

Bortoni-Ricardo, S. M. 1985. *The Urbanisation of Rural Dialect Speakers: a sociolinguistic study in Brazil*. Cambridge: Cambridge University Press.

Bott, E. 1971. *Family and Social Network*, revised edn. London: Tavistock.

Bourdieu, P. 1977. The economics of linguistic exchanges. *Social Science Information* 16, 6, 645–68.

Brown, G. 1982. The spoken language. In Carter, R. (ed.), *Linguistics and the Teacher*, London: Routledge and Kegan Paul, 75–87.

Brown, P. and Levinson, S. C. 1987. *Politeness*. Cambridge: Cambridge University Press.

Brown, R. and Gilman, A. 1960. Pronouns of power and solidarity. In Sebeok, T. (ed.), *Style in Language*, Boston: MIT Press, 253–75.

Brunner, K. 1963. *An Outline of Middle English Grammar*. Oxford: Basil Blackwell.

Bynon, T. 1977. *Historical Linguistics*. Cambridge: Cambridge University Press.

Cameron, D. 1990. Demythologizing sociolinguistics. In Joseph, J. E. and Taylor, T. J. (eds), *Ideologies of Language*, London: Routledge, 79–93.

Carter, R. (ed.) 1982. *Linguistics and the Teacher*. London: Routledge and Kegan Paul.

Catford, J. C. 1957. Vowel-systems of Scots dialects. *Transactions of the Philological Society*, 107–17.

Cedergren, H. and Sankoff, D. 1974. Variable rules: performance as a statistical reflection of competence. *Language*, 50, 333–55.

Cheshire, J. 1982. *Variation in an English dialect: a sociolinguistic study*. Cambridge: Cambridge University Press.

Chomsky, N. 1975. *Language and Responsibility*. Sussex: Harvester Press.

Clark, C. 1990. The myth of the Anglo-Norman scribe. Paper delivered to the International Conference on English Historical Linguistics, Helsinki.

Cohen, A. (ed.) 1982. *Belonging*. Manchester: Manchester University Press.

Crystal, D. (ed.) 1981. *Linguistic Controversies: festschrift for F. R. Palmer*. London: Edward Arnold.

Davenport, M., Hansen, E. and Nielsen, H.-F. (eds) 1983. *Current Topics in English Historical Linguistics*. Odense: Odense University Press.

Dennis, N., Henriques, F. M. and Slaughter, C. 1957. *Coal is our Life*. London: Eyre and Spottiswood.

Diaconis, P. 1985. Theories of data analysis: from magical thinking through classical statistics. In Hoaglin, D., Mosteller, M. and Tukey, J. (eds), *Exploring Data Tables*,

Trends and Shapes, New York: Wiley, 1–5.

Dittmar, N. and Schlobinski, P. (eds) 1988. *The Sociolinguistics of Urban Vernaculars*. Berlin: Mouton/de Gruyter.

Dittmar, N., Schlobinski, P. and Wachs, I. 1988. The social significance of the Berlin urban vernacular. In Dittmar, N. and Schlobinski, P. (eds), *The Sociolinguistics of Urban Vernaculars*, Berlin: Mouton/de Gruyter, 19–43.

Dobson, E. J. 1955. Early Modern Standard English. *Transactions of the Philological Society*, 25–54.

Dobson, E. J. 1968. *English Pronunciation: 1500–1700*, 2 vols, 2nd edn. Oxford: Clarendon Press.

Downes, W. 1984. *Language and Society*. Bungay, Suffolk: Fontana.

Eckert, P. 1980. The structure of a long-term phonological process: the back chain-shift in Souletan Gascon. In Labov, W. (ed.), *Locating Language in Time and Space*, New York: Academic Press, 179–219.

Edwards, V. 1985. *Language in a Black Community*. Clevedon, Avon: Multilingual Matters.

Edwards V. forthcoming. The grammar of Southern British English. In Milroy, J. and Milroy, L. (eds), *The Grammar of English Dialects of the British Isles*, London: Longman.

Ekwall, E. 1975. *A History of Modern English Sounds and Morphology*. Oxford: Basil Blackwell.

Fasold, R. and Shuy, R. W. (eds) 1977. *Studies in Language Variation*. Washington DC: Georgetown University Press.

Fischer, C. 1984. *The Urban Experience*, 2nd edn. New York: Harcourt, Brace, Jovanovitch.

Francis, W. Nelson 1983. *Dialectology: an introduction*. London: Longman.

Gal, S. 1979. *Language Shift: social determinants of linguistic change in bilingual Austria*. New York: Academic Press.

Gal, S. 1988. The political economy of code choice. In Heller, M. (ed.), *Codeswitching*, Berlin: Mouton/de Gruyter, 245–63.

Gans, H. J. 1962. *The Urban Villagers: group and class in the life of Italian-Americans*, 2nd edn. New York: Free Press.

Giddens, A. 1989. *Sociology*. Cambridge: Polity Press.

Giles, H. and St Clair, R. 1979. *Language and Social Psychology*. Oxford: Basil Blackwell.

Giles, H. and Smith, P. 1979. Accommodation theory: optimal levels of convergence. In Giles, H. and St Clair, R. (eds), *Language and Social Psychology*, Oxford: Basil Blackwell, 45–65.

Gimson, A. C. 1970. *Introduction to the Pronunciation of English*, 2nd edn. London: Edward Arnold.

Givón, T. (ed.) 1979. *Discourse and Syntax* (Syntax and Semantics, 12). New York: Academic Press.

Gleick, J. 1988. *Chaos*. London: Heinemann.

Goldthorpe, J. H. 1968–9. *The Affluent Worker in the Class Structure*, 3 vols. Cambridge: Cambridge University Press.

Granovetter, M. 1973. The strength of weak ties. *American Journal of Sociology*, 78, 1360–80.

Granovetter, M. 1982. The strength of weak ties: a network theory revisited. In Marsden, P. V. and Lin, N. (eds), *Social Structure and Network Analysis*, London: Sage.

Gregersen, F. and Pedersen, I. L. forthcoming. *The Copenhagen Study in Urban Sociolinguistics* (Universitetsjubilæets Danske Samfund, Serie A). Copenhagen: C. A. Reizel.

Gregg, R. J. 1964. Scotch-Irish urban speech in Ulster. In Adams, B. (ed.), *Ulster Dialects: a symposium*, Hollywood, Co. Down: Ulster Folk Museum, 163–91.

Gregg, R. J. 1972. The Scotch-Irish dialect boundaries in Ulster. In Wakelin, M. F. (ed.), *Patterns in the Folk Speech of the British Isles*, London: Athlone Press, 109–39.

Gumperz, J. J. 1982. *Discourse Strategies*. Cambridge: Cambridge University Press.

Gumperz, J. J. and Hymes, D. 1972. *Directions in Sociolinguistics*. New York: Holt, Rinehart and Winston.

Gunn, B. 1982. Prestige lengthening in Belfast English. Paper delivered to the Sociolinguistic Symposium, Sheffield.

Guy, G. 1980. Variation in the group and the individual: the case of final stop deletion. In Labov, W. (ed.), *Locating Language in Time and Space*, New York: Academic Press, 1–36.

Guy, G. 1988. Language and social class. In Newmeyer, F. (ed.), *Linguistics: the Cambridge Survey*, Cambridge: Cambridge University Press, vol. 4, 37–63.

Haas W. (ed.) 1982. *Standard Languages: spoken and written*. Manchester: Manchester University Press.

Hall, J. (ed.) 1920. *Early Middle English*. 2 vols. Oxford: Clarendon Press.

Harris, J. 1984. Syntactic variation and dialect divergence. *Journal of Linguistics*, 20, 2, 303–27.

Harris, J. 1985. *Phonological Variation and Change*. Cambridge: Cambridge University Press.

Harris, J., Little, D. and Singleton, D. (eds) 1986. *Perspectives on the English Language in Ireland*. Dublin: Trinity College.

Haugen, E. 1972. Dialect, language, nation. In Pride, J. B. and Holmes, J. (eds), *Sociolinguistics*, Harmondsworth: Penguin Books, 97–111.

Heller, M. (ed.) 1988. *Code-switching*. Berlin: Mouton/de Gruyter.

Henderson, E. 1971. *The Indispensable Foundation*. Oxford: Oxford University Press.

Hoaglin, D., Mosteller, M. and Tukey, J. (eds). 1985. *Exploring Data Tables, Trends and Shapes*. New York: Wiley.

Horvath, B. 1985. *Variation in Australian English*. Cambridge: Cambridge University Press.

Horvath, B. and Sankoff, D. 1987. Delimiting the Sydney speech community. *Language in Society*, 16, 179–204.

Houston, A. 1987. *Continuity and Change in English Morphology: the variable* (ING). PhD dissertation: University of Pennsylvania.

Højrup, T. 1983. The concept of life-mode: a form-specifying mode of analysis applied to contemporary western Europe. *Ethnologia Scandinavica*, 1–50

Jespersen, O. 1922. *Language: its nature, development and origin*. London: Allen and Unwin.

Johnston, P. 1983. Irregular style variation patterns in Edinburgh speech. *Scottish Language*, 2, 1–19.

Jones, D. 1955. *An English Pronouncing Dictionary*. London: Dent.

Jones, D. 1956. *The Pronunciation of English*, 4th edn. Cambridge: Cambridge University Press.

Joseph, J. E. and Taylor, T. J. 1990. *Ideologies of Language*. London: Routledge.

Kibrik, A. E. 1977. *The Methodology of Field Investigations in Linguistics* (Janua Linguarum, Series Minor). The Hague: Mouton.

Kiparsky, P. 1988. Phonological change. In Newmeyer, F. (ed.), *Linguistics: the Cambridge Survey*, Cambridge: Cambridge University Press, vol. 1, 363–416.

Knowles, G. 1978. The nature of phonological variables in Scouse. In Trudgill, P. (ed.), *Sociolinguistic Patterns in British English*, London: Edward Arnold, 80–90.

Kökeritz, H. 1953. *Shakespeare's Pronunciation*. New Haven: Yale University Press.

Kristensson, G. 1967. *Survey of Middle English dialects: the six northern counties and Lincolnshire*. Lund: Lund Studies in English.

Kroch, A. 1978. Toward a theory of social dialect variation. *Language in Society*, 7, 17–36.

Labov, W. 1966. *The Social Stratification of English in New York City*. Washington DC: Center for Applied Linguistics.

Labov, W. 1972a. *Language in the Inner City*. Philadelphia: Pennsylvania University Press.

Labov, W. 1972b. *Sociolinguistic Patterns*. Philadelphia: Pennsylvania University Press.

Labov, W. 1973. Where do grammars stop? In Shuy, R. W. (ed.), *Sociolinguistics: current trends and prospects*, Washington DC: Georgetown University Press, 43–88.

Labov, W. 1975. On the use of the present to explain the past. In Baldi, P. and Werth, R. N. (eds), *Readings in Historicall Phonology*, University Park: Pennsylvania State University Press, 275–312.

Labov, W. (ed.) 1980. *Locating Language in Time and Space*. New York: Academic Press.

Labov, W. 1981. Resolving the Neogrammarian controversy. *Language*, 57, 267–308.

Labov, W. 1982. Building on empirical foundations. In Lehmann, W. P. and Malkiel, Y. (eds), *Perspectives in Historical Linguistics*, Amsterdam: Benjamins, 79–92.

Labov, W. 1986. Language structure and social structure. In Lindenberg, S. et al. (eds), *Approaches to Social Theory*, New York: Russell Sage.

Labov, W. 1989. The child as linguistic historian. *Language Variation and Change*, 1, 85–98.

Labov, W. and Harris, W. 1986. De facto segregation of black and white vernaculars. In Sankoff, D. (ed.), *Diversity and Diachrony*, Amsterdam: Benjamins, 1–24.

Labov, W., Yaeger, M. and Steiner, R. 1972. A quantitative study of sound change in progress. Report on National Science Foundation Project no. GS–3287. Philadelphia: US Regional Survey.

Laing, M. 1989. Dialectal analysis and linguistically composite texts in Middle English. In McIntosh, A., Samuels, M. and Laing, M. (eds), *Middle English Dialectology: essays on some principles and problems*, Aberdeen: Aberdeen University Press, 150–169.

Lanegran, D. A. and Palm, R. (eds) 1978. *An Invitation to Geography*, 2nd edn. New York: McGraw Hill.

Lass, R. 1976. *English Phonology and Phonological Theory*. Cambridge: Cambridge

University Press.

Lass, R. 1980. *On Explaining Language Change*. Cambridge: Cambridge University Press.

Lass, R. 1987. *The Frame of English*. London: Dent.

Lavandera, B. 1978. The variable component in bilingual performance. In Alatis, J. (ed.), *International Dimensions of Bilingual Education*, Washington DC: Georgetown University Press, 391– 411.

Lehmann, W. P. 1962. *Historical Linguistics*. New York: Holt, Rinehart and Winston.

Lehmann, W. P. and Malkiel, Y. (eds) 1968. *Directions for Historical Linguistics*. Austin: University of Texas Press.

Lehmann, W. P. and Malkiel, Y. (eds) 1982. *Perspectives on Historical Linguistics*. Amsterdam: Benjamins.

Leith, Dick 1980. *The Social History of English*. London: Routledge and Kegan Paul.

Le Page, R. B. 1975. Projection, Focusing, Diffusion. MS: University of York.

Le Page, R. B. and Tabouret-Keller, A. 1985. *Acts of Identity*. Cambridge: Cambridge University Press.

Lightfoot, D. 1979. *Principles of Diachronic Syntax*. Cambridge: Cambridge University Press.

Lockwood, D. 1989. *The Black-coated Worker: a Study in Class-consciousness*, 2nd edn. Oxford: Clarendon Press.

Lomnitz, L. A. 1977. *Networks and Marginality*. New York: Academic Press.

Lutz, A. 1985. On the historical phonotactics of English. In Kastovsky, D. and Bauer, G. (eds). *Luick Revisited*, Tübingen: Gunter Narr, 221–39.

Macaulay, R. K. S. 1977. *Language, Social Class and Education: a Glasgow Study*. Edinburgh: Edinburgh University Press.

McIntosh A. and Wakelin, M. F. 1989. John Mirk's *Festial* and Bodleian MS Hatton 96. In McIntosh, A., Samuels, M., and Laing, M. (eds), *Middle English Dialectology: essays on some principles and problems*, Aberdeen: Aberdeen University Press, 170–8.

McIntosh, A., Samuels, M. and Benskin, M. 1986. *A Linguistic Atlas of Late Medieval English*, 4 vols. Aberdeen: Aberdeen University Press.

McIntosh, A., Samuels, M. and Laing, M. (eds) 1989. *Middle English Dialectology: essays on some principles and problems*. Aberdeen: Aberdeen University Press.

McKnight, G. 1928. *The Evolution of the English Language*. New York: Dover Publications.

Marsden, P. V. and Lin, N. (eds). 1982. *Social Structure and Network Analysis*. London: Sage.

Martinet, A. 1955. *Economie des changements phonétiques*. Bern: Francke.

Matthews, W. 1938. *Cockney Past and Present*. London: Routledge and Kegan Paul.

Mewett, P. 1982. Associational categories and the social location of relationships in a Lewis crofting community. In Cohen, A. (ed.), *Belonging*, Manchester: Manchester University Press, 101–130.

Miller J. forthcoming. The grammar of Scottish English. In Milroy, J. and Milroy, L. (eds), *The Grammar of English Dialects of the British Isles*, London: Longman.

Mills, C. Wright 1956. *The Power Elite*. Oxford: Oxford University Press.

Milroy, J. 1976a. Length and height variation in the vowels of Belfast vernacular. *Belfast Working Papers in Language and Linguistics*, 1.3, 69–110.

Milroy, J. 1976b. Synopsis of Belfast vowels. *Belfast Working Papers in Language and Linguistics*, 1.4, 111–15.

Milroy, J. 1977. *The Language of Gerard Manley Hopkins*. London: André Deutsch.

Milroy, J. 1978. Stability and change in non-standard English in Belfast. *Bulletin of the Northern Ireland Speech and Language Forum*, 2, 72–82.

Milroy, J. 1980. Lexical alternation and the history of English. In Traugott, E., Labrum, R. and Shepherd, S. (eds), *Papers from the Fourth International Conference on Historical Linguistics*, Amsterdam: Benjamins, 355–62.

Milroy, J. 1981 *Regional Accents of English: Belfast.* Belfast: Blackstaff.

Milroy, J. 1982a. On the problem of historical interpretation: Verner's Law in Gothic. In Ahlqvist, A. (ed.), *Papers from the 5th International Conference on Historical Linguistics*, Amsterdam: Benjamins, 223–9.

Milroy, J. 1982b. Probing under the tip of the iceberg: phonological normalisation and the shape of speech communities. In Romaine, S. (ed.), *Sociolinguistic Variation in Speech Communities*, London: Edward Arnold, 35–47.

Milroy, J. 1982c. Some connections between Galloway and Ulster speech. *Scottish Language*, 1, 9–20.

Milroy, J. 1983. On the sociolinguistic history of /h/-dropping in English. In Davenport, M., Hansen, E. and Nielsen, H.-F. (eds), *Current Topics in English Historical Linguistics*, Odense: Odense University Press, 37–53.

Milroy, J. 1984. Present-day evidence for historical change. In Blake, N. F. and Jones, C. (eds), *Progress in English Historical Linguistics*, Sheffield: University of Sheffield, 173–91.

Milroy, J. 1986. The methodology of urban language studies: the example of Belfast. In Harris, J., Little, D. and Singleton, D. (eds), *Perspectives on the English Language in Ireland*, Dublin: Trinity College, 31–48.

Milroy, J. 1989. The concept of prestige in sociolinguistic argumentation. *York Papers in Linguistics*, 13, 215–26.

Milroy, J. forthcoming. Middle English dialectology. In Blake, N. F. (ed.) *The Cambridge History of the English Language*, vol. 2, Cambridge: Cambridge University Press.

Milroy, J. and Harris, J. 1980. When is a merger not a merger?: the MEAT/MATE problem in a present-day English vernacular. *English World Wide*, 1, 2, 199–210.

Milroy, J. and Milroy, L. 1978. Belfast: change and variation in an urban vernacular. In Trudgill, P. (ed.) *Sociolinguistic Patterns in British English*. London: Edward Arnold.

Milroy, J. and Milroy, L. 1985a. *Authority in Language*. London: Routledge and Kegan Paul.

Milroy, J. and Milroy, L. 1985b. Linguistic change, social network and speaker innovation. *Journal of Linguistics*, 21, 339–84.

Milroy, J. and Milroy L. (eds) forthcoming. *The Grammar of English Dialects of the British Isles*. London: Longman.

Milroy, J., Milroy, L., Gunn, B., Harris, J., Pitts, A. and Policansky, L. 1983. Sociolinguistic variation and linguistic change in Belfast. Report to the Social Science Research Council. (Grant no. HR 5777).

Milroy, L. 1984. Comprehension and context: successful communication and communicative breakdown. In Trudgill, P. (ed.), *Applied Socialinguistics*. London:

Academic Press, 7–31.

Milroy, L. 1987. *Language and Social Networks*, 2nd edn. Oxford: Basil Blackwell.

Milroy, L. 1989. Gender as a speaker variable ... the glottalised stops in Tyneside. *York Papers in Linguistics*, 13, 227–36.

Milroy, L. and Li Wei forthcoming. A social network perspective on code-switching and language choice: the example of the Tyneside Chinese community. MS.

Milroy, L. and Milroy, J. 1977. Speech and context in an urban setting. *Belfast Working Papers in Language and Linguistics*, 2.1, 1–85.

Milroy, L. and Milroy, J. forthcoming. Social network and social class: towards an integrated sociolinguistic model.

Mitchell, J. C. 1986. Network procedures. In *The Quality of Urban Life*, Berlin: de Gruyter.

Morris, R. (ed.) 1873. *Genesis and Exodus*. Oxford: Early English Texts Society.

Mugglestone, L. 1990. Ladylike accents: female pronunciation and perceptions of prestige in nineteenth-century England. *Notes and Queries*, 37, 1, 44–52.

Müller, F. Max 1861. *Lectures on the Science of Language*, 1st series. London: Longmans, Green.

Müller, F. Max 1881. *Selected Essays on Language, Mythology and Religion*. London.

Newbrook, M. 1986. *Sociolinguistic Reflexes of Dialect Interference in West Wirral*. London: Peter Lang.

Newmeyer, F. (ed.) 1988. *Linguistics: the Cambridge Survey*, 4 vols. Cambridge: Cambridge University Press.

Ochs, E. 1979. Planned and unplanned discourse. In Givón, T. (ed.), *Discourse and Syntax*, New York: Academic Press, 51–80.

O'Connor, J. D. 1973. *Phonetics*. Harmondsworth: Penguin.

Oliphant, T. K. 1873. *The Sources of Standard English*. London: Macmillan.

Onions, C. T. 1966. *Oxford Dictionary of English Etymology*. Oxford: Clarendon Press.

Orton, H., Barry, M. V., Halliday, W. J., Tilling, P. M. and Wakelin, M. F. 1963–9. *Survey of English Dialects*, 4 vols. Leeds: E. J. Arnold.

Owens, E. 1977. *The Distribution of /l/ in Belfast Vernacular English*. MA dissertation, Queen's University, Belfast.

Palmer, F. 1965. *A Linguistic Study of the English Verb*. London: Longman.

Parsons, T. 1952. *The Social System*. London: Tavistock.

Patterson, D. 1860. *Provincialisms of Belfast*. Belfast: Mayne Boyd.

Pellowe, J., Nixon, G., Strang, B. and McNeany, V. 1972. A dynamic modelling of linguistic variation: the urban (Tyneside) linguistic survey. *Lingua*, 30, 1–30.

Phillipps, K. C. 1984. *Language and Class in Victorian England*. Oxford: Basil Blackwell.

Pitts, A. 1982. The elusive vernacular: an account of fieldwork techniques in urban sociolinguistic studies in Northern Ireland. *Belfast Working Papers in Language and Linguistics*, 6, 104–21.

Plutchik, R. 1974. *Foundations of Experimental Research*, 2nd edn. New York: Harper and Row.

Postal, P. 1968. *Aspects of Phonological Theory*. New York: Harper.

Pride, J. B. and Holmes, J. (eds) 1972. *Sociolinguistics*. Harmondsworth: Penguin Books.

Prokosch, E. 1939. *A Comparative Germanic Grammar*. Philadelphia: University of Pennsylvania Press.

Rickford, J. 1986. The need for new approaches to social class analysis in linguistics. *Language and Communication*, 6, 3, 215–21.

Rigg, L. 1987. *A Quantitative Study of Sociolinguistic Patterns of Variation in Adult Tyneside Speakers*. Undergraduate dissertation: University of Newcastle upon Tyne.

Rogers, E. M. and Shoemaker, F. F. 1971. *Communication of innovations*, 2nd edn. New York: Free Press.

Romaine, S. 1981. The status of variable rules in sociolinguistic theory. *Journal of Linguistics*, 17, 93–119.

Romaine, S. 1982a. *Socio-historical Linguistics*. Cambridge: Cambridge University Press.

Romaine, S. (ed.) 1982b. *Sociolinguistic Variation in Speech Communities*. London: Edward Arnold.

Romaine, S. 1984a. The sociolinguistic history of t/d deletion. *Folia Historica Linguistica*, 5, 2, 221–55.

Romaine, S. 1984b. The status of sociological models and categories in explaining linguistic variation. *Linguistische Berichte*, 90, 25–38.

Samuels, M. L. 1972. *Linguistic Evolution*. Cambridge: Cambridge University Press.

Sankoff, D. (ed.). 1978. *Linguistic Variation: models and methods*. New York: Academic Press.

Sankoff, D. (ed.) 1986. *Diversity and Diachrony*. Amsterdam: Benjamins.

Sankoff, D. and Laberge, S. 1978. The linguistic market and the statistical explanation of variability. In Sankoff, D. (ed.), *Linguistic Variation: models and methods*, New York: Academic Press, 239–50.

Sankoff, D., Cedergren, H., Kemp, W., Thibault, P. and Vincent, D. 1989. Montreal French: language, class and ideology. In Fasold, W. and Schiffrin, D. (eds), *Language Change and Variation*, Amsterdam: Benjamins.

Sapir, E. 1921. *Language*. New York: Harcourt, Brace.

Schegloff, E. 1979. The relevance of repair to syntax for conversation. In Givón, T. (ed.), *Discourse and Syntax*, New York: Academic Press, 261–86.

Scragg, D. 1974. *The History of English Spelling*. Manchester: Manchester University Press.

Sebeok, T. (ed.) 1960. *Style in Language*. Boston: MIT Press.

Shuy, R. W. (ed.) 1973. *Sociolinguistics: current trends and prospects*. Washington DC: Georgetown University Press.

Shuy, R. W., Wolfram, W. A. and Riley, W. K, 1968. *Field Techniques in an Urban Language Study*. Washington DC: Center for Applied Linguistics.

Sisam, K. (ed.) 1915. *The Lay of Havelok the Dane*, edited by W. W. Skeat, 2nd edn revised by K. Sisam.

Skeat, W. W. 1897. The proverbs of Alfred. *Transactions of the Philological Society*.

Smith, N. V. 1989. *The Twitter Machine*. Oxford: Basil Blackwell.

Smith N. V. and Wilson, D. 1981. *Modern Linguistics*. Harmondsworth: Penguin Books.

Staples, J. H. 1898. Notes on Ulster English dialect. *Transactions of the Philological*

Society, 357–87.

Sturtevant, E. H. 1917. *Linguistic Change*. Chicago: Chicago University Press.

Tarde, G. 1903. *The Laws of Imitation*, translated by E. Clews Parsons. New York: Holt.

Taylor, M. Vaiana 1973. The great southern Scots conspiracy: patterns in the development of northern English. In Anderson, J. and Jones, C. (eds), *Historical Linguistics*, Amsterdam: North-Holland Publishing Company, 403–26.

Traugott, E., Labrum, R. and Shepherd, S. (eds) 1980. *Papers from the Fourth International Conference on Historical Linguistics*. Amsterdam: Benjamins.

Trench, R. C. 1888. *On the Study of Words*, 20th edn. London: Macmillan.

Trudgill, P. 1974. *The Social Differentiation of English in Norwich*. Cambridge: Cambridge University Press.

Trudgill, P. (ed.) 1978. *Sociolinguistic Patterns in British English*. London: Edward Arnold.

Trudgill, P. 1981. On the limits of passive 'competence': sociolinguistics and the polylectal grammar controversy. In Crystal, D. (ed.), *Linguistic Controversies: festschrift for F. R. Palmer*, London: Edward Arnold.

Trudgill, P. 1983a. *Sociolinguistics*, 2nd edn. Harmondsworth: Penguin Books.

Trudgill, P. 1983b. *On Dialect*. Oxford: Basil Blackwell.

Trudgill, P. (ed.) 1984a. *Language in the British Isles*. Cambridge: Cambridge University Press.

Trudgill, P. (ed.) 1984b. *Applied Sociolinguistics*. London: Academic Press.

Trudgill, P. 1986a. *Dialects in Contact*. Oxford: Basil Blackwell.

Trudgill, P. 1986b. The apparent time paradigm: Norwich revisited. Paper presented at the 6th Sociolinguistics Symposium, University of Newcastle upon Tyne.

Tukey, J. 1977. *Exploratory Data Analysis*. Reading, Mass.: Addison Wesley.

Vennemann, T. 1989. Language change as language improvement. In *Modelli esplicativi della diachronia linguistica*, Pisa: Giardini editori.

Wakelin, M. F. (ed.) 1972. *Patterns in the Folk Speech of the British Isles*. London: Athlone Press.

Wakelin, M. F. and Barry, M. V. 1968. The voicing of initial fricative consonants in present-day dialectal English. *Leeds Studies in English*, new series, 2, 47–64.

Walker, J. 1791. *A Critical Pronouncing Dictionary*.

Wang, W. 1969. Competing changes as a cause of residue. *Language*, 45, 9–25.

Wardhaugh, R. 1986. *An Introduction to Sociolinguistics*. Oxford: Basil Blackwell.

Weinreich, U., Labov, W. and Herzog, M. 1968. Empirical foundations for a theory of language change. In Lehmann, W. P. and Malkiel, Y. (eds), *Directions for Historical Linguistics*, Austin: University of Texas Press, 95–189.

Wells, J. C. 1982. *Accents of English: an introduction*. Cambridge: Cambridge University Press.

West, S. 1988. *Aspects of the Phonology of Ballygawley*. MA dissertation: Queen's University, Belfast.

Williams, R. A. 1903. Remarks on Northern Irish pronunciation of English. *Modern Language Quarterly*, 6, 129–35.

Wirth, L. 1938. Urbanism as a way of life. *American Journal of Sociology*, 44, 1, 1–24

Woolard, K. 1985. Language variation and cultural hegemony: towards an integration of linguistic and sociolinguistic theory. *American Ethnologist*, 738–48.

Wright, J. 1954. *Grammar of the Gothic Language*, 2nd edn, revised by O. L. Sayce. Oxford: Clarendon Press.

Wyld, H. C. 1927. *A Short History of English*, 3rd edn. London: John Murray.

Wyld, H. C. 1936. *A History of Modern Colloquial English*. Oxford: Basil Blackwell.

Young, M. and Wilmott, P. 1962. *Family and Kinship in East London*. Harmondsworth: Penguin Books.

Index

한신문화사
☎ 244 – 1520
244 – 8905
HAN SHIN
PUBLISHING CO.